My
Messianic Jewish
Bar/Bat Mitzvah
Student Workbook

By Elisa Norman

THIS WORKBOOK BELONGS TO

_____

This workbook is designed to accompany the lessons included in the
Eitz Chaim Messianic Jewish Congregation Bnei Mitzvah Teacher's Guide.

All glory and honor and praise to Yeshua our Messiah.

CONTENTS

Section 4 – Holy Days and Daily Life

INTRODUCTION

What Does It Mean to Be a Bar or Bat Mitzvah?

A Bar or Bat Mitzvah is a step towards becoming a full and active participant in the congregational family. "Bar" or "Bat Mitzvah" literally means "son" or "daughter" of the Commandments, indicating your reverence for Adonai. As a long-standing family tradition, it is an important coming-of-age ceremony for the young person. The Messianic Jewish Bar or Bat Mitzvah specifically recognizes Yeshua as the prophesied Messiah.

What Is Involved in Preparing for my Bar or Bat Mitzvah?

To prepare for Bar or Bat Mitzvah, weekly class attendance for the lessons is expected. After the class and throughout the following days, you will continue studying the objectives for each lesson by completing the daily assignments in this Student Workbook. It is very important to focus on memorizing each week's Bible memory verse and each week's Hebrew word. Daily practice is necessary to accomplish these goals. There will be quizzes to take at the end of each section covering the lesson material, the Bible memory verses, and the Hebrew.

Outside of class, you will also be completing a service project using the gifts and talents that Adonai has given you. The service project should benefit you, the congregation, and our community.

As you get closer to your Bar or Bat Mitzvah date, you will be learning to cant your Torah parashah, and you will write and present your own mini-drash. Your parashah is the passage from the Torah that was read the week you were born. Many find personal prophetic significance in their parashah. For your mini-drash, you will prepare and present a five to ten minute message explaining either your parashah or another matter of spiritual consequence that Adonai places in your mind and on your heart to deliver to the congregation. Parents may help you edit and organize your message, but parents should not write it. This is your Bar or Bat Mitzvah; you are responsible for writing your mini-drash.

On your big day, you may carry the Torah, or you may enlist family member to carry it. You will cant your parashah, deliver your mini-drash, recite a few Bible memory verses, and share with the congregation how you used your unique gifts and talents to help build Messiah's kingdom through a service project. Your parents may pray over you, and after the service, you may choose to celebrate with a chavurah.

How Long Will It Take to Get Ready?

The program is designed to take two to three years to complete. It is possible to move at your own pace through it, taking as long as you like, or moving more quickly if you have already passed your 12th (girls) or 13th (boys) birthday, which are the traditional ages for a Bar or Bat Mitzvah.

PRAYER

Daily prayer is a great habit to establish at this point in your journey. You may already be in the habit of praying on your own, but for many of you, this time in your life may be the first time you have considered that you can pray on your own. Perhaps you are in the habit of praying regularly with your family, over meals, before bedtime, and when you go to shul, but now, at the start of your Bar/Bat Mitzvah journey, set aside a special time each day to pray.

If this is your first attempt to establish a prayer routine of your own, you may be wondering how to do that. You're in good company! Yeshua's disciples asked Him how they should pray. And this is what He taught them in Matthew 6:9-13:

Our Father, who is in heaven, blessed be your Name.
Your kingdom come, your will be done, on earth as it is in heaven.
Give us today our daily bread, and forgive us our sins, as we forgive those who sin against us.
And lead us not into temptation, but deliver us from evil,
for your is the kingdom and the power and the glory forever.
Amen.

This prayer praises God, aligns the person praying with God's will, asks God to provide for his or physical needs, acknowledges his or her sin and asks for God's forgiveness. Yeshua emphasizes that we must also forgive others. Praying to God means that we are actively engaged with Him and His work.

There are four main categories of prayer:

1) Acclamation. These are prayers that praise God, tell Him we love Him, and express wonder at the beauty of His works.
2) Thanksgiving. We give God thanks for everything! We develop an attitude of constant gratefulness.
3) Confession. We tell God our sins and ask for His forgiveness. This is like taking a daily shower, cleansing ourselves spiritually from the sin that makes us unclean. Confessing our sins to God helps us stay in fellowship with Him.
4) Supplication. This is when we ask God for help. Sometimes, we pray for our own requests, and other times, we pray for others' needs. Remember, though, that God is not a genie in a lamp! We cannot rub the lamp and expect Him to pop out and grant us our three wishes. He is God; we are not! He sees the bigger picture, and sometimes, His answer to our prayers is "no." However, often His answers are "yes," and He wants us to pray and be involved in His works.

BIBLE MEMORY

Memorizing Bible verses and passages may be the most important way to spend your time during this program. The Word of God is like a seed planted in your heart. As the Ruach waters it, the seed will grow, and it will eventually produce an abundant harvest in your life and in the growth of the Body of Messiah in the world. By memorizing the Words of God, you are welcoming the opportunity for it to change you from the inside out – forming you more into His image. Knowing the Word of God will help you know who you are in Him, help you have an answer ready for those who ask you questions about your faith, and help you strengthen and deepen your own faith in so many ways.

Tips for Successful Bible Memorization

1. Time – spend at least ten minutes every day working on your weekly memory verse or passage.
2. Repetition – practice your verse or passage over and over again. Repetition is what transfers your memory verse or passage from short-term memory to long-term memory.
3. Write it over and over again.
4. Say it out loud over and over again.
5. Use hand motions to act it out as you say it out loud.
6. Create a song melody that goes with the verse and sing it.
7. Write it on a sheet of paper, cut out all the words separately, and then fit them back together again in the correct order – like a puzzle.
8. Think about what the verse or passage means and why it is important.
9. Write the verse or passage on a dry erase board; then erase one word at a time, reciting it out loud with the missing words from memory. Continue this until all the words are erased and you are reciting only from memory.
10. Practice with a friend – recite to each other back and forth. You can start with just one word at a time, or one phrase, and then build up to the entire verse or passage.
11. Fold a piece of paper lengthwise. Write book, chapter, and verse on one side, and write the verse on the other side. With the paper folded, quiz yourself by looking at the book, chapter, and verse. If you can't recite it, turn the paper over or open the fold so that you can see the verse and see the words you missed. Fold the paper and try again. Add additional verses to the paper from week to week.
12. Say the verse frequently throughout the day. Look for situations in which your verse applies.
13. Have a conversation with a grown up about your verse or passage.
14. Race yourself – see how fast you can say the verse. Time yourself, and then next time, see if you can say it faster.
15. Say it slowly – think carefully about each word or phrase. Compare different translations of the same verse. Which words are the same? Which translations use different words? How does that affect your understanding of the verse or passage?
16. Make flash cards – book, chapter, and verse on one side; verse or passage written out on the other side.
17. Draw a picture that goes with your verse.
18. Teach your verse to someone else, maybe your younger brother or sister.
19. Practice opening your Bible and finding your verse. When you find it, read it. Do this again and again and see how much faster you can get.
20. Make a bookmark with your verse written on it. Give it as a gift, or start a collection with each verse's bookmark tucked into its page in your Bible.
21. As you learn more verses, keep practicing the old ones.
22. Refer to the Bible Memory Chart (next page) for a list of all the memory verses and passages you will learn throughout the course of this program. As you memorize each one, mark it with a checkmark in the box. Every week, practice all of the verses and passages that you have marked.

MEMORY VERSE CHART

Memory Verses: Place a check mark next to each verse or passage after you have successfully memorized it. Remember to keep practicing the verses you have memorized so that you do not forget them!	X
Genesis 2:2-3 By the seventh day, God had finished the work He had been doing; so on the seventh day, He rested from all His work. And God blessed the Sabbath day and made it holy, because on it He rested from all the work of creating that He had done.	
Genesis 3:15 And I will put enmity between you and the woman, and between your offspring and hers; He will crush your head, and you will strike His heel.	
Genesis 12:3 I will bless those who bless you, and whoever curses you I will curse; and all peoples on earth will be blessed through you.	
Genesis 17:7 I will establish my covenant as an everlasting covenant between me and you and your descendants after you for the generations to come, to be your God and the God of your descendants after you.	
Genesis 32:28 Then the man said, "Your name will no longer be Jacob, but Israel, because you have struggled with God and with men and have overcome."	
Genesis 49:10 The scepter will not depart from Judah, nor the ruler's staff from between his feet, until he comes to whom it belongs and the obedience of the nations is his.	
Exodus 12:13 The blood will be a sign for you on the houses where you are; and when I see the blood, I will pass over you. No destructive plague will touch you when I strike Egypt.	
Exodus 20:8 Remember the Sabbath day by keeping it holy.	
Exodus 20:14 You shall not commit adultery.	
Exodus 20:1-17 And God spoke all these words: I am the LORD your God, who brought you out of Egypt, out of the land of slavery. You shall have no other gods before me. You shall not make for yourself an idol in the form of anything in heaven above or on the earth beneath or in the waters below. You shall not bow down to them or worship them; for I, the LORD your God, am a jealous God, punishing the children for the sin of the fathers to the third and fourth generation of those who hate me, but showing love to a thousand generations of those who love me and keep my commandments. You shall not misuse the name of the LORD your God, for the LORD will not hold anyone guiltless who misuses his name. Remember the Sabbath day by keeping it holy. Six days you shall labor and do all your work, but the seventh day is a Sabbath to the LORD your God. On it you shall not do any work, neither you, nor your son or daughter, nor your manservant or maidservant, nor your animals, nor the alien within your gates. For in six days the LORD made the heavens and the earth, the sea, and all that is in them, but he rested on the seventh day. Therefore the LORD blessed the Sabbath day and made it holy. Honor your father and your mother, so that you may live long in the land that the LORD your God is giving you. You shall not murder. You shall not commit adultery. You shall not steal. You shall not give false testimony against your neighbor. You shall not cover your neighbor's house. You shall not covet your neighbor's wife, or	

his manservant or maidservant, his ox or donkey, or anything that belongs to your neighbor.	
Leviticus 23:2 Speak to the Israelites and say to them, "These are my feasts, the appointed feasts of the LORD, which you are to proclaim and sacred assemblies."	
Leviticus 23:24 Say to the Israelites, "On the first day of the seventh month, you are to have a day of rest, a sacred assembly commemorated with trumpet blasts."	
Numbers 15:39 These will serve as tassels for you to look at, so that you may remember all the Lord's commands and obey them and not become unfaithful by following your own heart and your own eyes.	
Deuteronomy 6:4-5 Hear, O Israel, the LORD our God, the LORD is one. Love the LORD your God with all your heart and with all your soul and with all your strength.	
Joshua 24:15b As for me and my house, we will serve the LORD.	
Esther 4:14 For if you remain silent at this time, relief and deliverance for the Jews will arise from another place, but you and your father's family will perish.	
Job 40:15 Look at the behemoth which I made along with you and which feeds on grass like an ox.	
Psalm 14:1 The fool says in his heart, "There is no God." They are corrupt, their deeds are vile; there is no one who does good.	
Psalm 56:3 When I am afraid, I will trust in you.	
Psalm 78:14 He guided them with the cloud by day and with light from the fire all night.	
Psalm 115:3 Our God is in heaven; he does whatever pleases him.	
Psalm 121:4 He who watches over Israel will neither slumber nor sleep.	
Proverbs 3:5-6 Trust in the LORD with all your heart, and do not lean on your own understanding. In all your ways, acknowledge Him, and He will make your paths straight.	
Proverbs 9:10 The fear of the LORD is the beginning of wisdom, and knowledge of the Holy One is understanding.	
Proverbs 16:9 In his heart, a man plans his course, but the LORD determines his steps.	
Proverbs 18:24 A man of many companions may come to ruin, but there is a friends who sticks closer than a brother.	
Proverbs 30:4 Who has gone up to heaven and come down? Who has gathered up the wind in the hollow of his hands? Who has wrapped up the waters in his cloak? Who has established all the ends of the earth? What is his name, and the name of his son? Tell me, for you know.	
Isaiah 5:20 Woe to those who call evil good and good evil, who put lightness for dark and dark for lightness, who put bitter for sweet and sweet for bitter.	
Isaiah 41:10 So do not fear, for I am with you; do not be dismayed, for I am your God. I will	

strengthen you and help you; I will uphold you with my righteous right hand.	
Isaiah 46:10 I make known the end from the beginning, from ancient times what is still to come. I say: My purpose will stand, and I will do all that I please.	
Isaiah 49:6b I will also make you a light for the Gentiles, that you may bring my salvation to the ends of the earth.	
Genesis 49:10 The scepter will not depart from Judah, nor the ruler's staff from between his feet, until he to whom it belongs shall come and the obedience of the nations shall be his.	
Isaiah 55:11 So is my word that goes out from my mouth: it will not return to me empty, but it will accomplish what I desire and achieve the purpose for which I sent it.	
Jeremiah 18:6b Like clay in the hand of the potter, so are you in my hand, O house of Israel.	
Jeremiah 29:11 For I know the plans I have for you, declares the LORD, plans to prosper you and not to harm you, plans to give you hope and a future.	
Jeremiah 31:33 This is the covenant I will make with the house of Israel after that time, declares the LORD. I will put my law in their minds and write it on their hearts. I will be their God, and they will be my people.	
Lamentations 3:40 Let us examine our ways and test them, and let us return to the LORD.	
Ezekiel 36:26 I will give you a new heart and put a new spirit in you; I will remove from you your heart of stone and give you a heart of flesh.	
Daniel 12:2 Multitudes who sleep in the dust of the earth will awake: some to everlasting life, others to shame and everlasting contempt.	
Joel 2:29 Even on my servants, both men and women, I will pour out my Spirit in those days.	
Amos 5:24 But let justice roll on like a river, righteousness like a never-failing stream!	
Micah 6:8 He has shown you, O man, what is good. And what does the LORD require of you? To act justly and to love mercy and to walk humbly with your God.	
Habakkuk 2:4b The righteous will live by his faith.	
Zechariah 12:10 And I will pour out on the house of David and the inhabitants of Jerusalem a spirit grace and supplication. They will look on me, the one they have pierced, and they will mourn for him as one mourns for an only child, and grieve bitterly for him as one grieves for a firstborn son.	
Zechariah 14:16 Then the survivors from all the nations that have attacked Jerusalem will go up year after year to worship the King, the LORD Almighty, and to celebrate the Feast of Sukkot.	
Matthew 4:1-11 Then Yeshua was led by the Spirit into the desert to be tempted by the devil. After fasting forty days and forty nights, he was hungry. The tempter came to him and said, "If you are the Son of God, tell these stones to become bread." Yeshua answered, "It is written: Man does not live on bread alone, but on every word that comes from the mouth of God." Then the devil took	

him to the holy city and had him stand on the highest point of the temple. "If you are the Son of God," he said, "throw yourself down. For it is written: 'He will command his angels concerning you, and they will lift you up in their hands, so that you will not strike your foot against a stone.'" Yeshua answered him, "It is also written: do not put the Lord your God to the test." Again, the devil took him to a very high mountain and showed him all the kingdoms of the world and their splendor. "All this I will give you," he said, "if you will bow down and worship me." Yeshua said to him, "Away from me, Satan! For it is written: Worship the Lord your God and serve him only." Then the devil left him and angels came and attended him.	
Matthew 4:19 "Come, follow me," Yeshua said, "and I will make you fishers of men."	
Matthew 5:8 "Blessed are the pure in heart, for they will see God."	
Matthew 5:13 "You are the salt of the earth. But if the salt loses its saltiness, how can it be made salty again? It is no longer good for anything, except to be thrown out and trampled by men."	
Matthew 5:14 "You are the light of the world. A city on a hill cannot be hidden."	
Matthew 5:17-18 Do not think that I have come to abolish the Law or the Prophets; I have not come to abolish them but to fulfill them. I tell you the truth, until heaven and earth disappear, not the smallest letter, not the least stroke of a pen, will by any means disappear from the Law until everything is accomplished."	
Matthew 5:19 "Anyone who breaks one of the least of these commandments and teaches others to do the same will be called least in the kingdom of heaven, but whoever practices and teaches these commands will be called great in the kingdom of heaven."	
Matthew 5:43-44 "You have heard that is was said, 'Love your neighbor and hate your enemy,' but I tell you: Love your enemies and pray for those who persecute you."	
Matthew 6:9-13 "This, then, is how you should pray: Our Father in heaven, hallowed by your name, your kingdom come, your will be done on earth as it is in heaven. Give us today our daily bread. Forgive us our debts, as we have also forgiven our debtors. And lead us not into temptation, but deliver us from the evil one."	
Matthew 7:7-8 "Ask and it will be given to you; seek and you will find; knock and the door will be opened to you. For everyone who asks receives; he who seeks finds; and to him who knocks, the door will be opened."	
Matthew 7:12 "So in everything, do to others what you would have them do to you, for this sums up the Law and the Prophets."	
Matthew 7:13-14 "Enter through the narrow gate. For wide is the gate and broad is the road that leads to destruction, and many enter through it. But small is the gate and narrow the road that leads to life, and only a few find it."	
Matthew 15:11 "What goes into a man's mouth does not make him unclean, but what comes out of his mouth, that is what makes him unclean."	

Luke 18:14b "For everyone who exalts himself will be humbled, and he who humbles himself will be exalted."	
John 1:14 The Word became flesh and made his dwelling among us. We have seen his glory, the glory of the One and Only, who came from the Father, full of grace and truth.	
John 3:14-16 Just as Moses lifted up the snake in the desert, so the Son of Man must be lifted up, that everyone who believes in him may have eternal life. For God so loved the world that he gave his one and only Son, that whoever believes in him shall not perish but have eternal life. For God so loved the world that He gave his one and only Son, that whoever believes in him should not perish but have eternal life.	
John 10:22-30 Then came the Feast of Dedication (Chanukah) at Jerusalem. It was winter, and Yeshua was in the temple area walking in Solomon's Colonnade. The Jews gathered around him, saying, "How long will you keep us in suspense? If you are the Messiah, tell us plainly." Yeshua answered, "I did tell you, but you do not believe. The miracles I do in my Father's name speak for me, but you do not believe because you are not my sheep. My sheep listen to my voice; I know them, and they follow me. I give them eternal life, and they shall never perish; no one can snatch them out of my hand. My Father, who has given them to me, is greater than all; no one can snatch them out of my Father's hand. I and the Father are one."	
John 11:25-26 Yeshua said to her, "I am the resurrection and the life. He who believes in me will live, even though he dies; and whoever lives and believes in me will never die. Do you believe this?"	
John 14:6 Yeshua answered, "I am the way and the truth and the life. No one comes to the Father except through me."	
John 15:16-17 You did not choose me, but I chose you and appointed you to go and bear fruit — fruit that will last. Then the Father will give you whatever you ask in my name. This is my command: Love each other.	
Acts 4:12 Salvation is found in no one else, for there is no other name under heaven given to men by which we must be saved.	
Acts 8:30-31 Then Philip ran up to the chariot and heard the man reading Isaiah the prophet. "Do you understand what you are reading?" Philip asked. "How can I," he said, "unless someone explains it to me?" So he invited Philip to come up and sit with him.	
Romans 8:28 And we know that God works all things together for good, for those that love God and are called according to his purpose.	
Romans 11:13-16 I am talking to you Gentiles. Inasmuch as I am the apostle to the Gentiles, I make much of my ministry in the hope that I may somehow arouse my own people to envy and save some of them. For if their rejection is the reconciliation of the world, what will their acceptance be but life from the dead? If the part of the dough offered as firstfruits is holy, then the whole batch is holy; if the root is holy, so are the branches.	
Romans 12:4-8 Just as each one of us has one body with many members, and these members do not all have the same function, so in Messiah we who are many form one body, and each member	

belongs to all the others. We have different gifts, according to the grace given us. If a man's gift is prophesying, let him use it in proportion to his faith. If it is serving, let him serve; if it is teaching, let him teach; if it is encouraging, let him encourage; if it is contributing to the needs of others, let him give generously; if it is leadership, let him govern diligently; if it is showing mercy, let him do it cheerfully.	
1 Corinthians 5:7 Get rid of the old yeast that you may be a new batch without yeast – as you really are. For Messiah, our Passover Lamb, has been sacrificed.	
1 Corinthians 10:2 They were all baptized into Moses in the cloud and in the sea.	
1 Corinthians 11:23-24 For I received from the Lord what I also passed on to you: Messiah Yeshua, on the night he was betrayed, took bread, and when he had given thanks, he broke it and said, "This is my body, which is for you; do this in remembrance of me."	
1 Corinthians 15:20 But Messiah has indeed been raised from the dead, the firstfruits of those who have fallen asleep.	
2 Corinthians 6:14 Do not be yoked together with unbelievers. For what do righteousness and wickedness have in common? Or what fellowship can light have with darkness?	
Galatians 3:28 There is neither Jew nor Greek, slave nor free, male nor female, for you are all one in Messiah Yeshua.	
Galatians 4:4-5 But when the time had fully come, God sent his Son, born of a woman, born under law, to redeem those under law, that we might receive the full rights of sons.	
Galatians 5:16 So I say, live by the Spirit, and you will not gratify the desires of the sinful nature.	
Galatians 5:22-23 But the fruit of the Spirit is love, joy, peace, patience, kindness, goodness, faithfulness, gentleness, and self-control. Against such things, there is no law.	
Ephesians 4:26 In your anger, do not sin: Do not let the sun go down while you are still angry.	
Ephesians 4:32 Be kind and compassionate to one another, forgiving each other, just as in Messiah, God forgave you.	
Hebrews 1:1-2 In the past God spoke to our forefathers through the prophets at many times and in various ways, but in these last days he has spoken to us by his Son, whom he appointed heir of all things, and through whom he made the universe.	
Hebrews 4:12 For the Word of God is living and active. Sharper than any double edged sword, it penetrates even to the dividing of soul and spirit, joints and marrow; it judges the thoughts and attitudes of the heart.	
Hebrews 10:14 Because by one sacrifice, He has made perfect forever those who are being made holy.	
Hebrews 11:7 By faith, Noah, when warned about things not yet seen, in holy fear built an ark to save his family. By his faith he condemned the world and became heir of the righteousness that	

comes by faith.	
James 1:22 Do not merely listen to the word and so deceive yourselves; do what it says.	
1 Peter 5:7 Cast all your anxiety on Him because He cares for you.	
1 John 1:9 If we confess our sins to God, He is faithful and just to forgive us our sins and to cleanse us from all unrighteousness.	
Revelation 20:11-15 Then I saw a great white throne and Him who was seated on it. Earth and sky fled from his presence, and there was no place for them. And I saw the dead, great and small, standing before the throne, and books were opened. Another book was opened, which is the Book of Life. The dead were judged according to what they had done as recorded in the books. The sea gave up the dead that were in it, and death and Hades gave up the dead that were in them, and each person was judged according to what he had done. Then death and Hades were thrown into the lake of fire. The lake of fire is the second death. If anyone's name was not found written in the Book of Life, he was thrown into the lake of fire.	

HEBREW

For your Bar or Bat Mitzvah, you will be canting your Torah portion from the Torah scroll. During the course of this program, you will learn the letters of the Hebrew alephbet, the vowel markings, and the cantillation marks that tell you how to cant ("sing") the words. Each week, you will have one Hebrew word as part of your lesson. This will be your vocabulary. As you study these words, use the following pages to help you learn the letters, vowels, and read the words. Practice at least five minutes each day.

The Hebrew Alephbet

All of the letters of the Hebrew alephbet are consonants. Vowels were added to the words by a group of Jewish scribes called the Masoretes between the 7th and 11th centuries. They realized that too few Jews knew how to read and pronounce Hebrew words. So that the added vowels would not interfere with the Hebrew as it is written in the scrolls, the Masoretes added vowels in the form of dots and dashes beneath, inside, or above the consonants.

Reading Hebrew

Hebrew reads right to left (whereas English reads left to right). When reading, read the consonant starting on the right, then read the vowel, then read the next consonant, and so on. The only exception to reading a vowel before a consonant is in the case of a "furtive" patach – it "sneaks" in before the chet, as in the word Ruach.

The Alephbet

Letter	Sounds Like	Practice Writing
Aleph א	Silent letter; it will take on the sound of the vowel with it	
Bet בּ ב	Sounds like "b" with the dagesh (the dot inside it) or like "v" if there is no dagesh	
Gimel ג	Sounds like "g" as in "go"	
Dalet ד	Sounds like "d"	

Hey ה	Sounds like "h"	
Vav ו	Sounds like "v" (anciently, it may have sounded like "w;" also, see the vowel chart below – the vav with a dot above it or a dot inside will not sounds like "v" – it will become a vowel)	
Zayin ז	Sounds like "z"	
Chet ח	sounds like "ch" as in clearing you throat (not like "ch" as in "chip" – we just write it that way because we do not have this sound in English)	
Tet ט	Sounds like "t"	
Yod י	Sounds like "y"	
Caf כ כ	Sounds like "ch" like the chet if there is no dot (dagesh) in the middle, or like "k" if there is a dagesh	
Caf Sofeet ך	This is the form found at the end of a word – sounds like "ch" like the Caf	

Lamed ל	Sounds like "l"	
Mem מ	Sounds like "m"	
Mem Sofeet ם	This is the form found at the end of a word – sounds like "m"	
Nun נ	Sounds like "n"	
Nun Sofeet ן	This is the form found at the end of a word – sounds like "n"	
Samech ס	Sounds like "s"	
Ayin ע	Silent letter; it will take on the sounds of the vowel with it. Anciently, it may have sounded like a very soft "g"	
Peh פ	Sounds like "p" with the dagesh, or "ph" without	
Peh Sofeet ף	This is the form found at the end of a word – sounds like "ph"	

Tzade צ	Sounds like "tz"	
Tzade Sofeet ץ	This is the form found at the end of a word – sounds like "tz"	
Qof ק	Sounds like "q/k"	
Resh ר	Sounds like "r"	
Shin שׁ	Sounds like "sh" Notice the dot is over the top right corner	
Sin שׂ	Sounds like "s" Notice the dot is over the top left corner	
Tav תּ ת	Sounds like "t" with the dagesh; theoretically sounds like "th" without it; however, the "th" sound is not pronounced in Hebrew today, so sounds like "t" all the time	

The Vowels

The vowels are introduced below using aleph as a vowel holder. Since aleph is a silent consonant, you can read the sound of the vowel below without also sounding a consonant. See also that vav becomes a vowel twice below:

Vowel	Sounds Like	Practice Writing
Kamatz ָ	"Ah" as in Father or "Oh" as in Rope when it closes a syllable (Shown here without a consonant)	
Patach אַ	"Ah" As in "Father" (Shown here with a consonant)	
Tsere אֵ	"Ay" As in "Say" In modern Hebrew, "eh"	
Segol אֶ	"Eh" As in "Red"	
Sheva אְ	Silent Or a very short "eh" As in Yeshua	
Cholam אֹ	"Oh" As in Rope	
Vav Holem וֹ	"Oh" As in Rope	
Chirik אִ	"Ee" or "Ih" As in Week or Wick	
Kibbutz אֻ	"Oo" as in Blue	
Vav Shuruk וּ	"Oo" as in Blue	

Hebrew Vocabulary Checklist

The following are the selected Hebrew words that you will learn throughout your lessons. Use this checklist as a way to track and review your growing Hebrew vocabulary. You will add the vowels to each Hebrew word, write the transliteration, and write the meaning of each word during the class time portion of this class.

Hebrew Word	Transliteration	Meaning
בְּרֵאשִׁית	Bereshit	In the beginning
ברא		
אלהים		
את		
השמים		
ואת הארץ		
ברית		
וירא		
ישראל		
מצרים		
שבט מיהודה		
ענן		
משכן		
אבן		

קרבן		
אש		
ציצית		
נחש		
דבר		
פינחס		
איש אישה		
שמע		
אחד		
לב		
אור		
יד		
נתן		
חיי עולם		
חיי עולם		
גם		
תיקון עולם		

תִּיקוּן עוֹלָם		
מֶלֶךְ		
אֱמוּנָה		
יְהוֹשֻׁעַ		
יהוה		
תַּלְמִיד		
עֶלֶם		
נְבוּאָה		
מָשָׁל		
נֵס		
יֵשׁוּעַ		

רוח		
אהבה		
תורה רוח		
ברוך		
שלח		
גויים		
אהבה		
טהרה		
שבת		
מועד		
מצה		
פסח		

בכורים		
שָׁבוּעוֹת		
תִּשְׁעָה בְּאָב		
יוֹם תְרוּעָה ראֹשׁ הַשָּׁנָה		
יוֹם כִּפֻּר		
סֻכּוֹת		
חֲנוּכָּה		
פּוּרִים		
טוֹב		
תִּקְוָה		
כִּי־אֲנִי		
תֵּנַשׁ		
הִנֵּה		
אַחֲרִית		
הַיּוֹם		
אֲשֶׁר		
וַיּאֹמֶר		

חרב־פיפיות		
זכר		
זכר		
יוסף		
עשׂר		
מגיד		

SECTION 1 – TORAH PORTION SELECTIONS

LESSON 1
BERESHIT PART 1

Lesson Objectives: See how Creation makes more sense than Evolution. Know that God's Word can be trusted.

Bible Memory: Genesis 2:2-3 By the seventh day, God had finished the work He had been doing. So on the seventh day He rested from all his work. Then God blessed the seventh day and made it holy, because on it He rested from all the work of creating that He had done.

Hebrew Word: בְּרֵאשִׁית   bereshit - in the beginning

Lesson Summary:

The opening verse of the Bible states: "In the beginning, God created the heavens and the earth." Let's look closely at that verse. Everything that God needed to do His work of creation is in that verse. To create this world, it was necessary to have Time, Space, Matter, and a Force that does the Action.

Time: In the beginning
Force: God
Action: created
Space: the heavens
Matter: and the earth.

Before this universe existed, there was no time. There was no space. There was no matter. God is above and outside of all of that. He created all of it. He is eternal and He is sovereign.

In contrast, Evolution states that in the beginning there was nothing. And then there was a Big Bang, and then stuff exploded and stretched out and became more stuff. Evolution does not believe in God. Evolution does not believe that there was a reason for the Big Bang; it just happened. Evolution believes that anything can happen if given enough time. In a way, Time becomes one of Evolution's gods. (Natural Selection is another of Evolution's gods.)

Evolution's view:
Time: began when the Big Bang happened billions of years ago
Force: nothing
Action: there was a Big Bang (but nothing cause it)
Space: appeared after the Big Bang
Matter: appeared after the Big Bang

Evolution says that it is the scientific viewpoint but Creation is the faith-based viewpoint. In other words, evolutionists believe that they are the "smart" people who follow the obvious rules and evidence of Science, while the Creationists are religious fanatics who choose faith in God over clear scientific evidence that proves He's not real. This is not true at all. Unfortunately, evolutionists are deceived. Creation is not at war with Science; in fact, the more we learn about Science, the more we see that Science confirms exactly what the Bible says. Science and the Bible are in agreement with each other; they are not at odds with each other, as evolutionists would have us all believe.

Let's take a look. A basic law of Physics is the law of cause and effect. There cannot be an effect without a cause. The cause makes the effect happen. For example, if I have a ball and I throw it across the room, I am the cause that produced the effect of the ball changing locations. The ball cannot throw itself.

Take a look at the fundamental requirements for the universe's existence above in the Creation list from Genesis 1:1 and from the Evolutionists list. What is the cause in Genesis 1:1? And what is the effect?

God
Created

God created everything out of nothing.

What is the evolutionists' cause?

Nothing!
Nothing created everything??

"Nothing" cannot create anything. "Nothing" cannot produce an effect.

Therefore, evolution is not scientific, and the beginning of the universe cannot possibly have happened that way.

Some people will try to combine Creation and Evolution is different ways. There are many different theories about this, but the believers of these theories all basically have one thing in common: they believe Science and the Bible do not agree with each other, but they want to believe both, so they try to explain creation in evolutionary ways. This is also neither Biblical nor Scientific. Science is not a god. Science and scientific laws were created by God and are subject to His authority.

One way that people try to combine creation with evolution's theories of very long periods of time (millions and millions of years) is by redefining the word "day." They will say that a "day" can be a long period of time. In some cases, this can be true. For example, if you have a conversation with your grandfather, and he says, "Back in my day," you know he is about to tell you a story from his younger years, a period of time longer than a 24 hour day. Also, when we read in the Bible about "the day of the Lord," we know that we are reading about a prophetic period of time that is still to come. Another way that "day" is used to mean something longer than a 24 hour day is when it is used in a phrase of figurative language. For example, 2 Peter 3:8 says that to the Lord, "a day is as a thousand years, and a thousand years is as a day." Do you see the key word "as"? That word tells us that this is a simile, which is a kind of metaphor. God is not saying that the word "day" really means one thousand years (or millions and millions of years). If we read the whole passage in context, then we understand that He is explaining that He, the creator of time, is not subject to time. He is outside of it.

Even though the word "day" can mean a longer period of time than a literal 24 hour day, we know that the work of creation in Genesis 1 happened in literal 24 hour days. We know this because Genesis 1 clearly defines "day" as "evening and morning," and each day is numbered: "day one," "the second day," and so on. It is as if Adonai knew that our generations today would doubt His work! So He made it very clear.

It is so clear that we must realize that rejection of God's Word is rebellion against Him. And, at the root of it, that is exactly evolutionists' intent. As we begin our journey into God's Word, let us remember that God's Word can be trusted.

Weekly assignments:

Day 1:

1) Bible Memory: Memorize Genesis 2:2-3. Refer to the Bible Memory Tip and Tricks page for ideas to aid in memorization.

2) Practice Hebrew:

When we read English, we start at the left and read across the page to the right. Hebrew goes the other direction. So, we start at the right side of the page and read across to the left.

In the Hebrew alphabet, which is called the aleph-bet, all the letters are consonants. Originally, Hebrew did not have vowels. A group of Jewish scribes called the Masoretes added vowel markings to the Hebrew text between the 6th and 10th centuries CE (AD). They did not want to change the text of the Scriptures, so they created vowel markings that were placed in, under, or over the letters that were already there. They look like dots and dashes.

Today we will practice the first two letters of the word בראשית bereshit, which means "in the beginning." It is the first word in the Bible.

בּ bet – sounds like "b" when the dot is in the center, and "v" if the dot is not there - בּ.

Practice writing bet: _____

ר resh – sounds like "r"

Practice writing resh: _____

בְּ Do you see the marking under the bet that looks like a colon? That is a vowel. It is called a sheva. The sheva can do two different things. First, it can sound like a short "eh." That's how it sounds here. Second, it can also be silent and just close a syllable. We'll see that later.

When we read a word in Hebrew, we read the consonant sound first and then the vowel (there is one exception where we read the vowel first, but we'll meet that one later.) So when we read the bet first and then the sheva, how does it sound?

בְּ sounds like "beh"

Now try it with the resh: בְּר sounds like "behr." (Did you remember to start on the right and read to the left?)

3) Think about the lesson:

Read Genesis 1. What does Adonai call His creation? _____

Day 2:

1) Bible Memory: Practice Genesis 2:2-3

2) Practice Hebrew:

Read the following from right to left:

בְּר   בְּ

ר The two side by side dots under the resh are the vowel sere. Sere sounds like "ay" in Biblical Hebrew (but more like "eh" in Modern Hebrew). So resh with sere sounds like "ray." Remember to read consonant first and then vowel.

א This letter is the aleph. It is the first letter of the Hebrew alephbet. It is silent. If it has a vowel, it will sound like the vowel.
Practice writing aleph: _____

Now let's put it all together:

בְּרֵא Beray. Practice reading this several times.

3) Think about the lesson:

Read Genesis 1 again.
Put this list in the correct order according to when Adonai created it:

Light
Sun, moon, and stars
Birds and sea creatures
Humans and land dwelling animals
Dry ground and plants
Sky, separation of water above from waters below

1._____
2._____
3._____
4._____
5._____
6._____

Evolutionists believe that there were simple, single-celled organisms that evolved into more complex life forms. Water creatures became amphibious and then turned into land animals, lizards grew wings and feathers and evolved into birds, and apes became humans. Does this fit with the order of creation you see in Genesis 1? Why or why not?
_____
_____
_____

Day 3:
1) Bible Memory: Practice Genesis 2:2-3

2) Practice Hebrew:

Review: בְּרֵא

New letter: Shin. שׁ Sounds like "sh." Notice the dot over the top right corner of the letter. (If the dot were on the left, it would be the sin, which sounds like "s.")

New vowel: שִׁ Hireq. It's the dot under the shin. Sounds like "ee." (In Modern Hebrew, can sound like "ih."

Putting it together: בְּרֵאשִׁ Sounds like "bereshee"

3) Think about the lesson: God made everything after its kind. Different species can change and develop within their kinds ("families" at the taxonomy level), but no new species become different kinds. For example, Darwin's finches change over time due to their environment and breeding, but they are still finches. There are no "transitional forms" in the fossil record that would support the theory of evolution. Evolutionists are puzzled because of the "Cambrian explosion" they see in the fossil record. The Cambrian explosion is a time period where multitudes of different types of animals suddenly show up in the fossil record. They all appear, without millions or billions of years between them. Does this support evolution? Or creation? Why?

_____

_____

_____

Day 4:

1) Bible Memory: Practice Genesis 2:2-3

2) Practice Hebrew:

Review: בְּרֵאשׁ

New letter: י Yod. Sounds like "y."

Putting it together: בְּרֵאשִׁי Sounds like "bereshee"

3) Think about the lesson: Dinosaurs that were land dwelling creatures were made on the sixth day along with the other land dwelling animals. This means that humans and dinosaurs lived at the same time, along with all the other animals. Dinosaurs that were birds or sea creatures were created on the fifth day, along with all the other creatures of the air and water. Read Job 40:15-41:34. What do you think Adonai is describing in these passages?

_____

_____

Day 5:

1) Bible Memory: Practice Genesis 2:2-3
2) Practice Hebrew:

Review: בְּרֵאשִׁי

New letter: ת Tav. Sounds like "t."

Putting it together: בְּרֵאשִׁית Sounds like "beresheet." Means "in the beginning." The bet at the front is a preposition that means "in."

3) Think about the lesson: Many different cultures around the world have stories about dragons. For example, ancient British tales often depict knights fighting dragons to save fair maidens, and the Chinese calendar has a year of the dragon. All of the other years are of known animals, which causes us to wonder if the dragon, which we do not see in existence today, might have been a real, living creature with which the ancient people were familiar. Also, we see cave drawings and carvings depicting dinosaurs such as the stegosaurus. How did the ancient people draw these if they'd never seen them? Considering the evidence, do you think it is reasonable to assume that the Bible is true when it says that God created all of these creatures in a literal six day period of time? And that dinosaurs were animals that lived alongside humans just like all the other animals? Why or why not?

_____

_____

Day 6:

1) Bible Memory: Practice Genesis 2:2-3. You should be able to recite it out loud from memory now.

2) Practice Hebrew: בְּרֵאשִׁית

Read your Hebrew word of the week out loud. What does it mean? _____

Which letter is the preposition that means "in?" _____

3) Think about the lesson: Read Genesis 1:27. What makes men and women special?

_____

LESSON 2
BERESHIT PART 2

Lesson Objectives: Sin enters the world, causing a separation between God and humans. God promises restoration through the Messiah. God proclaims His salvation all over the world.

Bible Memory: Genesis 3:15 And I will put enmity between you and the woman, and between your offspring and hers; He will crush your head, and you will strike His heel.

Hebrew Word: בָּרָא he created

Lesson Summary:

When the serpent tempted Eve in the garden, he promised that the fruit of the tree of the knowledge of good and evil would make them wise like God. Even though God had said not to eat it, Eve decided that she would. And then she gave some to Adam, and he ate. It seemed like such a small thing; however, it was the one rule that God gave them, and they broke it. They sinned.

Sin is disobedience to God.

When Adam and Eve sinned, they died spiritually, just as God said they would, and their bodies became mortal; their bodies would now grow old and die physically. What God warned against was exactly what happened. What the serpent said also happened; however, as the serpent does, he spoke words that were a little bit true, but he twisted the truth, and rather than becoming wise in a good way, the wisdom Adam and Eve gained was the wisdom of evil. Their sin affected them as well as the world God created for them to live in. The whole world changed. Because of sin, thorns grew on the earth. It became hard work to grow and harvest food to eat. Having children became painful. Humans, in choosing sin, became slaves to sin and suffered the consequences. Humanity was separated from God.

Throughout the ages, humans have dealt with the problem of separation from God in different ways.

Some people create or follow religions that require them to do a lot of good, religious things to earn their way back into God's graces.

Others deny that God exists. If there is no God, then there is no right or wrong, which means that there is no sin, so they don't have to try to bridge the separation between their sinful selves and the perfect God.

All around the world, people are born into different countries and cultures which each include a unique world view with either a religious or non-religious mindset. Many people never take the time or thought to seriously consider why they do what they do or why they think what they think; they just do what their parents have done forever and ever. Those who see that we are separated from God often believe that the path back to God is unique to them and others are not included unless they become like them.

27

This is all human wisdom, and human wisdom is tainted with evil.

God shows us a different way. God's way is the only way that works.

Adam and Eve used to walk with God in the garden, and when God showed up to meet them, they hid. When He called out to them, Adam blamed Eve, and Eve blamed the serpent. God cursed the serpent and told it that Eve's seed would crush its head and he would bite its heel. This verse foretells the Messiah. Messiah would be born of a woman through Adam and Eve's lineage, and although the serpent would kill Him ("bite his heel") this would not destroy Him; instead, the Messiah would crush the head of the serpent. Messiah would completely and totally destroy the plans of the serpent.

Sin came through a woman (Eve/Chavah); the Savior would come through a woman (Mary/Miriam).

The first Adam went along with what he knew was wrong; the Messiah, the "second Adam," would pay the penalty for all wrongdoing so that humanity could return to God.

God told the serpent, with Adam and Eve listening, what He would do. The serpent knows God's plans better than people do! The serpent, Satan, has tried throughout history to destroy God's plan of salvation, to destroy the Messiah and the people from whom the Messiah would be born. He does everything in his power to stop people from returning to God. He tells lies about God, and he confuses and deceives many.

As history progresses, confusion about God and religion increases. However, God makes sure that everyone, no matter where or when they are born, everyone can hear the truth about the Messiah. When we hear it, we are responsible for deciding whether we will accept it or reject it. If we accept Messiah's salvation, then He heals the separation from God that our sin causes, and we will be with Him for all eternity. If we reject Messiah's salvation, then we have chosen sides with the serpent, and we will be separated from God for all eternity. As God says in Deuteronomy 30, "See I have set before you life and death; choose life, so that you and your descendants may live!"

Weekly Assignments:

Day 1:

1) Bible Memory: Review Genesis 2:2-3 and begin memorizing Genesis 3:15.

2) Practice Hebrew: Last week, you learned the letters that are in this week's Hebrew word.

בָּרָא he created (sounds like "barah")

Point to each letter and say its name and its sound.
Read the word; remember to read consonant first and then the vowel.

3) Think about the lesson: In the beginning, when God created the heavens and the earth, He pronounced his creation good. Sin caused God's perfect world to lose its goodness. Death entered with the first sin. Think about the theory of evolution. Evolutionists believe that death, disease, and decay existed for millions of years before the first people ever appeared. Does this work with Genesis 1-3? (Read Genesis 1-3 before your answer.) Why or why not? Give reasons.

Day 2:

1) Bible Memory: Review Genesis 2:2-3 and memorize Genesis 3:15.

2) Practice Hebrew: Let's read last week's word and this week's word together:

בְּרֵאשִׁית ברא

How do you say it?
What does it mean?

3) Think about the lesson: Many religions teach that we can return to God if we follow all the religious rules, or if we are a good person, or if we do everything right in the right way. Is that what God says in Genesis 3? _____ What does God promise in Genesis 3:15?

Day 3:

1) Bible Memory: Review Genesis 2:2-3 and memorize Genesis 3:15.

2) Practice Hebrew: בְּרֵאשִׁית ברא

Point to each consonant and say its name and its sound.

3) Think about the lesson: In our culture, people get upset if they feel like someone is judging them. In general, people want to do whatever they want without someone else saying that it is wrong. Atheists deny that there is a God. If there is no God, then there is no right or wrong, and people really can do whatever they want without consequences. However, most thinking atheists realize that cultures can't exist without any laws at all, so they believe that the culture makes the laws. This means that right and wrong would vary from place to place and during different time periods. Can you think of some examples of cultures that have different rules for right and wrong?

Day 4:

1) Bible Memory: Review Genesis 2:2-3 and memorize Genesis 3:15.

2) Practice Hebrew: בְּרֵאשִׁית ברא

Point to each vowel and say its name and its sound.

3) Think about the lesson: Naturalists believe that only the world we can sense with our five senses exists, meaning that only the natural world that we can see, hear, smell, taste, and touch. Naturalists do not believe in anything supernatural; they do not believe that God exists or that anything outside the natural realm can happen. Yet they have faith in scientific laws. Think: how can there be scientific laws if there was no Lawgiver to make the laws?

Day 5:

1) Bible Memory: Review Genesis 2:2-3 and memorize Genesis 3:15.

2) Practice Hebrew: בְּרֵאשִׁית בּרא
   Write the Hebrew words:_____
   Circle the letter that is the preposition that means "in."

3) Think about the lesson: During the class time lesson, you heard an excerpt read from *Bruchko,* the missionary to the Motilone tribe in South America. How did God, through Bruchko's obedience and attentiveness to the Spirit, reveal Yeshua to the Motilone tribe?

   _____

   _____

Day 6:

1) Bible Memory: Review Genesis 2:2-3 and memorize Genesis 3:15.

2) Practice Hebrew: בְּרֵאשִׁית בּרא
   Read the words out loud in Hebrew.
   What do they mean?

3) Think about the lesson: There is only one way to the Father – through Yeshua His Son, our Messiah. Out of all the other books and sacred texts in the world, what is special about the Bible?

   _____

   _____

LESSON 3
NOACH PART 1

Lesson Objectives: Marriage is the first institution that God created. Who we marry is very important to God.

Bible Memory: 2 Corinthians 6:14 Do not be yoked together with unbelievers. For what do righteousness and wickedness have in common? Or what fellowship can light have with darkness?

Hebrew Word: אלהים Elohim - God

Lesson Summary:

In Genesis 2, we see that Adam is alone, and God says that it is not good for him to be alone. This is the first time after creation that God says anything is not good! So God causes Adam to fall asleep, and while he sleeps, God takes one of his ribs and creates a woman out of Adam's rib. Adam says about her, "This is now bone of my bones and flesh of my flesh; she shall be called woman, for she was taken out of man (Genesis 2:23)." When a husband and wife marry, they become "one flesh (Genesis 2:24)."

Adam and Eve begin having children. In Genesis 4, we meet Cain, and perhaps you already know the story of Cain and Abel. If not, read Genesis 4. After Cain kills Abel, he begins to have children of his own, and the violence that began with him increases with his offspring. In Genesis 4:24, Lamech, Cain's descendant, says, "If Cain is avenged seven times, that Lamech seventy-seven times."

Not all of Adam and Eve's children increased in evil, though. Seth, the child God gave them in place of Abel, had a son named Enosh, and Genesis 4:26 says that "at that time men began to call on the name of the LORD." Genesis 5 shows us the righteous line from Seth that resulted in Noah and his family.

At the beginning of this Torah portion, Genesis 6:1-4, we see that the sons of God are marrying the daughters of men, and they are producing Nephilim offspring.

There are two ways to understand this passage: 1) Some say that the sons of God are believers and the daughters of men are the unbelievers, and that if we are believers we should not marry unbelievers. That makes us "unequally yoked." This is a good lesson for us all to know. It is true that we should not be unequally yoked in marriage. A spouse who follows God wholeheartedly is the most important value we should look for when we are looking for someone to marry. There are many Bible verses and passages that illustrate the importance of this. 2) The second way to understand this passage is the way that it has been understood from ancient days: the sons of God were angels who rejected God's authority and took human women as wives, producing children that were half-angelic, half-human beings that grew to gigantic sizes and were wicked, violent, and evil. The Bible records the existence of giants, and so do many other ancient texts from around the world.

In Hebrew, Nephilim does not mean "giant," although this is how we understand it; it literally means "fallen ones."

In this week's assignments, we'll look at these two interpretations more closely. In the end, whether you agree with the first option or the second (or both), the main principle is the same:

Do not become unequally yoked with anyone evil or unrighteous.

When you are old enough and mature enough to consider marriage, look for someone who is following God, who recognizes that Yeshua is the Messiah, and who is wholeheartedly ready to give himself or herself to becoming one with you and raising children with you and who is devoted to training your children in the righteous ways of Adonai.

Weekly Assignments:

Day 1:

    1)   Bible Memory: Review Genesis 2:2-3 and Genesis 3:15. Memorize 2 Corinthians 6:14.

    2)   Practice Hebrew: אֶ

Aleph – silent letter; the three dots beneath it are the segol – sounds like "eh" so this is "Eh"

    3)   Think about the lesson:
       Read the following verses and write down what God says will happen if we marry people who are not following Him.
       Genesis 27:46 _____
       Exodus 34:16 _____
       Numbers 25:1-3 _____
       Numbers 31:16 _____
       Deuteronomy 7:3-4 _____

Day 2:

    1)   Bible Memory: Review Genesis 2:2-3 and Genesis 3:15. Memorize 2 Corinthians 6:14.

    2)   Practice Hebrew: לֹ

Lamed – sounds like "L" and the dot to the top right of the letter is the holem – sounds like "oh"
So, together, sounds like "Low"

    3)   Think about the lesson:
       Read the following verses and write down what happens to the leaders of God's people when they marry unbelievers.
       Joshua 23:12-13 _____
       1 Kings 11:1-11 _____
       2 Chronicles 18:1 _____
       Ezra 9:1-2 _____
       Nehemiah 13:23-27 _____

Day 3:

1) Bible Memory: Review Genesis 2:2-3 and Genesis 3:15. Memorize 2 Corinthians 6:14.

2) Practice Hebrew: הִ

Heh – sounds like "h" and the dot beneath it is the hireq – sounds like "ee" or "ih" so together this sounds like "hee"

3) Think about the lesson:
Read the following verses and write down what God says about Godly relationships and having Godly offspring.
Malachi 2:15 _____
Matthew 24:38 _____
1 Corinthians 7:39 _____
2 Corinthians 6:14-18 _____
James 4:4 _____
Revelation 2:14 _____

Day 4:

1) Bible Memory: Review Genesis 2:2-3 and Genesis 3:15. Memorize 2 Corinthians 6:14.

2) Practice Hebrew: י

Yod – sounds like "y"

3) Think about the lesson: There are many stories of ancient giants who terrorized the world. Consider these: 1) the Nephilim of the Bible, 2) the Titans of Greek mythology, 3) Peru's god who is said to have created stone giants that soon began to fight, 4) Marduk from Babylonian mythology, 5) the Montagnais people of Canada who believed that a race of giants was destroying the earth (causing God to become angry and so He commanded the people to build a large canoe!), 6) the Oklahoma Pawnee who believed that the first living creatures were giants who became very arrogant, 7) the Aztecs who believed that the first creatures were big ugly giants who refused to worship God, 8) the Celts who believed that the devil married women and had wicked giants for children, 9) Ymir from Norway who was a frost giant, 10) a group of ancient giants from England who were blamed for burning villages. The list goes on.
Spend some time researching these stories and finding others.
What do you notice?

_____

_____

Given the evidence from the Bible and from other ancient texts, do you think giants actually existed? Why or why not?

_____

_____

Day 5:

    1)   Bible Memory: Review Genesis 2:2-3 and Genesis 3:15. Memorize 2 Corinthians 6:14.

    2)   Practice Hebrew: ם

Final mem (or mem sofeet) – the form of this letter that is found at the end of a word - sounds like "m"

    3)   Think about the lesson:
       In the scriptures, the term "sons of God" sometimes means angels and sometimes means believers. For example, in Job 1:6, the sons of God are angels, and in Romans 8:14-17, the sons of God are believers in Yeshua. Do a word study by searching the phrase "sons of God" and looking up all the verses and passages you find. What do you notice?
       Verses you looked up:

_____

_____

       Your comments:

_____

_____

       Read Matthew 22:23-33. What does Yeshua's answer reveal to you?

_____

_____

       Also read Jude 6. How do you think Genesis 6:1-4 is best interpreted?

_____

_____

_____

_____

Day 6:

    1)   Bible Memory: Review Genesis 2:2-3 and Genesis 3:15. Memorize 2 Corinthians 6:14.

    2)   Practice Hebrew: אֱלֹהִים

Elohim – God; note that El by itself means God also and that Elohim is the plural form. There is only one God, and He exists in three persons: Father, Son, and Spirit.

    3)   Think about the lesson: Is it Godly love? Or is it sinful lust?
       Read 1 Corinthians 13:4-7. Fill in the chart with the missing words, using 1 Corinthians 13:4-7.

Love	Lust
	Impatient, in a hurry, wants it now
Kind	
	Bragging
	Prideful
Polite	
	Self-seeking, self-centered
	Easily angered
	Holds grudges; unforgiving
Tells the truth	
	Puts partner at risk
Trustworthy and can trust	
Hopeful	
	Gives up easily, fleeting, never satisfied

When you are looking for a spouse, what are some values you will look for in him or her?

_____

_____

What values should you have in order to be a good husband or wife?

_____

_____

LESSON 4
NOACH PART 2

Lesson Objectives: See salvation through the story of the Ark. See the evidence for a global flood that happened exactly as the Bible describes it.

Bible Memory: Hebrews 11:7 By faith, Noah, when warned about things not yet seen, in holy fear built an ark to save his family. By faith he condemned the world and became heir of the righteousness that comes by faith.

Hebrew Word: אֵת Et – this word does not have a translation in English. Grammatically, it points to the direct object in a sentence in Hebrew. It is called a direct object marker. Notably, this word consists of the first and last letters of the Hebrew alephbet – the aleph and the tav. Who else is called the first and the last?

Lesson Summary:

When we are young, we believe what people tell us. When we are told something over and over again, we believe it to be true. Correcting our beliefs later in life is very difficult, so it's important to understand the truth from as young an age as possible. Many children are read stories of dinosaurs and told that they lived "millions and millions of years ago." This idea of millions and millions of years gets ingrained in a child's head, and the belief that this is true lasts into adulthood. However, the evolutionist's tales and timelines do not line up with the Bible. Evolutionists do not believe there was a global flood, even though there is archeological evidence for a catastrophic flood found all over the world. Since this evidence does not make sense with their long-ingrained mantra of "millions and millions of years," they cannot accept what is clearly in front of them.

In Genesis 6, when God sees how great the wickedness of man on the earth had become, He tells Noah, the only one of his generation to find favor with the Lord, to build an ark and take himself and his family onto it. God also sends the animals, two of every unclean kind, and seven pairs of every clean kind, to join Noah and his family on the ark. God gives Noah the instructions on how to build the ark, which is large enough to be seaworthy in a storm and to house all those animals and the food they would need for a year.

We know that the Biblical account of the flood is true for three reasons: 1) We know that there was a flood because many cultures record the existence of one (and it's highly unlikely that they all spontaneously made up similar stories); 2) We know that the Biblical account of the flood is superior to the other stories of the flood because the details and dimensions are all realistic and practical (unlike tales of a boat that is cube-shaped, for example); and 3) the rock layers and the fossils they contain demonstrate a world-wide catastrophic flood event.

For so many cultures to have recorded a catastrophic flood story, we know that there must have been one. Native American tribes from both the northern and southern continents have stories that tell about how violence and arrogance led to the angering of God (whom they call by different names according to their languages) who then flooded the earth, destroying its inhabitants. These stories are not as detailed and specific as the Biblical account, nor do they make much practical sense. For example, one story says that there was one man saved from the flood because he was in a canoe, and after the flood, he repopulated the earth with his tribe. This leaves us with the question of how one man (without a wife) repopulated the earth?

Another story, this one from Asia, says that a family of eight escaped the flood waters in a cube-shaped boat. We know that a cube-shaped boat would not have been seaworthy; it would not have survived a catastrophic flood. Yet, the fact that these stories exist proves that there was an event that prompted the telling of these stories. Without a copy of the Biblical account in hand, it would have been easy for the stories to get corrupted over the years in the telling and retelling from generation to generation, somewhat like the telephone game.

The world is covered with rock layers. Some of these rock layers stretch across entire continents with matching layers found in continents across oceans. Evolutionists believe that these layers were laid down over millions and millions of years. However, none of the layers show any evidence of erosion. Therefore, the evolutionist's story does not make sense. We know from observing recent catastrophic floods that layers of earth are laid down in a matter of minutes, hours, or days and appear in the same types of formations that we see in layers that have been left by the Biblical flood. A modern day example of this is the flooding caused by the eruption of Mt. Saint Helen's in 1980. In contrast, the pre-flood earth floor layer that existed before the flood, the earth that Adam and Eve up until Noah walked on, shows evidence of erosion; the evolutionists do not understand why this layer shows erosion and the other layers do not. Evolutionists call this the Great Unconformity and they cannot explain it. The Bible explains it well!

We also know that fossils are formed rapidly, not over millions of years. For a fossil to form, it must be quickly encased in dirt and water. This kills it fast and prevents oxygen and scavengers from destroying its remains. The water flows through the dirt covered creature, leaving mineral deposits that calcify and create the fossil. Fossils are found all over the earth inside the layers left by the flood. Some of these fossils cut up through multiple layers; these are called polystrate fossils, and they disprove the evolutionist's idea that different creatures lived at different times in the layers that were supposedly laid down over millions and millions of years. Many animal fossils are discovered with their heads arched backwards. This is a death pose characterizing a death by flood. As the waters swept dirt over the creatures, rolling them under, they may have arched their backs in a struggle to find air, to escape, or because the waters rolled them into that position, breaking their necks. Some died so quickly that they have been fossilized in the act of giving birth!

How did Noah fit all those animals on the ark? Remember that God sent pairs of each kind. A kind is the family level of taxonomy; for example, the canine kind includes all the domestic dogs plus coyotes and wolves. There would not have to have been pairs of each species, just of each kind. God has designed DNA so that all the genetic information to develop different species is contained in the DNA of each kind. From one pair of canines on the ark, all the species of canines we see today developed. Also, Noah most likely took young animals on the ark. They would have been smaller, would have needed less food, and would have had more years to procreate later when they got off the ark and began to repopulate the earth.

Where there dinosaurs on the ark? Yes! All land-dwelling animals that breathed air were included. Most dinosaurs were not huge, and like giraffes and elephants, their young ones would have been a manageable size to board the ark. After the flood, many kinds of dinosaurs went extinct along with other kinds of animals due to various reasons: changes in habitat, food sources, predation, humans killing them, etc. There is evidence that humans and dinosaurs lived together up until about the Middle Ages. We hear stories of knights fighting dragons, and we see drawings and carvings of different dinosaurs like the Stegosaurus and the Brontosaurus, etc.

The story of the flood in Genesis 6-8 is certainly a story of judgment and of catastrophe, but it is also a story of love and grace and salvation. For God to continue to allow the evil that had grown on the earth to survive may have meant the elimination of the Godly line through which the Promised Messiah would come. God's grace and favor were not just for Noah but for all of humanity.

Weekly Assignments:

Day 1:

1) Bible Memory: Memorize Hebrews 11:7. Review Genesis 2:2-3.

2) Practice Hebrew: אֵת Et – this word does not have a translation in English. Grammatically, it points to the direct object in a sentence in Hebrew. It is called a direct object marker. Notably, this word consists of the first and last letters of the Hebrew alephbet – the aleph and the tav. Who else is called the first and the last? (Read Isaiah 44:6, Revelation 1:8, and Revelation 22:13-16 to find out)

_____

_____

3) Think about the lesson: Read Genesis 6:14-18. How big was the ark?

_____

_____

Day 2:

1) Bible Memory: Memorize Hebrews 11:7. Review Genesis 3:15.

2) Practice Hebrew: בְּרֵאשִׁית בָּרָא אֱלֹהִים

Bereshit bara Elohim

In the beginning God created

Notice that in Hebrew, the verb comes first and then the noun (which is the subject doing the action).

3) Think about the lesson: Read Genesis 6:19-7:3.
   a. _____ of every unclean animal, male and female
   b. _____ pairs, male and female, of every clean animal
        i. For food and for sacrifices
        ii. Genesis 7:2 Sheva sheva ish v'ishto – seven seven a male and his female – this is specific in Hebrew whereas there is some confusion in various English translations
   c. Kind = Family level in Taxonomy, so Canine = one Kind; Feline = one Kind
   d. ***Species developed from the Kinds***, so each kind was represented; there was no need to take a pair from each species.
   e. Young animals = smaller , to fit on the ark, and better suited for procreating after leaving the ark
   f. Animals with the "breath of life"
   g. Total number of animals: approximately 7000

Day 3:

1) Bible Memory: Memorize Hebrews 11:7. Review 2 Corinthians 6:14.

2) Practice Hebrew: אֵת Et – this word does not have a translation in English. Grammatically, it points to the direct object in a sentence in Hebrew. It is called a direct object marker. When we put this together with the rest of the verse, we know that there will be a direct object following it. In the beginning, God created . . .

בְּרֵאשִׁית בָּרָא אֱלֹהִים אֵת

3) Think about the lesson: What is the timeline? Adonai is very specific about the dates.

Genesis 7:6-10	7 days, animals gather
Genesis 7:11-16	17th day of the 2nd month; 40 days of heavy rains, flooding begins
Genesis 7:17-24	for 150 days the earth is flooded
Genesis 8:1-4	after another 150 days (17th day of the 7th month) ark rests over Ararat
Genesis 8:5	1st day of the 10th month, waters receding
Genesis 8:6-9	40 days, Noah sends out the raven and the dove
Genesis 8:10-11	7 days, the dove returns
Genesis 8:12	7 days, the dove does not return
Genesis 8:13-20	27th day of the 2nd month, they leave the ark

Day 4:

1) Bible Memory: Memorize Hebrews 11:7. Review Genesis 2:2-3.

2) Practice Hebrew: בְּרֵאשִׁית בָּרָא אֱלֹהִים אֵת

3) Think about the lesson: Was it a global flood?
   a. Read Genesis 6:7, 12-13, 17; 7:19-23
   b. Sedimentary rock layers cover vast swaths of the earth
   c. Fossils exist worldwide
   d. Marine fossils exist on the highest mountains
   e. Flood histories exist in all cultures around the world

Day 5:

1) Bible Memory: Memorize Hebrews 11:7. Review Genesis 3:15.

2) Practice Hebrew: בְּרֵאשִׁית בָּרָא אֱלֹהִים אֵת

3) Think about the lesson: Compare Genesis 1:2 to Genesis 8:1. What do you see?

_____

Day 6:

1) Bible Memory: Memorize Hebrews 11:7. Review 2 Corinthians 6:14.

2) Practice Hebrew: בְּרֵאשִׁית בָּרָא אֱלֹהִים אֵת

3) Think about the lesson:
   a. Read Genesis 8:6-12
   b. The raven and the dove: Which is clean? Which is unclean?
   c. The raven is a scavenger. It can happily feed on dead rotting things. Who else roams to and fro over the earth? _____Job 1:7, 1 Peter 5:8
   d. The dove symbolizes _____ John 1:32
   e. The olive **leaf** symbolizes _____ Romans 11:17-24 (branches), Zechariah 4:1-6 and 11-14 (trees and branches), Revelation 11:3-6 (trees)

LESSON 5
LECH LECHA PART 1

Lesson Objective: Interconnectedness: God's people are a blessing to the world.

Bible Memory Verse: Genesis 12:3 I will bless those who bless you, and whoever curses you I will curse; and all peoples on earth will be blessed through you.

Hebrew Word: הַשָּׁמַיִם hashamayim – the heavens

Lesson Summary:

After Noah and his family departed the ark, they began repopulating the earth. As new families grew and the population expanded, they grouped together at Babel. This was not good, since God had commanded them to spread out and fill the earth. Also, the tower they built was in opposition to what God had planned for them. Interestingly, the name in Babylonian means "gate of God," but in Hebrew it means "confusion." God confused the languages there so that people would not be able to communicate, to work against His commands, and would have to spread out as He had intended them to from the beginning. Before the flood, it's possible that the earth's continents were one huge massive continent that then split during the catastrophic flood period. So, in addition to the confusion of the languages, the continents were drifting away from each other, so people were spreading out over the entire globe.

As multiple languages appeared and people groups began drifting away from one another, the stories of their history began to change; that's why we see differences in flood stories, stories of giants, creation stories, etc. From the beginning, people have had the choice to follow the one Creator God or to follow a god of their making. Of all the seemingly abundant religious choices on this earth and in our time, this is really what our choices boil down to: God's way or not-God's way. Anything that is not God's way is idolatry. In fact, in German, the word for idolatry is literally "not-God" – Abgott. Idolatry abounded, because then, like now, we want to do our own thing rather than be obedient to the will of God. In Abraham's day, idols looked like statues; today, idols look like self-centered narcissism and/or adoption of religious practices and beliefs that are against the Bible. Many people today are outspoken followers of Satan, while others are unknowing followers. Satan's mantra is "Do what you will." Our idolatrous culture has eaten that up to the full! Abraham's culture looked a little different, but Satan's tactics were the same, and in this Torah portion, God calls Abraham out of idolatry, out of the land where he was, and calls him into a new land and a covenantal relationship with Him. From Abraham's line, the Messiah would be born.

This is what makes the Jewish people special. This is the line, the tribe, to whom God gave the words of scripture and from whom the Messiah would be born. In this way, the Jewish people are a blessing to all the peoples of the earth.

Weekly Assignments:

Day 1:

1) Bible Memory: Memorize Genesis 12:3.

2) Hebrew Practice: ‏הַ‎ ha – the

‏הַ‎ hey – sounds like "h;" with the patach vowel beneath it sounds like "ha;" and attached to the front of a word, it means "the"

3) Think about the lesson: Read Genesis 12:1-3. What does God tell Abram (Abraham's name before God changed his name to Abraham) to do? And what does God promise Abram?

_____

_____

Day 2:

1) Bible Memory: Memorize Genesis 12:3.

2) Hebrew Practice: ‏שׁ‎ shin – sounds like "sh"

3) Think about the lesson: Read Exodus 19:5-6. If the Israelites obey God commandments and keep His covenant, what will they be to God?

_____

Day 3:

1) Bible Memory: Memorize Genesis 12:3.

2) Hebrew Practice: ‏מַיִם‎ mayim – the first mem is the form found at the beginning or in the middle of a word; the second mem is the final form (mem sofeet) found at the end of a word. With the yod in the middle, this word means "water."

3) Think about the lesson: Read Exodus 19:5-6 again. What will the Israelites be for the world? A _____ nation that is a kingdom of _____.

Day 4:

1) Bible Memory: Review Genesis 12:3, Hebrews 11:7, 2 Corinthians 6:14.

2) Hebrew Practice: ‏הַשָּׁמַיִם‎ hashamayim – the heavens

3) Think about the lesson: Read Isaiah 49:6. God will make the Jewish people to be a _____ for the _____ that they may bring _____ to the ends of the earth.

Day 5:

1) Bible Memory: Review Genesis 12:3, Genesis 3:15, and Genesis 2:2-3.

2) Hebrew Practice: בְּרֵאשִׁית בָּרָא אֱלֹהִים אֵת הַשָּׁמַיִם

       In the beginning, God created the heavens

3) Think about the lesson: Read Romans 3:1-2. What advantage is there is being Jewish?

_____

Day 6:

1) Bible Memory: Review Genesis 12:3, Genesis 2:2-3, Genesis 3:15, 2 Corinthians 6:14, Hebrews 11:7.

2) Hebrew Practice: בְּרֵאשִׁית בָּרָא אֱלֹהִים אֵת הַשָּׁמַיִם

       In the beginning, God created the heavens

3) Think about the lesson: Many in our world today are Anti-Semitic, which means that they don't like Jews. What does Genesis 12:3 say about that? When we hear Anti-Semitic comments or observe Anti-Semitic actions, what should our response be?

_____

_____

LESSON 6
LECH LECHA PART 2

Lesson Objective: Calling: what's your calling? What are your gifts and talents? How can you build God's kingdom?

Memory Verse: John 15:16-17 You did not choose me, but I chose you and appointed you to go and bear fruit – fruit that will last. Then the Father will give you whatever you ask in my Name. This is my command: Love each other.

Hebrew Words: וְאֵת הָאָרֶץ v'et haaretz – and the earth

Lesson Summary:

God called Abram out of Haran. Abram's name means "exalted father;" later God changed Abram's name to Abraham because He would make him a father of many nations. The funny thing is, Abraham and Sarah (whose name was Sarai before God changed it) didn't have any children. How would Abraham become the father of many nations if he wasn't a father? Even though things didn't always make sense, Abraham trusted God.

In addition to trusting God, Abraham had other qualities that made him a good leader. He was not afraid to stand up for his faith and to act on his faith by leaving everything he knew behind him to set out for a new land. He exercised good discernment when determining right from wrong. He was gracious in his dealings with Lot, and he loved Lot and took care of him. He handled his affairs well, and he gave God the glory for his successes. However, the Bible shows his faults as well. The Bible does this for every hero! Nobody is perfect (except for Yeshua). The Bible gives us a good picture of heroes we can follow as well as warnings about which actions not to repeat!

Just like Abraham, we have character qualities given to us by God that help make us who we are. Each one of us is unique and uniquely created by God for a purpose. When God reveals His purpose to us, we call that a "calling." Abraham was called to step out in faith and become a father of many nations. From him would come the promised son Isaac, who would have Jacob, who have the twelve sons who became the twelve tribes of Israel. From Israel would come the Messiah. All this started with Abraham!

Like Abraham, we have a unique calling. You may not know what your calling is yet, but if you stay connected to God through reading His Word, through prayer, through fellowship with Godly friends and mentors, and through obedience to His Word, then you will grow in Him and He will reveal your calling to you at the right time. If you recognize and accept Yeshua as the Messiah, then He sends the Ruach HaKodesh (Holy Spirit) to live in you and gift you with all the necessary gifts that you will need to accomplish the purpose He has for your life. The gifts of the Spirit combined with the talents that you were born with (given to you by God) and have developed, will enable you to be a part of building His kingdom.

Weekly Assignments:

Day 1:

1) Memory Verse: Memorize John 15:16-17.

2) Hebrew Words: וְאֵת v'et. The ו vav attached to the front of a word means "and." Many verses in Hebrew begin with "and." Here, the "and" is not at the beginning, though, but in the middle of the verse. It is followed by the direct object marker אֵת et, so we know that another direct object will come after it.

3) Think about the lesson: Read Genesis chapter 12. After reading the chapter, write down some your observations about Abram. What did he do well?

_____

_____

What did he handle poorly?

_____

_____

Day 2:

1) Memory Verse: Memorize John 15:16-17.

2) Hebrew Words: הָאָרֶץ haaretz –the earth

  הַ hey – sounds like "h;" with the patach, sounds like "ha"

  אָ aleph – silent letter; with the patach, sounds like "ah"

  רֶ resh – sounds like "r;" with the segol, sounds like "reh"

  ץ final tzade (tzade sofeet) – sounds like "tz" and is the form of the letter found at the end of a word

3) Think about the lesson: Read Genesis chapter 13. After reading the chapter, answer the following: What happened between Abram's herdsmen and the herdsmen of Lot?

_____

_____

How did Abram handle this?

_____

_____

Day 3:

1) Memory Verse: Review John 15:16-17 and Genesis 2:2-3.

2) Hebrew Words: בְּרֵאשִׁית בָּרָא אֱלֹהִים אֵת הַשָּׁמַיִם וְאֵת הָאָרֶץ

Beresheet bara Elohim et hashamayim v'et ha'aretz
In the beginning, God created the heavens and the earth.
This is Genesis 1:1 in Hebrew.

3) Think about the lesson: Read Genesis chapter 14. After reading the chapter, answer the following: What happened to Lot and his men?

_____
_____

How did Abram respond?

_____
_____

Day 4:

1) Memory Verse: Review John 15:16-17 and Genesis 3:15.

2) Hebrew Words: בְּרֵאשִׁית בָּרָא אֱלֹהִים אֵת הַשָּׁמַיִם וְאֵת הָאָרֶץ

In the beginning, God created the heavens and the earth.
Genesis 1:1.

3) Think about the lesson: Read John chapters 15-16. Read the chapters a second time, and pray that God would reveal to you what He has for you in this passage. Write down your thoughts here:

_____
_____
_____
_____

Day 5:

1) Memory Verse: Review John 15:16-17 and 2 Corinthians 6:14.

2) Hebrew Words: בְּרֵאשִׁית בָּרָא אֱלֹהִים אֵת הַשָּׁמַיִם וְאֵת הָאָרֶץ

In the beginning, God created the heavens and the earth.
Genesis 1:1.

3) Think about the lesson: Make a list of heroes from the Bible that you admire. What are the qualities about them that you find admirable?

_____

_____

_____

_____

Day 6:

1) Memory Verse: Review John 15:16-17, Hebrews 11:7, and Genesis 12:3.

2) Hebrew Words: בְּרֵאשִׁית בָּרָא אֱלֹהִים אֵת הַשָּׁמַיִם וְאֵת הָאָרֶץ

In the beginning, God created the heavens and the earth.
Genesis 1:1.

3) Think about the lesson: List the abilities and talents that God has given you.

_____

_____

Have you recognized and accepted Yeshua as the Messiah? _____

If not, pray that God would reveal His salvation to you.

If so, then the Spirit has given you spiritual gifts to be used for the building of His kingdom.
Brainstorm ways that you might be uniquely suited for building God's kingdom here on earth:

_____

_____

LESSON 7
LECH LECHA PART 3

Lesson Objectives: Know what a covenant is and know the covenants that God makes.

Memory Verse: Genesis 17: 7 I will establish my covenant as an everlasting covenant between me and you and your descendants after you for the generations to come, to be your God and the God of your descendants after you.

Hebrew Word: בְּרִית b'reet – covenant

Lesson Summary:

In our last lesson, we saw that God called Abraham, and Abraham responded in faith and obedience. In this lesson, we'll see that God made a covenant with Abraham. A covenant is like a promise that two people make to each other, but it's stronger than a promise. If we break a promise to a friend, their feelings may be hurt and our relationship may be damaged. A covenant, in contrast, is more like a legal document. There are serious consequences for breaking a covenant that stretch beyond just the two people who made it. For example, a marriage is a covenant. When a husband and wife decide to break that covenant by getting a divorce, it doesn't just affect them; if affects their children, and when enough people in a society get divorced, it affects the entire society. Covenants are meant to be kept.

The covenant that God makes with Abraham in Genesis 17 includes something that God will do and something that Abraham will do. It is at this time that God changes Abram's name to Abraham; Abram means "exalted father," but Abraham means "father of many." God says that He will make Abraham a father of many nations. In this covenant, God promises to give Abraham and his descendants the whole land of Canaan. Since God promised this, the land is called the Promised Land. It is the physical land of Israel, but in the Bible, the Promised Land also reminds us that we are looking forward to living in heaven with God. The Promised Land is symbolic of heaven. After God promises to give Abraham and his descendants the land for all generations to come, He tells Abraham what he must do. Abraham and all the male descendants after him must be circumcised. Since ancient days, the sign of circumcision is a sign of belonging to the chosen people of God. It is a sign of the covenant.

Consider other covenants in the Bible as we proceed through this week's reading assignments.

Weekly Assignments:

Day 1:

Bible Memory: Memorize Genesis 17:7. Write down all the verses you have memorized so far and place them in a jar. Each day this week, work on Genesis 17:7 and also pull out two verses from the jar for review.

Hebrew Word: בְּרִית b'reet – covenant

בְּ bet – sounds like "b" and the two dots beneath it that look like a colon is the vowel sheva, which here sounds like a very short "eh," so this together sounds like "beh"

רְ resh – sounds like "r" and the dot beneath it is the vowel hireq, which sounds like "ee" when it rolls in with the yod following it

י yod – sounds like "y," read with the resh and hireq before it and they all sounds like "ree"

ת tav – sounds like "t"

Think about the lesson: Read Genesis 9:8-17. What covenant does God make?

_____

What is the sign of this covenant?

_____

Day 2:

Bible Memory: Memorize Genesis 17:7. Pull two other verses from your verse jar and recite them for review.

Hebrew Word: בְּרִית b'reet – covenant

Think about the lesson: Read Exodus 19:5-6 and Exodus 24:7. What are the stipulations (rules) of this covenant? (Hint: See the chapters and verses in between what you read. Pay close attention to Exodus chapter 20)

_____
_____
_____
_____
_____

Day 3:

Bible Memory: Memorize Genesis 17:7. Pull two other verses from your verse jar and recite them for review.

Hebrew Word: בְּרִית b'reet – covenant

Think about the lesson: Read Deuteronomy chapters 29 and 30.
What is different about this covenant?
(Hint: see Deuteronomy 30:6) _____

Day 4:

Bible Memory: Memorize Genesis 17:7. Pull two other verses from your verse jar and recite them for review.

Hebrew Word: בְּרִית b'reet – covenant

Think about the lesson: Read Jeremiah 31:31-34. After reading the passage, write down what you notice about it:

_____

_____

_____

Day 5:

Bible Memory: Memorize Genesis 17:7. Pull two other verses from your verse jar and recite them for review.

Hebrew Word: בְּרִית b'reet – covenant

Think about the lesson: Matthew 26:27-28. What do you think Yeshua is talking about?

_____

Day 6:

Bible Memory: Memorize Genesis 17:7. Pull two other verses from your verse jar and recite them for review.

Hebrew Word: בְּרִית b'reet – covenant

Think about the lesson: Read Galatians 4 and Hebrews 8.

What was the shortcoming of the first covenant?

_____

_____

What makes the second covenant better?

_____

_____

Does God ever say to stop obeying Him? _____

Abiding by all covenants God gives us is good. Obedience shows our love for God, in that we want to please Him and to be in fellowship with Him. The superiority of the second covenant is that Yeshua's sacrifice on our behalf is the only way to have forgiveness for our sins and to bring us into salvation. He saves us from slavery to sin and death. He conquers the curse. We do not place our faith in ourselves and the work that we do; we place our faith in the work that He did.

LESSON 8
VAYERA

Lesson Objective: See God incarnate through the scriptures.

Memory Verse: John 1:14 The Word became flesh and made His dwelling among us. We have seen his glory, the glory of the one and only who came from the Father, full of grace and truth.

Hebrew Word: וַיֵּרָא vayera – and he appeared

Lesson Summary:

The name of this Torah portion is Vayera. It means "and he appeared." In this Torah portion, God appears to Abraham. He visits Abraham and Sarah with two angels accompanying him. In this visit, he tells Abraham that Abraham and Sarah will have a son. He also tells Abraham that he is going to destroy the cities of Sodom and Gomorrah for their sins. Abraham, knowing that his nephew Lot was living there, tries to save Lot by asking Adonai if He would spare the city if it had a certain number of righteous people in it. While they talk, the two angels leave and go rescue Lot's family from the coming destruction. To read the whole story, read Genesis 18-22.

What's really interesting about the name of this Torah portion and Lots' three visitors is that Adonai actually appears to Abraham. He and Abraham speak face to face! It is said that no one can see God and live. Yet Abraham speaks with Adonai face to face, and this is not the only time in the scriptures that this happens. When Adonai appears in bodily form, it is said that He is "incarnate." Incarnate means that God appears in human form. In your daily readings, you'll read about other places in the scriptures where Adonai appears to people in bodily form. The most amazing, of course, is when Adonai is born into this world as a baby, grows up as a perfect example for us to follow, dies for our sins, and resurrects to return to heaven and intercede for us. Adonai is Yeshua, God incarnate. He is the Word who became flesh and made His dwelling among us!

This can be difficult to understand, but God gives us little glimpses into what He is doing. Later in this Torah portion, God tells him to take Isaac, the son that God promised to Abraham and Sarah, and go sacrifice him. Abraham doesn't understand, but he is willing to obey God no matter what. When the time comes, Adonai stops Abraham and tells him that He will provide the lamb. And then Abraham sees the ram caught in the thicket that God provided for the sacrifice. This is in Genesis chapter 22, and this chapter is called the Akeida, or the binding of Isaac. It is central to understanding Judaism and understanding Yeshua. Yeshua is ultimately the Passover lamb that takes away the sins of the world. He is the salvation that God provides. A human cannot perform or be a sacrifice that can remove sin. Only Yeshua can, since He is the Word made flesh. He is both fully man and fully God. He is the only one in the world who can be our savior.

Day 1:

    1)   Bible Memory: Memorize John 1:14.

    2)   Hebrew Word: וַיֵּרָא vayera – and he appeared

        וַ vav – sounds like "v" and patah – sounds like "ah," so "Vah" The vav means "and."

        יֵּ yod – sounds like "y" and sere – sounds like "ay," so "yay"

        רָא resh – sounds like "r" and kametz – sounds like"ah," and the aleph is silent, so "rah"

    3)   Think about the lesson: Read the following passages and write down the names of the people to whom the LORD appears:
        a. Genesis 16:9-13 _____
        b. Genesis 18:1-3 _____
        c. Genesis 22:11-14 _____

Day 2:

    1)   Bible Memory: Memorize John 1:14. Choose three other verses to review.

    2)   Hebrew Word: וַיֵּרָא vayera – and he appeared

    3)   Think about the lesson: Read Genesis 32:24-43.
        a. With whom did Jacob wrestle? _____
        b. What did Jacob name the place? _____
        c. Why did Jacob give the place that name?

        _____

        _____

Day 3:

    1)   Bible Memory: Memorize John 1:14. Choose three other verses to review.

    2)   Hebrew Word: וַיֵּרָא vayera – and he appeared

    3)   Think about the lesson: Read Judges 6:11-24. In your own words, describe what happened:

        _____

        _____

        _____

Day 4:

1) Bible Memory: Memorize John 1:14. Choose three other verses to review.

2) Hebrew Word: וַיֵּרָא vayera – and he appeared

3) Think about the lesson: Read Judges 13:2-23.
   a. Why were Samson's parents afraid? _____
   b. Did they die? _____

Day 5:

1) Bible Memory: Memorize John 1:14. Choose three other verses to review.

2) Hebrew Word: וַיֵּרָא vayera – and he appeared

3) Think about the lesson: Read Daniel 3:23-29. Who was in the furnace with Shadrach, Meshach, and Abednego? _____

Day 6:

1) Bible Memory: Memorize John 1:14. Review all your verses.

2) Hebrew Word: וַיֵּרָא vayera – and he appeared

3) Think about the lesson: Read Joshua 5:13-15.
   a. What is the question that Joshua asks the commander of the LORD's army?

   _____

   _____

   b. And what is his response?

   _____

   _____

LESSON 9
TOLDOT, VAYETZEI, VAYISHLACH

Lesson Objective: Know about Jacob's life and understand the importance of birthrights and relationships.

Bible Memory Verse: Genesis 32:28 Then the man said, "Your name will no longer be Jacob, but Israel, because you have struggled with God and with men and have overcome."

Hebrew Word: ישראל Israel – he struggles or persists with God

Lesson Summary:

Abraham and Sarah finally had the son that God had promised them. They named him Isaac, which means "laughter," since Sarah had laughed when she heard that they would have a son in their old age. As Isaac grew up, his older half-brother Ishmael, the son of Sarah's maid Hagar, tormented him, causing his mother Sarah to send Hagar and Ishmael away. Ishmael later became the father of many tribes, and so did Isaac's other half-brothers, those born to Abraham and Keturah after Sarah died. Isaac, however, was the child that God hads promised through Abraham and Sarah, and Isaac became the father of Jacob, from whom the twelve tribes of Israel came. Abraham, Isaac, and Jacob are the patriarchs, or fathers of Israel, and their wives, Sarah, Rivkah (Rebecca), Rachel, and Leah are the matriarchs, or mothers.

Isaac and Rebecca had twins: Jacob and Esau. When they were inside Rebecca's womb, the babies were struggling with each other. Rebecca asked God why, and He told her the prophecy that the older would serve the younger. When they were born, Esau came out first, but Jacob was grasping Esau's heel. Jacob's name means "supplanter," meaning that he was trying to take his brother's place as firstborn. Being the firstborn child in this culture meant that he would receive twice the inheritance and the blessings.

Esau didn't seem to value his rights as firstborn, as we can see later when the boys grow up. Esau liked to hunt, but Jacob liked to stay home. Jacob was home one day making a pot of stew when Esau came in from a long hunt very hungry. He wanted some of the stew. Jacob didn't want to share it with him for free; he had a price. He asked Esau to sell him his birthright for a bowl of stew. Esau agreed.

Think about that for a moment. A birthright is a long-term, permanent inheritance. Esau sells it for a bowl of stew. A bowl of stew is quickly eaten and does not keep us full for more than a few hours. It is not long-term or permanent. Why on earth would Esau sell his birthright for a bowl of stew? Because he is hungry at that moment and he loses sight of the long-term picture. He is focused on his perceived needs in that moment, and he is not focused on the future of his life.

What is our long-term picture? What are some ways that we in our culture "sell" our long-term blessings from God for a momentary pleasure?

Later, Isaac their father planned to bestow blessings on Esau. His wife, their mother Rebecca, found out what his plans were, and she told Jacob to go get a lamb and prepare it for dinner and pretend to be Esau so that he, Jacob, could get the blessings meant for Esau from their father Isaac.

Since Isaac was blind, Rebecca told Jacob to cover his arms with the lamb's fur so that when Isaac felt his arms, he would think that Jacob was his hairy brother Esau.

Jacob did all that his mother had recommended, and Isaac blessed him with the blessings of the firstborn, thinking the whole time that he was blessing Esau.

When Esau found out what happened, he swore to kill Jacob, so Jacob ran away.

Jacob stopped for the night at a place he later named Bethel, for in this place, he had a dream. He used a stone for his pillow. Imagine: after running away from his brother who wanted to kill him, Jacob was surely experiencing tiredness of body and soul, and he used a stone for a pillow! That doesn't sound very comfortable at all! Yet, he slept with his head on this stone and dreamt of a ladder reaching up to the heavens with angels ascending and descending on it. When we woke, he realized the importance of his dream and named the place Bethel, or house of God.

Jacob continued his journey the next day and came to a well where he met shepherds from Haran. He asked them if they knew his relative Laban. They did! And they told him that the shepherdess that was coming over to the well was Laban's daughter, and this is how Jacob met Rachel.

Jacob returned with Rachel to Laban's house and proposed to work seven years for Laban in return for Rachel because he wanted to marry her. Laban agreed. Jacob worked hard for Laban and helped his herds prosper and become very fruitful. At the end of the seven years, Laban tricked Jacob into marrying Leah, Rachel's older sister, instead of Rachel. And then he gave Rachel to Jacob as well, in exchange for another seven years of work.

While Jacob worked, Rachel and Leah competed with each other for children. Leah was able to have children, but Rachel was not. So Rachel gave her maid to Jacob to have children with on her behalf, and so Leah did the same with her maid. Finally, Rachel was able to conceive two sons of her own. In this way, Jacob had a total of twelve sons between the four women.

After fourteen years of working for Laban, who wasn't the best of bosses, Jacob was ready to leave. He and his wives and children and herds set off for Canaan.

On the way, Jacob heard news that Esau was coming to meet him. Jacob feared that Esau might still want to kill him, even after all those years, so he sent gifts to Esau ahead of him to soften his heart. The night before they met, Jacob went down to the river Jabbock and had a strange experience. There was a man there, and Jacob and the man wrestled all night long. Apparently, this was no ordinary man, for after he touched Jacob's hip socket and wrenched it, Jacob insisted that he would not let go until the man blessed him. The man said that Jacob's name would be Israel, for he had wrestled with God and with man and had overcome. Then he blessed him.

Day 1:

1) Bible Memory: Memorize Genesis 32:28.

2) Hebrew Word: יִשְׂרָאֵל Israel – he struggles or persists with God

   יִ   yod – sounds like "y"

   שְׂ   sin – sounds like "s"

   רָ   resh– sounds like "r"

   אֵ   aleph – silent

ל lamed – sounds like "l"

3) Think about the lesson: Read Genesis chapters 25-27.

The Bible doesn't show people as superheroes who never make mistakes; it shows people the way we really are. Even when we follow God, we still make mistakes. Sometimes, we do what our parents did. Isaac did something that his father did also regarding his wife. What was it?

_____

Isaac and Rebekah each had a favorite son. Which one favored which son and why?

_____

How do you think this favoritism might have affected family life?

_____

Day 2:

1) Bible Memory: Memorize Genesis 32:28. Choose three other verses to review.

2) Hebrew Word: ישראל Israel – he struggles or persists with God

3) Think about the lesson: Read Genesis 28-30. In the chart below, fill in the names of each of Jacob's sons and daughter beneath the names of their mothers.

Leah	Bilhah	Zilpah	Rachel
1)	1)	1)	1)
2)	2)	2)	2) Benjamin Gen 35:18
3)			
4)			
5)			
6)			
7) (daughter)			

Day 3:

1) Bible Memory: Memorize Genesis 32:28. Choose three other verses to review.

2) Hebrew Word: ישראל Israel – he struggles or persists with God

3) Think about the lesson: Read Genesis 31 and 32.

What did Rachel take from her father's house?

_____

Who is the man that Jacob wrestled with at the Jabbock river?

_____

Day 4:

1) Bible Memory: Memorize Genesis 32:28. Choose three other verses to review.

2) Hebrew Word: יִשְׂרָאֵל Israel – he struggles or persists with God

3) Think about the lesson: Read Genesis 33 and 34.

Why do you think Jacob didn't want to travel with Esau?

_____

What happened to Dinah? What lessons can we learn from her story?

_____

_____

_____

Day 5:

1) Bible Memory: Memorize Genesis 32:28. Choose three other verses to review.

2) Hebrew Word: יִשְׂרָאֵל Israel – he struggles or persists with God

3) Think about the lesson: Read Genesis 35.

What happened to Rachel?

_____

What did she name her second son? _____

What did Jacob rename him? _____

Think: These two names may represent the two comings of Messiah:
Son of my suffering and
Son of my right hand.

Day 6:

1) Bible Memory: Memorize Genesis 32:28. Choose three other verses to review.

2) Hebrew Word: יִשְׂרָאֵל Israel – he struggles or persists with God

3) Think about the lesson: Jacob wrestled with God physically by a river. Some say that his new name, Israel, also suggests that he wrestled with God in prayer. God confirmed His covenant with Jacob twice in these chapters, once at Bethel and again at Peniel. God showed Jacob that He is actively involved in our lives, and that our lives have a purpose.

LESSON 10
VAYESHEV, MIKETZ, AND VAYIGASH

Lesson Objective: Joseph in Egypt appeared to be an Egyptian – his brothers did not recognize him. In a similar way, Yeshua's brothers do not recognize Him today.

Memory Verse: Romans 8:28 And we know that God works all things together for good, for those that love God and are called according to his purpose.

Hebrew Word: מצרים Mitzraim – Egpyt

Lesson Summary:

We learned about Jacob in the last lesson, and we saw that he had twelve sons. These twelve sons became the twelve tribes of Israel. In this lesson, we'll see how Jacob's son, Joseph, who was Rachel's firstborn, saved the world from a famine.

Jacob loved Joseph more than his other sons, and they knew it. It made them jealous.

Joseph had dreams that indicated that his brothers and even his mother and father would someday bow down to him. This was unheard of! In this culture, older children did not bow to younger children, and parents would never have bowed to their children. This upset the proper order. So when Joseph shared his dreams, his brothers became even more jealous than before.

One day, when Joseph went out to find his brothers, they saw him coming and decided to throw him in a pit. He was sold to traveling merchants, and in this way, he was brought to Egypt and sold as a slave to a man named Potiphar, who was the captain of the guard. Joseph's brothers robbed him of his special cloak that his father Jacob had given him, and they brought the cloak back to Jacob. They dipped the cloak in blood and gave it to their father, allowing him to believe that Joseph had been killed by wild animals. This broke his father's heart.

In Egypt, Joseph worked hard and well for Potiphar, and Potiphar prospered as a result. So Potiphar put Joseph in charge of everything in his household. However, Potiphar's wife lied about him to her husband, actually accusing him of what she had tried to do. Although Joseph was totally innocent, Potiphar did not investigate. He believed his wife's lies and threw Joseph into prison.

While in prison, Joseph interpreted dreams for the pharaoh's chief baker and cupbearer. His interpretations came true.

Later, when the Pharaoh had some disturbing dreams, he called for his wise men, but no one could interpret his dreams. The cupbearer suddenly remembered Joseph, and he told Pharaoh that Joseph could interpret dreams. After Pharaoh sent for Joseph, Joseph was quick to correct that God interpreted dreams, not him.

Joseph delivered God's interpretation of the dreams to Pharaoh. The world would experience seven years of good harvests and then seven years of famine. Pharaoh was so delighted to have his dreams explained that he put Joseph in charge of everything under him.

Joseph acted wisely on the interpretation of the dreams. As the seven years of plenty progressed, Joseph saved all the extra grain that would be needed for the coming seven years of famine.

As the famine progressed and the world became hungry, everyone traveled to Egypt to buy grain. In this way, Joseph's wisdom and good management kept the world's population from starving to death during that time.

Joseph's brothers were some of the people who came to Egypt to buy food. When they first arrived, they did not recognize him, but he recognized them right away. He did not tell them who he was. He questioned them and found out that his brother Benjamin was alive. He told his brothers to go home and get Benjamin and bring him back. They still did not recognize Joseph, and now they were terrified. Their father Jacob had grieved so deeply for the loss of Joseph, and now Benjamin was his favorite. What would happen if they brought Benjamin to Egypt? Yet Joseph insisted.

The brothers returned home with heavy hearts. They had the food they needed for a while, but how would they go back for more? They couldn't deprive their father of Benjamin, nor could they show up before Joseph without him. To make matters worse, the money they had used to pay for the grain from Egypt somehow showed up in each brother's pack! They were so afraid.

When the grain ran out and it was time to return to Egypt to buy more, Judah convinces his father to let him bring Benjamin, and he takes personal responsibility. Jacob agrees, although he doesn't like it, and the brothers pack gifts along with twice the silver they will need.

When they arrive in Egypt, they are taken immediately to Joseph's house. The brothers have no idea that this is for the purpose of eating dinner at Joseph's house. They fear they will be made slaves. They quickly take their silver out of their sacks and explain that they do not know how it came to be back in their sacks after their last purchase. The steward assures them that he received their payment in full last time. What a miracle!

Joseph tests his brothers twice to see if they can be trusted. First, he favors Benjamin with more food than any of the other brothers. Then he secretly has his own silver cup placed in Benjamin's sack.

Are his brothers still jealous? Will they get rid of Benjamin as readily as they got rid of him?

When Benjamin is discovered to have the silver cup, all the brothers rush to volunteer themselves to be slaves. They beg Joseph not to keep Benjamin, for it would kill their father.

At this, Joseph dismisses all the servants and reveals himself to his brothers. It is a joyful and tearful reunion! Joseph sends them home to get their father and their families and move to Egypt for the remainder of the famine.
Joseph's life shows us that God has a plan for each one of us, and even if things don't look great, God can have a purpose in that. God used the awful situations that Joseph endured to bring good out of it. Because of Joseph's obedience to God, Joseph was able to save the world at the time from dying in the famine.

Yeshua's first coming as the Messiah ben Joseph, the Suffering Servant, was like this. His brothers, the Jewish people, do not recognize who He is. Just as Joseph was unrecognizable to his brothers because he looked

60

Egyptian, so Yeshua looks to his brothers and sisters like someone from a different family – the Jesus that so many see today does not look Jewish at all! But Yeshua was and is Jewish. He is the Messiah. Yeshua saved the entire world from the eternal death that sin causes by dying for the sins of the world on the cross. He laid down His life for us. We are the ones who have done wrong; we deserve to die. He was perfect, and he bought our salvation with the sacrifice of His perfect life. He is the right hand of salvation that brings us out of spiritual death! Romans 11 tells us that there will be a reunion in the future with His Jewish brothers and sisters!

Day 1:

1) Bible Memory: Memorize Romans 8:28.

2) Hebrew Word: מצרים Mitzraim – Egpyt

3) Think about the lesson: Think about Romans 8:28. How does this verse prove true in Joseph's life?

_____

_____

_____

_____

Day 2:

1) Bible Memory: Review Romans 8:28. Write all your memory verses on slips of paper and put them in a jar. Each day, review this week's memory verse and pull out three more from the jar to review.

2) Hebrew Word: מצרים Mitzraim – Egpyt

3) Think about the lesson: Read Genesis chapter 37. Consider the favoritism that Jacob shows to Joseph. Many of us live life the same way we were taught as children. Why do you think Jacob showed favoritism?

_____

_____

Day 3:

1) Bible Memory: Review Romans 8:28. Shuffle the verses in your jar, and pull out three more from the jar to review.

2) Hebrew Word: מצרים Mitzraim – Egpyt

3) Think about the lesson: Read Genesis 39-40. List some adjectives that describe what you can see of Joseph's character in these chapters:

_____   _____   _____

_____   _____   _____

Day 4:

1) Bible Memory: Review Romans 8:28. Shuffle the verses in your jar, and pull out three more from the jar to review.

2) Hebrew Word: מצרים Mitzraim – Egpyt

3) Think about the lesson: Read Genesis 41-42. How do Joseph's childhood dreams come true?

_____

_____

_____

Day 5:

1) Bible Memory: Review Romans 8:28. Shuffle the verses in your jar, and pull out three more from the jar to review.

2) Hebrew Word: מצרים Mitzraim – Egpyt

3) Think about the lesson: Read Genesis 43-44. Why did all the brothers eat separately from Joseph who was eating separately from the Egyptians?

_____

_____

Read Acts 13:26-41 and Luke 24:15-16. What connections do you see between Joseph and Yeshua?

_____

_____

Day 6:

1) Bible Memory: Review Romans 8:28. Shuffle the verses in your jar, and pull out three more from the jar to review.

2) Hebrew Word: מצרים Mitzraim – Egpyt

3) Think about the lesson: Read Genesis 45-47. Pray about this week's lessons. And then journal your thoughts:

_____

_____

_____

_____

_____

LESSON 11
VAYECHI

Lesson Objective: Know that Adonai has a plan, He has a way for us to be a part of His plan, and He provides us the choice to take our places in His plan.

Memory Verse: Genesis 49:10 The scepter will not depart from Judah, nor the ruler's staff from between his feet, until he to whom it belongs shall come and the obedience of the nations shall be his.

Hebrew Word: שבט מיהודה scepter from Judah

Lesson Summary:

In this chapter, Genesis 49, Jacob speaks prophetic words over his sons. Many consider these his blessings for them, but not all that he has to say is a blessing! He goes down the line in birth order. He recounts the things that they have done, and he is not pleased with some of their actions. But when he gets to Judah, we truly see a blessing.

Do you remember what King Achashverosh held in his hand when Esther dared to visit him uninvited? A scepter. If he lowered it before her, she would be forgiven and invited to speak, but if not, she would die. A scepter is a staff that represents that the holder is the King.

In Genesis 49:10, Jacob prophesies that Judah's line will be the line of the Messiah who will be King over all the nations.

Later in verse 18, Jacob says, "I wait for your salvation, O Lord." The word in Hebrew that means "salvation" is Yeshua.

Day 1:

1) Bible Memory: Memorize Genesis 49:10.
2) Hebrew Word: שבט מיהודה scepter from Judah

3) Think about the lesson: God has a plan for history. Read Genesis 49. Pray that God shows you what you need to know about His plan for history.

Day 2:

1) Bible Memory: Review Genesis 49:10 and three previous verses.
2) Hebrew Word: שבט מיהודה scepter from Judah
3) Think about the lesson: God has a plan specifically for us within His plan for history. Read Jeremiah 29:11. Pray and ask God what plans He has for you.

Day 3:

1) Bible Memory: Review Genesis 49:10 and three previous verses.

2) Hebrew Word: מיהודה שבט scepter from Judah

3) Think about the lesson: God's plan is focused on Yeshua. Yeshua is a direct descendant of the tribe of Judah. Read Matthew 1. Read Luke 19:28-40. Riding a donkey is a symbol of being King. Read Genesis 49:8-12 and compare it to Revelation 19:11-16. What do you notice?

_____

_____

Day 4:

1) Bible Memory: Review Genesis 49:10 and three previous verses.

2) Hebrew Word: מיהודה שבט scepter from Judah

3) Think about the lesson: To share in God's blessings, we must be followers of Yeshua within God's plan. If you have not already recognized and accepted Yeshua as the Messiah, take a few moments to pray and ask God to reveal Himself to you in a way that you can understand. If you are already following Yeshua, pray for Him to be revealed to others who need to know Him as savior.

Day 5:

1) Bible Memory: Review Genesis 49:10 and three previous verses.

2) Hebrew Word: מיהודה שבט scepter from Judah

3) Think about the lesson: We saw last week that Joseph's life is a picture of Yeshua as Messiah ben Joseph, the Suffering Servant. Yeshua came the first time to die for us, that we might be forgiven of our sins. The second time he comes, he will come as King, Messiah ben David, and he will rule all the nations from Jerusalem. Read about Judah's repentance in Genesis 44, specifically verse 16, but read the context, too. Do you remember why Judah needed to repent?

_____

_____

Day 6:

1) Bible Memory: Review Genesis 49:10 and three previous verses.

2) Hebrew Word: מיהודה שבט scepter from Judah

3) Think about the lesson: Read Psalm 110:1 and Matthew 22:44. What is Yeshua saying in Matthew 22?

_____

_____

_____

LESSON 12
BESHALACH

Lesson Objective: Adonai is our provider, protector, and guide.

Memory Verse: 1 Corinthians 10:2 They were all baptized into Moses in the cloud and in the sea.

Hebrew Word: עָנָן cloud

Lesson Summary:

After Joseph and his brothers were reunited, he invited the entire family to join him in Egypt for the remainder of the famine. They ended up staying about 400 years. At that time, a new Pharaoh arose who did not have respect for Joseph or the tribe of Israel. He enslaved the Israelite people. They cried out to God, and God heard them.

God sent Moses to bring his people out of Egypt. God sent ten terrible plagues (we'll learn more about these at Pesach). Until the last plague, the death of the firstborn, when Moses asked the Pharaoh to let them go, the Pharaoh said no. After the death of the firstborn, the Pharaoh allowed the Israelites to leave, but he quickly changed his mind and pursued them.

As the Israelites fled, they were led not only by Moses but by a great pillar moving ahead of them. During the day, it was a pillar of cloud; during the night, it was a pillar of fire. The Angel of God takes the form of a pillar of cloud and a pillar of fire. Why? Consider that the cloud is made of water particles. Water and fire are both life-sustaining and life-threatening. Both are life-sustaining for those who are following God, but life-threatening for those who are against God's people. In addition to leading the people, the pillars also separate God's people from their enemies, provide protection from the sun during the day (cloud), the cold during the night (fire), and hide the people from the Egyptians.

Day 1:

1) Bible Memory: Memorize 1 Corinthians 10:2.

2) Hebrew Word: עָנָן cloud

3) Think about the lesson: Read Exodus 14:19-20. How does God take care of Israel?

_____

_____

Day 2:

1) Bible Memory: Review 1 Corinthians 10:2 and three other verses.

2) Hebrew Word: עָנָן cloud

3) Think about the lesson: Read 1 Corinthians 10:1-4. What do you think it means to be baptized into Moses and into the sea?

_____
_____

Day 3:

1) Bible Memory: Review 1 Corinthians 10:2 and three other verses.

2) Hebrew Word: עָנָן cloud

3) Think about the lesson: How does God lead us today? Read Psalm 43:3 and 143:8.

_____
_____

Day 4:

1) Bible Memory: Review 1 Corinthians 10:2 and three other verses.

2) Hebrew Word: עָנָן cloud

3) Think about the lesson: How does God provide for us today? Read Philippians 4:19 and Matthew 6:33.

_____
_____

Day 5:

1) Bible Memory: Review 1 Corinthians 10:2 and three other verses.

2) Hebrew Word: עָנָן cloud

3) Think about the lesson: How does God protect us today? Read Psalm 121:4 and Psalm 138:7.

_____
_____

Day 6:

1) Bible Memory: Review 1 Corinthians 10:2 and three other verses.

2) Hebrew Word: עָנָן cloud

3) Think about the lesson: Spend some time today in prayer, asking for God's guidance in your life, and for His provision and protection.

LESSON 13
TERUMAH, TETZAVEH

Lesson Objective: We can learn about Yeshua from studying the Tabernacle.

Memory Verse: Hebrew 1:1-2 In the past, God spoke to our forefathers through the prophets at many times and in various ways, but in these last days he has spoken to us by his Son; whom he appointed heir of all things and through whom also he made the universe.

Hebrew Word: מִשְׁכָּן tabernacle (tent, place to dwell)

Lesson Summary:

As the Israelites followed Adonai into the wilderness, God gave them instructions for building a tabernacle for worship. The Israelites were coming out of Egypt, out of slavery. They wanted to follow God but didn't know how. They had been familiar with the gods of Egypt. Adonai had to show them how He wanted them to worship Him. So He told Moses how to build a tabernacle. The tabernacle was portable; they could move it around with them as they wandered in the wilderness. Later, the pattern for the Tabernacle would become the pattern for the Temple in Jerusalem.

The Tabernacle, or Mishkan, became the resting place for the pillar. The pillar of cloud rested over the Tabernacle when it was completed. This was Adonai in their midst.

Each part of the Tabernacle teaches us about Yeshua.

Here is a diagram of how the Tabernacle was designed:

Label each part of the Mishkan as you complete this week's assignments.

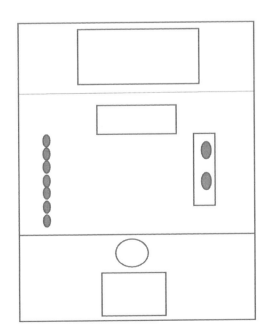

Day 1:

1) Bible Memory: Memorize Hebrews 1:1-2.

2) Hebrew Word: מִשְׁכָּן tabernacle (tent, place to dwell)

3) Think about the lesson: The mishkan is where Adonai meets with His people. It is where the cloud rested. This is a picture of Yeshua dwelling with His people. Read John 1:14 and Revelation 21:1-3. What do you see? _____

Upon entering the mishkan, worshippers approached the curtain. The curtain was woven of thread made of four colors: red, white, purple, and blue. The curtain represents Yeshua. The red symbolizes earth, blood, and the humanity of Yeshua. The white represents the righteousness of Yeshua. The purple signifies His royalty, and the blue reminds us that He came from heaven. We enter through the doorway that is Messiah. Read Hebrews 10:19-22. What do you see?

_____

Read Exodus 38:1-7. The bronze altar. This is where sacrifices were made. The animal sacrifices that occurred on this altar teach us about Yeshua. Sin is disobedience to God. The consequence of sin is death. They animal sacrifices represented atonement for sin. They were a representation only; a symbol of the coming Messiah. The blood of bulls and goats couldn't actually atone for human sins. Read Isaiah 1:11-18. Yeshua's blood, His death on the cross, atoned for us. The altar reminds us of this. Read Psalm 51:6-17, Hebrews 13:15, and 1 John 1:7-9. What do you see?

_____

_____

_____

Day 2:

1) Bible Memory: Memorize Hebrews 1:1-2.

2) Hebrew Word: מִשְׁכָּן tabernacle (tent, place to dwell)

3) Think about the lesson: Read Exodus 38:8. The bronze basin. The basin, or laver, was a big bowl of water. The metal the bowl was made of was made from the bronze mirrors the women used. They donated their mirrors for the building of this basin. The metal bowl and the water were both reflective, so looking into it to wash their hands the people could see their reflections. Water symbolizes the Word of God. As we enter the mishkan, we first enter through the curtain that represents Yeshua. Then we encounter the altar; we accept that He died for our sins. Then, we wash in the water of His Word. His Word purifies and cleanses us. Read James 1:22-25, Ephesians 5:26, Titus 3:5, Hebrews 10:22, and Deuteronomy 32:2. What do you see?

_____

_____

_____

Day 3:

1) Bible Memory: Memorize Hebrews 1:1-2 and review three other verses.

2) Hebrew Word: מִשְׁכָּן tabernacle (tent, place to dwell)

3) Think about the lesson: Read Exodus 37:17-23. The menorah. The outer court includes the altar and the basin. From here, the worshipper proceeds to the inner court. The inner court represents growing closer to Messiah. Inside the inner court, we find light, food, and sweet smelling incense. The menorah has the light. The menorah is a candlestick with one strong base and seven branches holding light in each. The base represents Yeshua (He is the light of the world), and the branches that hold His light represent those of us who carry His good news to the world. Our fire burns in oil, and the oil represents the Holy Spirit, or Ruach HaKodesh. May we all be on fire for God! This has been God's plan from the beginning. Read Isaiah 49:6, which is quoted in Acts 13:47, so read that, too. Also read John 8:12, John 15:1-8, and Revelation 1:12-20. What do you see?

_____

_____

_____

Day 4:

1) Bible Memory: Memorize Hebrews 1:1-2 and review three other verses.

2) Hebrew Word: מִשְׁכָּן tabernacle (tent, place to dwell)

3) Think about the lesson: Read Exodus 37:10-16. The table for the bread. Yeshua is the bread of life. Read John 6:30-35. What do you see?

_____

_____

Day 5:

1) Bible Memory: Memorize Hebrews 1:1-2 and review three other verses.

2) Hebrew Word: מִשְׁכָּן tabernacle (tent, place to dwell)

3) Think about the lesson: Read Exodus 37: 25-29. The altar of incense. The incense represents the prayers of the saints. (The "saints" as defined in Revelation 12:17 and 14:12, are those who hold to the testimony of Yeshua and to His commandments; they are not defined in the Bible as the "saints" of any religious denomination that proclaims sainthood upon people) Read Psalm 141:2 and Revelation 5:8. What do you see?

_____

_____

Day 6:

1) Bible Memory: Memorize Hebrews 1:1-2 and review three other verses.

2) Hebrew Word: מִשְׁכָּן tabernacle (tent, place to dwell)

3) Think about the lesson: Read Exodus 37:1-9. The Ark of the Covenant. As worshippers progressed from the outer court to the inner court, we see the walk of faith: first comes salvation through the sacrifice of Yeshua, then comes the washing of the water of His Word. After that, spiritual growth occurs through a deepening relationship with Yeshua. He is the light of the world and the bread of life, and when we dwell with Him, our prayers are a sweet smelling incense to Him. This is the Holy

Place. The next room is the Holy of Holies. This represents the presence of God. It was over the Holy of Holies that the pillar rested. The Ark of the Covenant was inside. No one was allowed in except for the High Priest, and he was only able to enter one time per year – on Yom Kippur. Read Revelation 4:1-6 and Revelation 5:9-10. What do you see?

_____

_____

Spend some time in prayer today.

LESSON 14
KI TISA

Lesson Objective: As Moses broke the tablets when he saw the golden calf, so Yeshua, who is the Word, was broken for us because of our sins.

Memory Verse: 1 Corinthians 11:23-24 For I received from the Lord what I also passed on to you: Messiah Yeshua, on the night he was betrayed, took bread, and when he had given thanks, he broke it and said, "This is my body, which is for you; do this in remembrance of me."

Hebrew Word: אֶבֶן even (pronounced eh-ven) stone. Interestingly, if you look at just the first two letters – the aleph and the bet – they spell the word av/father; if you look at just the last two letters – the bet and the nun – they spell the word ben/son. The Father and the Son are in one word. This word, stone, is important. Remember that there was a stone that went with the Israelites in the wilderness and provided them water? And do you remember the "stone that men rejected (Matthew 21:42)"? That's Yeshua!

Lesson Summary:

Read Exodus 31:18 - 32:35. God used his own finger to inscribe His laws into the stone tablets. Then, after He revealed Himself through numerous miracles, including the plagues, the crossing of the Red Sea, the pillars of fire and cloud, and the providing of manna, His people panic and leave Him, creating and worshiping their own false god. When Moses went up the mountain to meet with Adonai, he was there for 40 days, and that was a long time! Maybe the Israelites feared he was dead or wasn't coming back. They wanted to worship, so they did what they knew how to do. They worshipped in a pagan way – they took their jewelry, melted it down, and formed a golden calf. God is understandably upset. He informs Moses that He will destroy them for their sin, but Moses intercedes on their behalf.

Moses paints a beautiful picture of the coming Messiah when he says, "Now, if you would only forgive their sin. But if not, please erase me from the book you have written (Exodus 32:32)." Moses is offering to take the people's place, just as Yeshua did for us. Moses is foreshadowing Yeshua. Read more about God's Book of Life in verse 33 and in the following verses: Psalm 69:28, Malachi 3:16, Luke 10:20, Philippians 4:3, Revelation 3:5, 13:8, 17:8, 20:11-15, 21:27. Think about how Yeshua is foreshadowed by the finger of God who writes the law, the tablets themselves that are broken, and Moses' intercession for the people and his offer to take their place in punishment for their sin.

Day 1:

1) Bible Memory: Memorize 1 Corinthians 11:23-24.

2) Hebrew Word: אֶבֶן even (pronounced eh-ven) stone

3) Think about the lesson: Read Exodus 31:18-32:35. Who wrote the law on the tablets? How and why did the tablets break? What were the people doing? Why? How did God feel about this? Why? Notice that Moses offered to take their place. Why did he do this? Who else did this?

_____

_____

Day 2:

1) Bible Memory: Review 1 Corinthians 11:23-24 and review three other verses.

2) Hebrew Word: אֶבֶן even (pronounced eh-ven) stone

3) Think about the lesson: Read these verses about the Book of Life: Revelation 20:15, Luke 10:20, Hebrews 12:22-23. What do you see?

Day 3:

1) Bible Memory: Review 1 Corinthians 11:23-24 and review three other verses.

2) Hebrew Word: אֶבֶן even (pronounced eh-ven) stone

3) Think about the lesson: Read these verses about the Book of Life: Daniel 12:1, Phil 4:3, Rev 3:5, Rev 21:27. Pray. What does it mean to be written in the Lamb's Book of Life?

Day 4:

4) Bible Memory: Review 1 Corinthians 11:23-24 and review three other verses.

5) Hebrew Word: אֶבֶן even (pronounced eh-ven) stone

6) Think about the lesson: Read these verses about the Book of Life: Psalm 69:27-28, Rev 13:8, Rev 17:8. Pray and discuss with your parents.

Day 5:

7) Bible Memory: Review 1 Corinthians 11:23-24 and review three other verses.

8) Hebrew Word: אֶבֶן even (pronounced eh-ven) stone

9) Think about the lesson: Read Psalm 56:8 and Malachi 3:16. Pray and discuss with your parents.

Day 6:

10) Bible Memory: Review 1 Corinthians 11:23-24 and review three other verses.

11) Hebrew Word: אֶבֶן even (pronounced eh-ven) stone

12) Think about the lesson: When you and your family open Shabbat tonight, say the blessing over the challah. What does this mean? Who is the Bread of Life? Discuss as a family.

LESSON 15
VAYIKRA, TZAV

Lesson Objective: We can learn about Yeshua from studying the offerings. We can also learn about how Adonai defines worship.

Memory Verse: Hebrews 10:14 Because by one sacrifice He has made perfect forever those who are being made holy.

Hebrew Word: קָרְבָּן a sacrificial offering

Lesson Summary:

Since we have all sinned and fall short of the glory of God, we cannot enter His presence without our sin being covered, or atoned for. We saw last week that the only way into the presence of God in the tabernacle begins with a sacrifice on the altar. It is the blood that atones for sin. These Torah portions tell us about the different types of sacrifices that were made in the Tabernacle, and later, the Temple. These sacrifices are designed for the worshipper to repent of his or her sins and draw near to God. What God is looking for is not just the blood of bulls or goats, but a broken and contrite heart. He wants our repentance. He wants changed hearts. Sacrificing a perfect animal in those days and in that culture represented sacrificing something expensive, valuable, and dear to the worshipper. He had to count the cost of his sin. The blood of bulls and goats cannot take away our sin, but these sacrifices taught the worshippers about the coming prophesied Messiah who would be our atoning sacrifice. His blood covered the sins of everyone in the entire world. Since Yeshua is God, He has the power to forgive our sins, and since He lived as a perfect man, He was qualified to offer Himself as a perfect, sinless sacrifice. We'll look closely at each of the types of sacrifice as we study our daily assignments this week.

Here in Leviticus, God defines the first step of worship as a sacrifice. Sacrificing animals is not how we worship today for a few reasons. First, Yeshua's sacrifice covered all our sins, and His story is recorded. We can look back and see the fulfillment of the prophecies. There is no need for the sacrifices of bulls and goats to teach us about what is coming, because He already came. Second, there is no Temple. If there is no Temple with an altar and no established priesthood working in it, then we cannot have legitimate sacrifices today. Finally, we need to focus on what God's focus is for us now – our hearts. He wants our repentance. He wants to circumcise out hearts to follow Him.

Worship today is often defined in our culture as singing and dancing to the Lord. These are beautiful ways to praise the Lord and enter into His presence, and these are ways that He was worshipped anciently as well, but we know that the sacrifices came first and were the primary and central focus of the mishkan. Have we repented of our sins and accepted Yeshua's sacrifice on our behalf? If so, then we can enter into the presence of God with singing and dancing. If not, then that is the altar we must approach first.

Day 1:

1) Bible Memory: Memorize Hebrews 10:14.

2) Hebrew Word: קָרְבָּן a sacrificial offering

73

3) Think about the lesson: The Burnt Offering. Read Leviticus 1:1-17 and 6:8-13, Philippians 2:5-11, and Romans 12:1-2. Fill in the following:

The Burnt Offering Olah	What was offered?	Why was it offered?	What does it teach us about Yeshua?

Day 2:

1) Bible Memory: Review Hebrews 10:14 and choose three other verses to review.

2) Hebrew Word: קָרְבָּן a sacrificial offering

3) Think about the lesson: The Grain Offering. Read Leviticus 2:1-16 and 6:14-23. Read Hebrews 4:15 and 1 John 3:5.

The Grain Offering Minchah	What was offered?	Why was it offered?	What does it teach us about Yeshua?

Day 3:

1) Bible Memory: Review Hebrews 10:14 and choose three other verses to review.

2) Hebrew Word: קָרְבָּן a sacrificial offering

3) Think about the lesson: The Fellowship, or Peace, Offering. Read Leviticus 3:1-17 and 7:11-38 and 1 Corinthians 5:7-8.

Fellowship Offering Shalem	What was offered?	Why was it offered?	What does it teach us about Yeshua?

Day 4:

1) Bible Memory: Review Hebrews 10:14 and choose three other verses to review.

2) Hebrew Word: קָרְבָּן a sacrificial offering

3) Think about the lesson: The Sin Offering. Read Leviticus 4:1-5, 5:13, and 6:24-30 and 2 Corinthians 5:21.

The Sin Offering Chattah	What was offered?	Why was it offered?	What does it teach us about Yeshua?

Day 5:

1) Bible Memory: Review Hebrews 10:14 and choose three other verses to review.

2) Hebrew Word: קָרְבָּן a sacrificial offering

3) Think about the lesson: The Guilt, or Trespass, Offering. Read Leviticus 5:14-6:7 and 7:1-10 and Colossians 2:13.

The Guilt Offering Asham	What was offered?	Why was it offered?	What does it teach us about Yeshua?

Day 6:

1) Bible Memory: Review Hebrews 10:14 and choose three other verses to review.

2) Hebrew Word: קָרְבָּן a sacrificial offering

3) Think about the lesson: Discuss with your parents what you have learned about the offerings this week. Pray that Yeshua reveals Himself to you through your study of these offerings.

LESSON 16
BEHA'ALOTCHA

Lesson Objective: Contrast the differences between the fruits of following our own hearts versus following God.

Memory Verse: Psalm 78:14 He guided them with the cloud by day and with light from the fire all night.

Hebrew Word: אֵשׁ aish - fire

Lesson Summary:

Occasionally, the idea of following God doesn't seem like all that much fun. At times, we have ideas of other things we would rather do, but think about this: God made you. If God made you, then God knows what will be best for you, what will keep you safe, and what will give you the most joy. Since Yeshua died for us, is it too much for us to consider dying to our own desires so that we can follow Him? In the end, the things we think we really want right now probably won't satisfy us after a time, but when we follow God, we will be fully loved, fully satisfied, and cleansed from all sin. We will be living a life that glorifies our Creator.

In Numbers chapters 8-12, we see that the Israelites were following Adonai through the wilderness as He led them by the pillar of cloud by day and of fire by night. When the pillar moved, they moved. When the pillar stopped, they stopped.

He led them, and he fed them. He fed them manna every day. However, the Israelites got tired of manna and began complaining. They wanted some meat. Now, God doesn't mind that we like meat or eat it, as long as it's the kind of meat that He says is ok to eat, but in this case, God is disappointed with His people because their rejection of the manna is rejection of God's provision for them. They want what they were used to eating when they were in slavery. They didn't want God's food; they wanted the world's food. God let them have it, and in this case, it wasn't good for them at all!

Day 1:

1) Bible Memory: Memorize Psalm 78:14.

2) Hebrew Word: אֵשׁ aish - fire

3) Think about the lesson: Read Numbers 9:15-22.
   What were the Israelites following and why?

   _____

   _____

Day 2:

1) Bible Memory: Review Psalm 78:14 and choose three other verses to review.

2) Hebrew Word: אֵשׁ aish - fire

3) Think about the lesson: Read Numbers 11:4-34.

What did the Israelites want, and what happened when they got it?

_____

_____

Day 3:

1) Bible Memory: Review Psalm 78:14 and choose three other verses to review.

2) Hebrew Word: אֵשׁ aish - fire

3) Think about the lesson: Pray, and discuss with your parents: Why was God so upset with the Israelites' request for meat?

Day 4:

1) Bible Memory: Review Psalm 78:14 and choose three other verses to review.

2) Hebrew Word: אֵשׁ aish - fire

3) Think about the lesson: Read Romans 1:18-32. Discuss this passage with your parents. How much of this passage is applicable to our culture today?

Day 5:

1) Bible Memory: Review Psalm 78:14 and choose three other verses to review.

2) Hebrew Word: אֵשׁ aish - fire

3) Think about the lesson: Read Matthew 6:24-35. How does this apply to us today? What are some things we want that wouldn't be good for us to have? How do we line up what we want with what God wants for us? Why is it important to follow God? We don't see His cloud or fire today, so how can we follow Him now?

_____

_____

_____

Day 6:

1) Bible Memory: Review Psalm 78:14 and choose three other verses to review.

2) Hebrew Word: אֵשׁ aish - fire

3) Think about the lesson: Pray, and discuss with your parents: Why is it important to follow God? We don't see His cloud or fire today, so how can we follow Him now?

LESSON 17
SHLACH AND KORACH

Lesson Objective: Adonai establishes authority, and we should not covet someone else's position.

Memory Verse: Numbers 15:39 These will serve as tassels for you to look at, so that you may remember all the Lord's commands and obey them and not become unfaithful by following your own heart and your own eyes.

Hebrew Word: צִיצִית tzitzit – tassels worn at the corners of the tallit (prayer shawl)

Lesson Summary:

In Numbers chapters 13-18, we see the twelve spies entering the land of Canaan. Ten bring back a bad report, and two bring back a good report. The land is good, and God intends to give it to them, but the people choose to fear the land's inhabitants rather than the God who promised them this land. Therefore, God punishes their disobedience with forty years more in the wilderness.

The lesson? God expects us to obey Him immediately without fearing what men can do to us.

After a subsequent Sabbath violation, God instructs His people to wear tassels as a reminder of His commandments. Once again, the lesson is to keep God and His wishes foremost over our own.

Motivated by jealousy, Korah incites rebellion. His wishes have usurped God's wishes, and God kills him and all who are with him. While the whole community is holy to God (Korah's statement mirrors Satan's mixture of half-truth in the Garden of Eden), the facts are that God calls different people to different stations in life. The lesson is that we should be satisfied with our own calling and not be jealous of another's. This is coveting (and insurrection). The budding of Aaron's staff is a divine miracle clearly showing the people that Aaron's family is chosen for priestly duties.

Day 1:

1) Bible Memory: Memorize Numbers 15:39.
2) Hebrew Word: צִיצִית
3) Think about the lesson: Read Numbers 13:26-33. What do you notice?

_____

_____

Day 2:

1) Bible Memory: Review numbers 15:39 and three other verses.
2) Hebrew Word: צִיצִית

3) Think about the lesson: Read Numbers 15:32-36. What do you notice?

_____

_____

Day 3:

   1) Bible Memory: Review numbers 15:39 and three other verses.
   2) Hebrew Word: צִיצִת
   3) Think about the lesson: Read Numbers 15: 37-41. What do you notice?

_____

_____

Day 4:

   1) Bible Memory: Review numbers 15:39 and three other verses.
   2) Hebrew Word: צִיצִת
   3) Think about the lesson: Read Numbers 16:1-5. What do you notice?

_____

_____

Day 5:

   1) Bible Memory: Review numbers 15:39 and three other verses.
   2) Hebrew Word: צִיצִת
   3) Think about the lesson: Read Numbers 16:31-33. What do you notice?

_____

_____

Day 6:

   1) Bible Memory: Review numbers 15:39 and three other verses.
   2) Hebrew Word: צִיצִת
   3) Think about the lesson: Numbers 17:1-5, 8. What do you notice?

_____

_____

Discuss what you have noticed in all these passages with your parents. Have family prayer time☺

LESSON 18
CHUKAT

Lesson Objective: Yeshua is represented as a rock and also as a snake in order to save His people.

Memory Verse: John 3:14-16 Just as Moses lifted up the snake in the desert, so the Son of Man must be lifted up, so that everyone who believes in Him may have eternal life. For God so loved the world that He gave his one and only Son, so that everyone who believes in Him will not perish but have eternal life.

Hebrew Word: נחש nachash - serpent

Lesson Summary:

In the Torah portion Chukat (Numbers 19:1-22:1) and in John 3, we see two key symbols that teach us about Yeshua: the rock and the snake.

In Exodus 17:6, God told Moses to strike the rock so that water would gush out for the people to drink. Moses obeyed. Then in Numbers 20:11, God tells Moses to speak to the rock, but Moses strikes it. For this act of disobedience, Moses is not permitted to enter into the Promised Land with the people. Why is it so important that he speak to it, not strike it, the second time?

The rock is symbolic of Yeshua (1 Corinthians 10:4) and his two comings. The first time he came bodily to earth, he was struck down, providing eternal salvation for us. The second time, he will not be struck. He will come as the conquering King, and he will set up His Kingdom here on earth. We will speak to him. In striking the rock the second time, Moses disobeyed God's instructions which were meant to paint a picture of the coming Messiah.

The second story, that of Yeshua as the snake, is an interesting one. The people were grumbling (surprise, surprise!) so God sent poisonous snakes into their midst. The snakes bit them and many of them died.

The lesson? Sin kills.

The solution? Yeshua became our sin sacrifice. He was lifted onto a pole for our salvation. The lifting of the snake on the pole represents the lifting of the second Adam (the sinless One) on the cross. Our sins are as deadly as the poisonous snakes, but if we lift our eyes to Yeshua, he will save us.

Day 1:

1) Bible Memory: Memorize John 3:14.

2) Hebrew Word: נחש nachash - serpent

3) Think about the lesson: Read Numbers 19:1-22:1 and discuss with your parents.

Day 2:

1) Bible Memory: Memorize John 3:15. Review John 3:14.

2) Hebrew Word: נחש nachash - serpent

3) Think about the lesson: Read John 3 and discuss with your parents.

Day 3:

1) Bible Memory: Memorize John 3:16. Review John 3:14-15.

2) Hebrew Word: נחש nachash - serpent

3) Think about the lesson: Consider the readings you have done so far this week – Chukat and John 3 – and the discussions you have had with your parents. Summarize what you have learned:

_____

_____

_____

Day 4:

1) Bible Memory: Review John 3:14-16.

2) Hebrew Word: נחש nachash - serpent

3) Think about the lesson: What is a symbol?

_____

Why do you think God uses symbols to teach us?

_____

_____

Day 5:

1) Bible Memory: Review John 3:14-16.

2) Hebrew Word: נחש nachash - serpent

3) Think about the lesson: Isn't it interesting that God chose the symbol of the serpent to save the people from the poisonous snakes? It was the serpent in the Garden of Eden who tempted Eve to disobey God. The serpent is considered to represent Satan. Satan wants to take God's place; He wants to be worshipped as God. Therefore, he is a great impersonator of God, but we know that the entire universe is God's and He has dominion over all that is in it. Whatever poison Satan offers, God has the antidote. Discuss with your parents. Pray that God would always bless you with His protection and good discernment.

Day 6:

1) Bible Memory: Review John 3:14-16.

2) Hebrew Word: נחש nachash - serpent

3) Think about the lesson: Spend some time in prayer today.

LESSON 19
BALAK

Lesson Objective: Nothing can stop God's Word from being accomplished.

Memory Verse: Isaiah 55:11 So is my Word that goes out from my mouth: it will not return to me empty, but it will accomplish what I desire and achieve the purpose for which I sent it.

Hebrew Word: דָּבָר davar – in noun form: word; in verb form: speak

Lesson Summary:

Balak is a regional king who sees the Israelites as a threat. So he hires Balaam to curse the Israelites. However, God has a better plan. Unfortunately for Balak, even though Balaam tries to earn his pay, curses will not leave his lips. Every time he opens his mouth, blessings come out!

This passage is fascinating and prompts so many questions. Why does Balak want to curse Israel? What kind of man/prophet is Balaam? God talks through a donkey!?!?!?! If Balak wants curses, and Balaam wants to be paid, why is it that only blessings can come out of his mouth, despite multiple attempts? Why does Balaam continue his course even when he knows he will not be able to accomplish what Balak wants?

The basic message God has for us in this story is that His Word will not return to Him void (Isaiah 55:11). His people are blessed, He will bless them, and those who bless them will also be blessed (Genesis 12:2). The hearts of kings are as water in His hands, and He turns them however He chooses (Proverbs 21:1). Ultimately, this is a lesson in God's sovereignty.

A second lesson is that God can and does talk through unexpected vessels - are we humble enough to accept that?

Think about how this lesson can apply to you.

How can we make sure that we are following God's direction for our lives?

What are some of the ways that God speaks to us?

How does our memory verse for this week apply to this lesson?

Day 1:

1) Bible Memory: Memorize Isaiah 55:11.

2) Hebrew Word: דָּבָר davar – in noun form: word; in verb form: speak

3) Think about the lesson: Read Balaam's first oracle in Numbers 23:7-10. Summarize what you have read.

_____

_____

Day 2:

    1)   Bible Memory: Review Isaiah 55:11 and review three other verses.

    2)   Hebrew Word: דבר davar – in noun form: word; in verb form: speak

    3)   Think about the lesson: Read Balaam's second oracle in Numbers 23:18-26. Summarize what you have read:

_____

_____

Day 3:

    1)   Bible Memory: Review Isaiah 55:11 and review three other verses.

    2)   Hebrew Word: דבר davar – in noun form: word; in verb form: speak

    3)   Think about the lesson: Read Balaam's third oracle in Numbers 24:3-9. Summarize what you have read:

_____

_____

Day 4:

    1)   Bible Memory: Review Isaiah 55:11 and review three other verses.

    2)   Hebrew Word: דבר davar – in noun form: word; in verb form: speak

    3)   Think about the lesson: Read Balaam's fourth oracle in Numbers 24:15-24. Summarize what you have read:

_____

_____

Day 5:

    1)   Bible Memory: Review Isaiah 55:11 and review three other verses.

    2)   Hebrew Word: דבר davar – in noun form: word; in verb form: speak

    3)   Think about the lesson: Is Balaam a godly man? Why or why not? What is the difference between Balaam's asking for confirmation of God's direction and Gideon asking for confirmation of God's direction in Judges 6:36-40?

_____

_____

83

Day 6:

1) Bible Memory: Review Isaiah 55:11 and review three other verses.
2) Hebrew Word: דבר davar – in noun form: word; in verb form: speak
3) Think about the lesson: What does God say in Genesis 12:2? How does that apply here?

_____

_____

LESSON 20
PINCHAS

Lesson Objective: Our emotions can cause us to take actions that may or may not be righteous. We need to carefully consider our emotions before we act.

Memory Verse: Ephesians 4:26 In your anger, do not sin: do not let the sun go down while you are still angry.

Hebrew Word: - פּינחס Pinchas – his name, sometimes translated Phinehas

Lesson Summary:

Read Numbers 25:1-13 and Matthew 21:12-13. Consider how anger produces action. Often, our anger produces wrong action, but in these examples Pinchas and Yeshua exhibited righteous anger that produced violent but righteous actions. Many of you are entering your middle school years, and your emotions may up, down, and all over the place. You may not be able to define your emotions at any given moment or know why you are feeling the way that you do.

When we are experiencing anger, that emotion often clouds our judgment. Therefore, anger can be dangerous to our spiritual walk. Ephesians 4:26 warns us not to sin when we are angry and instructs us not to let the sun go down on our anger. In Genesis 4, we see that Cain's anger, sprouted from jealousy, spurs him to murder his brother.

Consider how we might discern the difference between righteous and unrighteous anger.

Righteous anger preserves the Word of God, while unrighteous anger involves self-preservation and self-justification. One is God-centered while the other is self-centered. This is the difference.

Day 1:

1) Bible Memory: Memorize Ephesians 4:26.
2) Hebrew Word: פּינחס Pinchas – his name, sometimes translated Phinehas
3) Think about the lesson: Read Numbers 25:1-13. What do you notice?

   _____

   _____

Day 2:

1) Bible Memory: Review Ephesians 4:26 and review three other verses.
2) Hebrew Word: פּינחס Pinchas – his name, sometimes translated Phinehas
3) Think about the lesson: Read Matthew 21:12-13. What do you notice?

   _____

   _____

Day 3:

1) Bible Memory: Review Ephesians 4:26 and review three other verses.

2) Hebrew Word: פּינחס Pinchas – his name, sometimes translated Phinehas

3) Think about the lesson: Consider this week's memory verse – Ephesian 4:26. When is anger righteous? And when is anger a sin?

_____

_____

Day 4:

1) Bible Memory: Review Ephesians 4:26 and review three other verses.

2) Hebrew Word: פּינחס Pinchas – his name, sometimes translated Phinehas

3) Think about the lesson: Read Genesis 4:6-8. What do you think it means that "sin is crouching at your door?"

_____

_____

Day 5:

1) Bible Memory: Review Ephesians 4:26 and review three other verses.

2) Hebrew Word: פּינחס Pinchas – his name, sometimes translated Phinehas

3) Think about the lesson: Think about times that you have felt angry. Was it righteous anger or sinful anger? Why? Pray about this.

Day 6:

1) Bible Memory: Review Ephesians 4:26 and review three other verses.

2) Hebrew Word: פּינחס Pinchas – his name, sometimes translated Phinehas

3) Think about the lesson: Discuss this week's lesson with your parents and pray together as a family.

LESSON 21
MATOT AND MASEI

Lesson Objective: God values women much more highly than the ancient pagan cultures did.

Memory Verse: Galatians 3:28 There is neither Jew nor Greek, slave nor free, male nor female, for you are all one in Messiah Yeshua.

Hebrew Words: אִישׁ ish – man, husband; אִישָׁה ishah – woman, wife

Lesson Summary:

Matot and Masei include great lessons on how to order the Israelite community as it prepares to enter the Promised Land. This passage sets the boundaries of Israel (timely for today!), declares the cities of refuge, and deals with issues regarding women's inheritance and vows. In fact, the beginning of our reading and the end of our reading open and close with a discussion of women.

The question of women's inheritance within the tribes arises in Numbers 27:1-11 and is re-addressed and clarified in Numbers 36. Numbers 30 addresses vows that women make. This is groundbreaking for ancient cultures in which women are primarily seen as property, having no rights of their own. So what is the Biblical view of women?

Let's go back to the beginning to look for an answer. In Genesis 1:27, God says, "So God created man in his own image; he created him in the image of God; He created them male and female." Male and female are both created in the image of God. As image bearers, both males and females possess infinite worth. And in the beginning, God pronounced this good. Genesis chapter 2 provides a little more detail as to how He made humans male and female. The man is made first from the earthy dirt, and then the woman is crafted from the man's rib. Adam says of Eve, she is "bone of my bone and flesh of my flesh" (Gen 2:23). As she is crafted from him, she is neither worth more nor less. They are of equal value and are made from the same material "stuff." All is well.

Then, sin enters and skews perfection.

After dining on forbidden fruit, Adam and Eve suffer the consequences. They play the blame game, and God issues His judgements. To the woman, He says, "I will intensify your labor pains; you will bear children in anguish. Your desire will be for your husband, yet he will rule over you" (Genesis 3:16).

From this point on, humanity is under a curse, and for women, the equal partnership that God originally created changes. Now, she will be subject to her husband.

God has a purpose for setting up a chain of command, but the ungodly of the world take this, twist this, and create systemic abuse of women that sees women as lesser than men, of lesser value, of lesser worth.

These passages in the book of Numbers show the ancient cultures that women have worth and value.

We see later that after Yeshua comes in the flesh and sacrifices himself on behalf of humanity that he, the second Adam, restores the order that God created in the beginning. God is no respecter of person (Acts 10:34, Romans 2:11), we see that Paul worked side by side with women in ministry (Romans 16 provides a few examples), and in Galatians 3:28, he sums up this perspective in the verse "There is neither Jew nor Greek, slave nor free, male nor female, for you are all one in Christ Jesus." In Yeshua, under the reign of His Kingdom, we are again equal in God's eyes.

However, God's kingdom is not yet manifest over all the earth, and the remaining vestiges of unbiblical mindsets still pervade our cultural understandings. Yeshua and Paul dealt with this as well in their culture which rested on slave labor. The Bible does not advocate slavery, but it sets laws that prevent the grossest abuses of it. Likewise, the Bible does not advocate misogyny, but it sets laws like the ones we find here in our passage that prevent the grossest abuses of it. While slavery is wrong and is not what God originally created, sexism is also wrong and is not what God originally created. The curse is defeated in Yeshua, but we still live in a cursed world, and we function the best that we can under the reign of God in our personal lives. When Yeshua returns, He will set up His Kingdom over all the earth, and we will return to an Eden-like state where everyone respects everyone else and recognizes their God-given gifts and talents as male reflecting the image of God or as female reflecting the image of God.

Day 1:

1) Bible Memory: Memorize Galatians 3:28.

2) Hebrew Word: אִישׁ ish – man, husband; אִישָׁה ishah – woman, wife

3) Think about the lesson: Read Numbers 27:1-11.
Who inherited the land in this passage? _____
Why did they inherit it? _____
What were the stipulations (rules) for them to inherit the land?

_____

_____

Day 2:

1) Bible Memory: Review Galatians 3:28, and choose three other verses to review.

2) Hebrew Word: אִישׁ ish – man, husband; אִישָׁה ishah – woman, wife

3) Think about the lesson: Read Numbers 36. What do you notice?

_____

_____

Day 3:

1) Bible Memory: Review Galatians 3:28, and choose three other verses to review.

2) Hebrew Word: אִישׁ ish – man, husband; אִישָׁה ishah – woman, wife

3) Think about the lesson: Read Numbers 30. What do the lessons on vows teach us about God's order in our homes?

_____

_____

Day 4:

1) Bible Memory: Review Galatians 3:28, and choose three other verses to review.

2) Hebrew Word: אִישׁ ish – man, husband; אִישָׁה ishah – woman, wife

3) Think about the lesson: Compare Numbers 30 with 1 Corinthians 11:3 "But I want you to know that Christ is the head of every man, and the man is the head of the woman, and God is the head of Christ." In Numbers 30, a divorced or widowed woman who is living alone is the head of her household (she makes her own vows and is held to them), while other women are either subject to their husbands or their fathers (either of them can nullify her vow). The chain of command in 1 Corinthians adds the man under Christ and Christ under God. This syncs with the picture in Numbers; if the man is missing from the picture, then the woman is directly under Christ. This is a chain of command, not a statement of worth. Read these passages, pray, and discuss with your parents.

Day 5:

1) Bible Memory: Review Galatians 3:28, and choose three other verses to review.

2) Hebrew Word: אִישׁ ish – man, husband; אִישָׁה ishah – woman, wife

3) Think about the lesson: During your grandparents' time, it was popular for men to make fun of women. People thought women couldn't be as smart as men, couldn't drive as well as men, etc. Today, it is more popular for women to make fun of men. For example, they say men are clueless, can't figure anything out, etc. Neither of these views is Biblical. God created each one of us in His image, and we all have individual gifts and talents that complement one another. Together, when men and women function within their individually God-given gifts and talents, the whole body of Christ is built up and we present a unified witness to the world. May your generation be the one to get it right! Spend some time today thinking about what you have seen or noticed in your culture today that either confirms or denies Biblical manhood or womanhood. Discuss with your parents what they have seen in their generation.

Day 6:

1) Bible Memory: Review Galatians 3:28, and choose three other verses to review.

2) Hebrew Word: אִישׁ ish – man, husband; אִישָׁה ishah – woman, wife

3) Think about the lesson: Spend some time in prayer today.

LESSON 22
DEVARIM AND VAETCHANAN

Lesson Objective: The Shema is a defining prayer.

Memory Verse: Deuteronomy 6:4-5 Hear, O Israel, the LORD our God, the LORD is one. Love the LORD your God with all your heart and with all your soul and with all your strength.

Hebrew Word: שְׁמַע shema - hear (with the understanding that to hear will be to obey)

Lesson Summary:

"Devarim" in Hebrew means "words;" whereas the name for this same book "Deuteronomy" comes from the Greek translation and means "second law," or a repetition of the giving of the law. Both names of this book remind us of the giving of the Torah at Mount Sinai (the Ten Commandments are called the ten words in Hebrew), and much of this book repeats the laws and information already given, hence given a second time.

Moses recounts the Israelites' history and repeats the instructions (the Torah) as they prepare to enter the Promised Land. Why does he do this? Why do we have a book in the Bible that basically repeats what we've already heard?

First of all, recall that this is the second generation. The first generation, the generation that came out of Egypt, died in the wilderness. To pass on our faith to the next generation, we have to teach them. As you work through this workbook, the is one way my generation (your teachers) are passing the Torah on to you. Your job is to live it, and then to pass it on to your children.

In order to learn something well, we have to hear it, see it, and experience it for ourselves. We have to take ownership of what we are learning.

Also, we learn through repetition. If we hear something once, there is an 80% chance that we will forget it within 24 hours. However, through repetition, what goes into our short term memory can be transferred to our long term memory and become a part of us.

The key focus of these two portions is the Shema. The Shema establishes that we will hear and obey, that we acknowledge the God of the Bible as our God, that we recognize that there is only One God, that will love Him with all that we are – heart, soul, and strength, and that we will live as witnesses to our next generation as well as to ourselves and to those with whom we come into contact - a good lesson to recall and live out on a daily basis!

Day 1:

1) Bible Memory: Memorize Deuteronomy 6:4-5.
2) Hebrew Word: שְׁמַע shema - hear
3) Think about the lesson: Read Deuteronomy 1:1-3:22. What do you notice?

_____

_____

Day 2:

1) Bible Memory: Review Deuteronomy 6:4-5 and review three other verses.

2) Hebrew Word: שְׁמַע shema - hear

3) Think about the lesson: Read Deuteronomy 3:23-7:11. What do you notice?

_____

_____

Day 3:

1) Bible Memory: Review Deuteronomy 6:4-5 and review three other verses.

2) Hebrew Word: שְׁמַע shema - hear

3) Think about the lesson: How do you know when your teacher is saying something important? Maybe something you need to remember or even take notes over? We listen for teacher cues. List some of the cues that clue you in to the need to focus: _____

_____

_____

Day 4:

1) Bible Memory: Review Deuteronomy 6:4-5 and review three other verses.

2) Hebrew Word: שְׁמַע shema - hear

3) Think about the lesson: What "teacher cues" does Moses give in these passages? Re-read Deuteronomy 6:1-9. List the "teacher cues" that you find: _____

_____

_____

Day 5:

1) Bible Memory: Review Deuteronomy 6:4-5 and review three other verses.

2) Hebrew Word: שְׁמַע shema - hear

3) Think about the lesson: Read the Shema passage again. (Deuteronomy 6:1-9) How do we love the LORD our God with all our heart, soul, and strength?

_____

_____

_____

Day 6:

1) Bible Memory: Review Deuteronomy 6:4-5 and review three other verses.

91

2) Hebrew Word: שמע shema - hear

3) Think about the lesson: Spend some time in prayer.

LESSON 23
KI TEITZEI

Lesson Objective: Students will see the importance of commitment in marriage.

Memory Verse: Exodus 20:14 You shall not commit adultery.

Hebrew Word: אֶחָד echad - one

Lesson Summary:

Does the idea of marriage seem like a faraway dream to you at your age? Believe it or not, this is a time to carefully consider what you will look for in a future husband or wife, a time to prayerfully prepare yourself to one day be a good husband or wife, and a time to establish the understanding that once you make that commitment to your future spouse, you will hold tight to your commitment to him or her. It is important to pay close attention to the responsibility a husband and wife must show to their commitment to one another, because there will come times when husbands and wives disagree and have troubles with each other.

In this Torah potion, we'll focus especially on Deuteronomy 24:1-5. Due to our modern cultural context, we are seeing more and more couples living together without getting married. They want to live together as husband and wife without making a lifetime commitment to each other. We are seeing an entire generation questioning why they should get married, especially considering the high rates of divorce and the consequences of broken families.

It is important for us to understand the selfless love, commitment, and responsibility a good marriage demonstrates to God, to our future spouse, and to our future children.

We live in a society where everything seems instant and expendable. People, however, are created in the image of God, and therefore, we are not expendable. Our commitments matter; the people in our lives matter; and our decisions have eternal consequences.

Day 1:

1) Bible Memory: Memorize Exodus 20:14.

2) Hebrew Word: אֶחָד echad – one

3) Think about the lesson: Discuss with your parents: What are some purposes for marriage? Can you think of some reasons why some people choose not to get married?

Day 2:

1) Bible Memory: Review Exodus 20:14 and review three other verses.

2) Hebrew Word: אֶחָד echad - one

3) Think about the lesson: Read Deuteronomy 24:1-5.
What laws did Moses give us regarding marriage here in our passage?

Did Moses allow a husband to divorce his wife? _____

Can he remarry her later? _____

Day 3:

1) Bible Memory: Review Exodus 20:14 and review three other verses.

2) Hebrew Word: אֶחָד echad - one

3) Think about the lesson: Read Matthew 5:27-32. What does Yeshua say about marriage and divorce? Whose law is stricter?

_____

_____

Day 4:

1) Bible Memory: Review Exodus 20:14 and review three other verses.

2) Hebrew Word: אֶחָד echad - one

3) Think about the lesson: Read Matthew 19:3-11. What do you notice?

_____

_____

_____

Day 5:

1) Bible Memory: Review Exodus 20:14 and review three other verses.

2) Hebrew Word: אֶחָד echad - one

3) Think about the lesson: Do you think God NEVER approves of divorce? Let's read something shocking - Jeremiah 3:8. What happened here? Who is the husband and who is the wife? Why did He issue Israel a certificate of divorce?

_____

_____

_____

_____

Day 6:

1) Bible Memory: Review Exodus 20:14 and review three other verses.

2) Hebrew Word: אֶחָד echad - one

3) Think about the lesson: After reading yesterday's passage, do you see any hope for Israel's return? Read Jeremiah 3:12-13. How can Israel be redeemed? Who is the Redeemer?

_____

At Shavuot, God made a promise, a commitment, to His people. He betrothed them; that means he gave Israel an engagement ring. God and Israel are symbolically engaged to be married (Shabbat is the engagement ring - the sign between God and Israel - Ezekiel 20:12). Keeping God's laws is like wearing His engagement ring - it shows others that Israel belongs to Adonai. When Israel breaks God's laws, it's like she took off her engagement ring and went on dates with other guys. Idolatry is like adultery. Do you think God was upset? After He divorces her, can He ever remarry her? Moses says, no, BUT God has a surprise. He does not give up on Israel. He DIES for her, and when He is resurrected, then he can marry her again. All we have to do is repent!

LESSON 24
KI TAVO AND NITZAVIM

Lesson Objective: The new covenant involves Adonai circumcising our hearts to follow Him. It is His work. It does not negate previous covenants.

Memory Verse: Jeremiah 31:33 This is the covenant I will make with the house of Israel after that time, declares the LORD. I will put my law in their minds and write it on their hearts. I will be their God, and they will be my people.

Hebrew Word: לב lev - heart

Lesson Summary:

Read the Torah portions – Deuteronomy 26:1-30:20. Notice that God is making an additional covenant with the Israelites in Deuteronomy 29:1, "These are the words of the covenant the Lord commanded Moses to make with the Israelites in the land of Moab, *in addition* to the covenant He had made with them in Horeb." As we continue to read, the stipulations of this covenant look pretty much the same on the part of what is required of the people. So, what is the difference? What is the addition?

The difference is found in Deuteronomy 30:6, "The Lord your God will circumcise your heart and the hearts of your descendants, and you will love Him with all your heart and soul and live." Contrast this with what He said earlier in Deuteronomy 10:16 when God tells them, "Circumcise your hearts and don't be stiff-necked any longer." He tells them to circumcise their own hearts, but they could not do it. That's the difference. The addition to the covenant is that God will circumcise our hearts for us.

He does the work. Circumcision of the heart is much more difficult than circumcision of the flesh because it entails a choosing to do things God's way, not ours. Without His power, we cannot make the right choices. We cannot circumcise our own hearts. We need Him to do it for us. This is His promise that He will.

Adam and Eve chose their own way, not God's, and we've had difficulty with sin ever since. What was God's solution for them? He sacrificed an animal and clothed Adam and Eve (in forgiveness and in His righteousness).

What is His solution for us? He circumcises our hearts so that we are able to make the right choice – to follow Him. Read Jeremiah 31:31-33. Yeshua is the innocent lamb He sacrificed, and He clothes us with forgiveness and His righteousness, and through Him, we have a circumcised heart. He actually changes us from the inside out – as we grow in him, our desires gradually change from being self-centered to being God-centered. Our very hearts change. They become circumcised. This is the "new covenant." Hebrews 10:12-18 makes this clear.

Day 1:

1) Bible Memory: Memorize Jeremiah 31:33.

2) Hebrew Word: לֵב lev - heart

3) Think about the lesson: Read Deuteronomy 29:1, 30:6, and 30:11-16. What do you notice?

_____

_____

Day 2:

1) Bible Memory: Review Jeremiah 31:33 and review three other verses.

2) Hebrew Word: לֵב lev - heart

3) Think about the lesson: Compare Deuteronomy 10:16 with Deuteronomy 30:6. What is the difference?

_____

_____

Day 3:

1) Bible Memory: Review Jeremiah 31:33 and review three other verses.

2) Hebrew Word: לֵב lev - heart

3) Think about the lesson: Read Jeremiah 31:31-33. What will God do with our hearts?

_____

_____

Day 4:

1) Bible Memory: Review Jeremiah 31:33 and review three other verses.

2) Hebrew Word: לֵב lev - heart

3) Think about the lesson: Read Hebrews 10:12-18. What do you notice?

_____

_____

Day 5:

1) Bible Memory: Review Jeremiah 31:33 and review three other verses.

2) Hebrew Word: לֵב lev - heart

3) Think about the lesson: There are some who say that the New Covenant replaces the old one, but Deuteronomy 29:1 says that the new covenant is in addition to the old one. Has the "old covenant" disappeared? What is "new" about the new covenant? Read and discuss Hebrews 8:6-13 with your parents.

Day 6:

1) Bible Memory: Review Jeremiah 31:33 and review three other verses.
2) Hebrew Word: לב lev - heart
3) Think about the lesson: Spend some time in prayer today.

SECTION 2 – PROPHETS

LESSON 25
ISAIAH

Lesson Objective: Adonai calls the Jewish people to be a light to the Gentiles.

Memory Verse: Isaiah 49:6b I will also make you a light for the Gentiles, that you may bring my salvation to the ends of the earth.

Hebrew Word: אוֹר or - light

Lesson Summary:

In this section, we are moving from the Torah to the writings of the Prophets. Isaiah was a prophet who lived in Judea from 740-680 BC. In 722BC, the northern kingdom of Israel was conquered by the Assyrians, and it looked like the southern kingdom of Judah might also be in danger. They were pursuing idolatry, and when we follow other gods, the real God removes His protection.

However, God does nothing without first revealing it to His prophets, so He called Isaiah to tell Judah to repent.

Isaiah wrote many prophecies to Judah and to the world. Most of his prophecies pointed out what they were doing wrong that they needed to change and do right. He warned about the coming of the LORD and urged them to be ready. He prophesied judgement on other nations besides his own, as well, for God is God over all the earth. Isaiah prophesied blessing upon Israel's restoration, upon the remnant, upon the nations, and upon the entire creation.

One of the most beautiful themes of Isaiah is that of Israel's role to be light to the nations.

Isaiah prophesied the coming of the Messiah through Israel – the promised Messiah who would make atonement for His people – and through Him bring salvation to the entire world.

Day 1:

1) Bible Memory: Memorize Isaiah 49:6b.

2) Hebrew Word: אוֹר or - light

3) Think about the lesson: Read Isaiah 48. What do you notice?

_____

_____

Day 2:

1) Bible Memory: Review Isaiah 49:6b and review three other verses.

99

2) Hebrew Word: אוֹר or - light

3) Think about the lesson: Read Isaiah 49. What do you notice?

_____

_____

Day 3:

1) Bible Memory: Review Isaiah 49:6b and review three other verses.

2) Hebrew Word: אוֹר or - light

3) Think about the lesson: Read Isaiah 50. What do you notice?

_____

_____

Day 4:

1) Bible Memory: Review Isaiah 49:6b and review three other verses.

2) Hebrew Word: אוֹר or - light

3) Think about the lesson: Read Isaiah 51. What do you notice?

_____

_____

Day 5:

1) Bible Memory: Review Isaiah 49:6b and review three other verses.

2) Hebrew Word: אוֹר or - light

3) Think about the lesson: Read Isaiah 52. What do you notice?

_____

_____

Day 6:

1) Bible Memory: Review Isaiah 49:6b and review three other verses.

2) Hebrew Word: אוֹר or - light

3) Think about the lesson: Read Isaiah 53. What do you notice?

_____

_____

_____

_____

LESSON 26
JEREMIAH

Lesson Objective: We are like clay in the hands of our Creator.

Memory Verse: Jeremiah 18:6b Like clay in the hand of the potter, so are you in my hand, O house of Israel.

Hebrew Word: יָד yad - hand

Lesson Summary:

Jeremiah was a prophet who faced fierce opposition, as so many other prophets did, but even when he wanted to give up, he didn't. He stayed true to what God had called him to do.

The job of a prophet was tough. The prophet's job was to bring God's Word to the people (whereas a priest's job was to bring the people to God). This was tough because so much of the time, God's Word brings direction and correction to the people who prefer going their own way and doing their own thing, even if it is sinful and is bringing them negative consequences. When they didn't want to hear God's Word through a prophet, they would ridicule, not listen to, or even imprison or kill the prophets.

Jeremiah lived from 627-585 BC. He prophesied to the Jews in Judea as well as to those who were taken to Babylon. He also had prophecies for other nations, because God is God of all the peoples on the earth, and God's laws govern all of creation.

The sovereignty of God can be clearly seen in Jeremiah's prophecies. One way that Jeremiah depicted the people was as clay in the hands of the potter. He described God as the potter who formed the clay into the vessels of His choosing.

Day 1:

1) Bible Memory: Memorize Jeremiah 18:6b.

2) Hebrew Word: יָד yad - hand

3) Think about the lesson: Read about Jeremiah's calling from God to be a prophet in Jeremiah 1:1-10. What do you notice?

_____

_____

_____

Day 2:

1) Bible Memory: Review Jeremiah 18:6b and review three other verses.

2) Hebrew Word: יָד yad - hand

3) Think about the lesson:

What was a prophet's job?_____

What was a priest's job?_____

Day 3:

1) Bible Memory: Review Jeremiah 18:6b and review three other verses.

2) Hebrew Word: יָד yad - hand

3) Think about the lesson: Read Jeremiah 46:13-26. Jeremiah is prophesying the coming of the Babylonians to defeat Egypt. What do you notice?

_____
_____
_____

Day 4:

1) Bible Memory: Review Jeremiah 18:6b and review three other verses.

2) Hebrew Word: יָד yad - hand

3) Think about the lesson: Read Jeremiah 46:27-28. What do you notice in this prophecy?

_____
_____
_____

Day 5:

1) Bible Memory: Review Jeremiah 18:6b and review three other verses.

2) Hebrew Word: יָד yad - hand

3) Think about the lesson: Read Jeremiah 18:1-10. What do you notice?

_____
_____
_____
_____

Day 6:

1) Bible Memory: Review Jeremiah 18:6b and review three other verses.

2) Hebrew Word: יָד yad - hand

3) Think about the lesson: Read Jeremiah 18:11-18. What sins are the people committing?

_____
_____
_____
_____

Spend some time in prayer today.

LESSON 27
EZEKIEL

Lesson Objective: Ezekiel passed on Adonai's messages to the people in unconventional ways.

Memory Verse: Ezekiel 36:26 I will give you a new heart and put a new spirit in you; I will remove from you your heart of stone and give you a heart of flesh.

Hebrew Word: נתן natan - give

Lesson Summary:

Ezekiel was known as the prophet who taught with "pictures;" he physically acted out images that taught God's message.

The northern kingdom of Israel had been conquered by Assyria in 722BC. The southern kingdom of Judah was finally conquered by the Babylonians in 586 BC, after multiple attacks and a total of three deportations.

A deportation is a forced movement from one location to another. This was a Babylonian practice after conquering a people. They did this for a couple of reasons. First, it would be tough for the people they had conquered to rise up against them again if those people were separated from their family and friends and relocated to another place where they were unfamiliar with the language and didn't know their way around the land. Secondly, when the Babylonians deported the youth, they had a plan for them – to make them into Babylonians. They took the strongest and smartest youth, gave them Babylonian names, and taught them Babylonian culture, language, and religion. This was a way that they increased and built their empire.

Ezekiel was called by God to be a prophet in 593 BC, just before the Babylonians conquered Judah. He was deported along with Daniel, Shadrach, Meshach, and Abednego, although maybe not all at the same time, since there were three deportations before Jerusalem finally fell.

Ezekiel taught using graphic pictures and images, and sometimes, he was like a mime acting out the lessons. His actions were so strange they must have caught the people's attention and were probably very memorable.

What can you think of that catches our attention today? Which messages do we remember best and why? How were those messages delivered?

Day 1:

1) Bible Memory: Memorize Ezekiel 36:26.
2) Hebrew Word: נתן natan - give
3) Think about the lesson: Read each passage; then fill in the sign and the teaching in the chart.

Passage	What was the sign?	What was the teaching?
Ezekiel 4:1-3		
Ezekiel 4:4-8		

Day 2:

1) Bible Memory: Review Ezekiel 36:26 and review three other verses.

2) Hebrew Word: נתן natan - give

3) Think about the lesson: Read each passage; then fill in the sign and the teaching in the chart.

Passage	What was the sign?	What was the teaching?
Ezekiel 4:9-17		
Ezekiel 5:1-17		

Day 3:

1) Bible Memory: Review Ezekiel 36:26 and review three other verses.

2) Hebrew Word: נתן natan - give

3) Think about the lesson: Read each passage; then fill in the sign and the teaching in the chart.

Passage	What was the sign?	What was the teaching?
Ezekiel 12:1-16		
Ezekiel 12:17-20		

Day 4:

1) Bible Memory: Review Ezekiel 36:26 and review three other verses.

2) Hebrew Word: נתן natan - give

3) Think about the lesson: Read each passage; then fill in the sign and the teaching in the chart.

Passage	What was the sign?	What was the teaching?
Ezekiel 21:1-32		
Ezekiel 22:1-31		

Day 5:

1) Bible Memory: Review Ezekiel 36:26 and review three other verses.

2) Hebrew Word: נתן natan - give

3) Think about the lesson: Read each passage; then fill in the sign and the teaching in the chart.

Passage	What was the sign?	What was the teaching?
Ezekiel 24:15-27		
Ezekiel 37:15-28		

Day 6:

1) Bible Memory: Review Ezekiel 36:26 and review three other verses.

2) Hebrew Word: נתן natan - give

3) Think about the lesson: Ezekiel saw visions. One of the most famous is his vision of dry bones. Read Ezekiel 37:1-10. Pray about this passage. What do you notice?

_____

_____

_____

_____

LESSON 28
DANIEL – PART 1

Lesson Objective: Young Jews like Daniel and his friends maintained their integrity in Babylon, despite every attempt to make them conform to Babylonian religion and practice.

Memory Verse: Daniel 12:2 Multitudes who sleep in the dust of the earth will awake: some to everlasting life, others to shame and everlasting contempt.

Hebrew Word: חיי עולם chayei olam – eternal life

Lesson Summary:

Nebuchadnezzar has a dream, and he finds it so disturbing that he calls all the wise men of the country to interpret it for him, but he will not tell them what the dream was. He insists that they must tell him the dream and its interpretation, and, if they cannot, he will kill them, brutally. Of course, they cannot.

Daniel to the rescue! Well, actually, Daniel's God, the Creator of heaven and earth, who knows the thoughts and the hearts of everyone He created on this earth! He knows Nebuchadnezzar's dream, of course, because He caused him to dream it! God is intending to proclaim a message through the dream He sent this King of Babylon.

Read Daniel 2.

Dream	Interpretation
Head of Gold	Kingdom of Babylon
Chest and Arms of Silver	Kingdom of the Medes and Persians
Stomach and Thighs of Bronze	Kingdom of Greece
Legs of Iron; Feet of Partly Iron and Partly Clay	Rome
The Stone that breaks off and destroys the statue	Yeshua
And grows to become a mountain	Ruler over the Kingdom of God

Many people think that if we pray, God has to answer us, meaning that we expect Him to do whatever we say. It's like the genie in the lamp in the story of Aladdin – if you rub the lamp three times, the genie pops out and has to grant you three wishes. That's not how God works. God is Sovereign – that means He is in charge

106

of everything. He is the ultimate Ruler – just like the dream that Daniel interpreted for Nebuchadnezzar showed. God answers our prayers because He loves us, and sometimes, His answer is no. Sometimes, God says no to our prayers because He sees the bigger picture. We think we know what we want, what will make us happy, or what we think should happen, but God knows better than we do. And, sometimes, He plans for us to walk hard paths. Sometimes, it is ultimately for His glory. As long as we are fulfilling our call to be lights in the world, to build His Kingdom, then it doesn't matter if our path is hard or easy. It's usually hard because we're in the midst of spiritual war. We fight daily battles – God against everything that is Not-God. Shadrach, Meshach, and Abednego knew this.

Nebuchadnezzar was so pleased to be the head of the statue in his dream – the head of gold – the best of all the kingdoms, that he got proud. He forgot that there would be a Stone break off that would destroy all the other kingdoms, including his own, which would establish God's reign. Nebuchadnezzar forgot about the real God. He built himself a statue of gold and told everyone to bow down and worship it. Since this is idolatry, Shadrach, Meshach, and Abednego refused. They knew the king could kill them. They also knew that God could save them. For them, it did not matter whether or not God saved them. They wanted to follow God wholeheartedly, to be a good witness of Him, and they did not care if they died for their faith. They told Nebuchadnezzar that God could save them if He wanted to. Nebuchadnezzar got so mad that he threw them into a fiery furnace that was so hot it killed the men who threw them in. However, it did not kill them. Instead, Nebuchadnezzar saw four men walking in the fire, not just the three he had thrown in, and when they came out, the fire had not even touched them. What a miracle! Who do you think was walking with them in the furnace? And, in addition to their lives being saved, how many Babylonians watching all this were saved spiritually because of the faithfulness of these three?

God is Sovereign.

Salvation is real.

And Daniel 12:2 teaches us that our salvation or destruction has eternal consequences. This verse, our memory verse for this week, is a good verse to remember from for people who think hell might not be real. It is.

Day 1:

1) Bible Memory: Memorize Daniel 12:2.
2) Hebrew Word: חיי עולם chayei olam – eternal life
3) Think about the lesson: Shadrach, Meshach, and Abednego understood that there were eternal consequences to temporal life. They knew that God could save them from the fiery furnace if He wanted to, but they did not care whether or not He did. They knew that they would be with Him forever, whether in this life or the next. To be with God forever, to spend eternity with Him, we need only to believe that Yeshua paid the penalty for our sins. He died for us so that we may live. Believe in Him today, and He will walk through all of life's fiery furnaces with you and bring you from death to eternal life at the end of this temporal life.

Day 2:

1) Bible Memory: Review Daniel 12:2 and review three other verses.

2) Hebrew Word: חיי עולם chayei olam – eternal life

3) Think about the lesson: Read Daniel 1. What do you notice?

_____

_____

Day 3:

1) Bible Memory: Review Daniel 12:2 and review three other verses.

2) Hebrew Word: חיי עולם chayei olam – eternal life

3) Think about the lesson: Read Daniel 2. What do you notice?

_____

_____

Day 4:

1) Bible Memory: Review Daniel 12:2 and review three other verses.

2) Hebrew Word: חיי עולם chayei olam – eternal life

3) Think about the lesson: Read Daniel 3. What do you notice?

_____

_____

Day 5:

1) Bible Memory: Review Daniel 12:2 and review three other verses.

2) Hebrew Word: חיי עולם chayei olam – eternal life

3) Think about the lesson: What do you think are some of the most important lessons we can learn from Daniel, Shadrach, Meshach, and Abednego?

_____

_____

_____

_____

Day 6:

1) Bible Memory: Review Daniel 12:2 and review three other verses.

2) Hebrew Word: חיי עולם chayei olam – eternal life

3) Think about the lesson: In our culture today, there is often intense pressure to conform to the unbiblical world views around us. How can we be equipped to withstand these outside pressures and stand firm in our faith? Pray and discuss with your parents and write your ideas below.

_____

LESSON 29
DANIEL – PART 2

Lesson Objective: God is in control of all history. He sees the big picture. For us, it does not matter if we live or die in this life; if we are in Him, we will be with Him for all eternity.

Memory Verse: (same as last week) Daniel 12:2 Multitudes who sleep in the dust of the earth will awake: some to everlasting life, others to shame and everlasting contempt.

Hebrew Word: (same as last week) חיי עולם chayei olam – eternal life

Lesson Summary:

Remember the dream Nebuchadnezzar had in the last chapter? His kingdom was the head of gold, and he sure let that go to his head! He built a giant golden statue and commanded that everyone worship it. Worshipping the statue meant that the people were worshipping him as their leader. Shadrach, Meshach, and Abednego refused, so they were thrown into the fiery furnace, yet they did not die, and in fact, there was someone, probably pre-incarnate Yeshua, walking around in the fire with them. God will discipline Nebuchadnezzar for his sin of pride.

In Daniel chapter 4, God humbles Nebuchadnezzar. Nebuchadnezzar goes wild. God sends him out into the wild to eat grass and grow wild hair and nails. At the end of that year, Nebuchadnezzar's mind returns, and he gives God the glory.

The exile to Babylon lasted 70 years. If teenage Daniel and his friends were taken to Babylon at age 15, how old were they when some of them were permitted to return?

If Babylon is the head of gold, who is next? The Medes and Persians will be the arms of silver. Daniel chapter 5 shows us the night that the Medes conquered Babylon. By this time, Nebuchadnezzar is no longer the king; Belshazzar is. During a great feast in which Belshazzar has offended God one time too many, God's hand appears and writes on the wall. His time is up; that night, Darius the Mede conquers Babylon.

Darius the Mede appoints Daniel as one of his satraps (one of the 120 people in charge under the authority of three main administrators in the kingdom). Daniel is maintaining his faith and praying openly three times per day. A plot is formed against him that lands him in the lion's den. You are probably already familiar with this story from Daniel chapter 6. Notice Daniel's commitment to following God no matter what. Note also that because of Daniel's strong faith he is comfortable accepting whatever consequences there are, while the king has a sleepless night. Lack of faith results in lack of comfort for the king, while Daniel's strong faith allows him to rest easy even though his situation is not ideal.

There are many prophecies in Daniel that reinforce the historical overview we saw last week with the statue. Some of these give us more clarity on what happens when the Greeks are in charge, and we see prophecies concerning the end times as well. We don't need to get too in depth into this at this point, but do review the order of reigning kingdoms: Assyria, Babylon, Medes and Persians, Greece, Rome. Rome, in a way, is still "in charge," since Rome is still the epicenter of the Roman Catholic church, and millions of people today look to the Pope for a "word from God." Eventually, Yeshua will return and set up His kingdom: He is the rock that causes men to stumble, and His kingdom will grow to smash all other kingdoms and fill the earth.

Daniel has much to teach us about the existence of heaven, hell, spiritual warfare, the Book of Life, and the resurrection. Some people teach that these are "New Testament" concepts, but here they are, and they've been here all this time!

Day 1:

1) Bible Memory: Choose five Bible memory verses or passages to review.

2) Hebrew Word: חיי עולם   chayei olam – eternal life

3) Think about the lesson: Read Daniel chapter 4. What do you notice?

_____

_____

_____

Day 2:

1) Bible Memory: Choose five Bible memory verses or passages to review.

2) Hebrew Word: חיי עולם   chayei olam – eternal life

3) Think about the lesson: Read Daniel chapter 5. What do you notice?

_____

_____

_____

Day 3:

1) Bible Memory: Choose five Bible memory verses or passages to review.

2) Hebrew Word: חיי עולם   chayei olam – eternal life

3) Think about the lesson: Read Daniel chapter 6. What do you notice that maybe you haven't seen before?

_____

_____

_____

Day 4:

1) Bible Memory: Choose five Bible memory verses or passages to review.

2) Hebrew Word: חיי עולם   chayei olam – eternal life

3) Think about the lesson: Read Daniel chapters 7-8. What do you notice?

_____

_____

_____

Day 5:

1) Bible Memory: Choose five Bible memory verses or passages to review.

2) Hebrew Word: חיי עולם chayei olam – eternal life

3) Think about the lesson: Read Daniel chapter 9. He knows that the 70 years of exile are coming to a close, and he looks forward to his people's return to the land of Israel. What do you find striking about Daniel's prayer on behalf of his people in this chapter?

_____

_____

_____

Day 6:

1) Bible Memory: Choose five Bible memory verses or passages to review.

2) Hebrew Word: חיי עולם chayei olam – eternal life

3) Think about the lesson: Read Daniel chapter 12. We see the Book of Life mentioned in Daniel, and we also see salvation and resurrection. We can have salvation and be written in the Lamb's Book of Life, no matter how bad our situation is. From the prophecies, we know that Yeshua's kingdom will conquer all other kingdoms, and to be a part of His kingdom, we need to trust in Him for our salvation. To be with God forever, to spend eternity with Him, we need only to believe that Yeshua paid the penalty for our sins. He died for us so that we may live. Believe in Him today, and He will write your name in His Book of Life and resurrect you to eternal life with Him.

LESSON 30
HOSEA AND JOEL

Lesson Objectives: Hosea: God loves Israel, even when Israel is unfaithful. Joel: The coming Day of the Lord includes both destruction and deliverance.

Memory Verse: Joel 2:29 Even on my servants, both men and women, I will pour out my Spirit in those days.

Hebrew Word: גַּם gam - also

Lesson Summary:

We've studied the time period of the destruction of Israel (722 BC Assyrian invasion) and deportation of Judah (586 BC Babylonian invasion), and we've met some of the main prophets of those times. Today, we're going to take a look at a couple of "minor" prophets who also prophesied during these times. First, Hosea, who prophesied to Israel before the Assyrian invasion, approximately 753 BC, and Joel, who prophesied around 835 BC, during the reign of Joash, King of Judah.

Remember how God told Ezekiel to prophesy by acting out events, sometimes in crazy ways? God tells Hosea to do something a little crazy, too, just to get His point across to the nation of Israel. God tells Hosea to get married. That's not crazy, of course, but the crazy part is that God tells Hosea to marry a woman who is going to cheat on him. She will be an adulteress. Who wants to marry someone who is going to run away and live with someone else? This must have been hard for Hosea. This must have broken his heart, over and over again. This is God's point: when we say we will follow Him, and then we don't, we are acting like Gomer, Hosea's cheating wife, and we break God's heart. God is like our husband, and we are like His wife. He wants us to love Him more than anything else.

The consequences of sin hurt us as well as our families. When husbands or wives cheat on each other today, they often get divorced, and that hurts their children. It's hard to live in divorced homes. Even if they choose not to get divorced, there may be a lot of fighting in the home, or there may be tension that is not discussed but is very uncomfortable. The home should be a nice place to be, but sin can make it unbearable. This is how adultery can hurt children in the family.

When we read our scriptures from Hosea (above), we see the consequences of Gomer's sin, but we also see Hosea's faithfulness. Hosea is acting like God acts towards Israel. Israel was unfaithful, and so Israel had to suffer the consequences of idolatry, but God has a plan to save Israel. In our readings, we'll see what God's plan is.

I love how Joel starts: Tell it to your children, and let your children tell it to their children, and their children to the next generation. Yes! Pass it on! Pass on the good news of salvation every generation.

What is the Day of the Lord? This is the time when Yeshua returns. He will defeat His enemies and set up His Kingdom. For those who follow Him, this will be a wonderful time, but for those who are His enemies, it will be a terrifying time.

Day 1:

1) Bible Memory: Memorize Joel 2:29.

2) Hebrew Word: **גַם** gam - also

3) Think about the lesson: Read Hosea 1:2 and 3:1. What do you notice?

_____

_____

Day 2:

1) Bible Memory: Review Joel 2:29 and review three other verses.

2) Hebrew Word: **גַם** gam - also

3) Think about the lesson: Read Hosea 4:6. What do you notice?

_____

_____

Day 3:

1) Bible Memory: Review Joel 2:29 and review three other verses.

2) Hebrew Word: **גַם** gam - also

3) Think about the lesson: Read Hosea 13:4 and 13:14. Also read Hosea 14:1-2. What do you notice?

_____

_____

_____

_____

God is our Savior; there is no other Savior. God can bring the dead to life. To be restored, all we need to bring to Him is the "fruit of our lips" – which is our confession of faith.

Day 4:

1) Bible Memory: Review Joel 2:29 and review three other verses.

2) Hebrew Word: **גַם** gam - also

3) Think about the lesson: Read Joel 1:3, Joel 2:1-2, Joel 2:11-13, and Joel 2:28-32. Who are we supposed to tell about the Day of the Lord?

_____

Describe the Day of the Lord:

_____

_____

_____

In this ancient culture, ripping one's clothing was a sign of sorrow. What is the significance of rending our hearts rather than our garments? Pray about this and discuss this with your parents.

_____

_____

What will happen after the Day of the Lord?

_____

_____

_____

Day 5:

1) Bible Memory: Review Joel 2:29 and review three other verses.

2) Hebrew Word: גַּם gam - also

3) Think about the lesson: The physical application of Hosea's story is do not commit adultery. The spiritual point that God is making through Hosea, the real point of the story, is do not commit idolatry – do not have anything more important to you than following God. In what ways might we commit idolatry today?

_____

_____

Joel reminds us that the Day of the Lord, which is real and is coming, will be a day of destruction for those who do not follow God and a day of deliverance and restoration for those who do follow God. May we be among those who follow God! Pray and discuss with your parents.

Day 6:

1) Bible Memory: Review Joel 2:29 and review three other verses.

2) Hebrew Word: גַּם gam - also

3) Think about the lesson: Sin separates us from God. God loves us and wants us to come come back to Him. He gives us every opportunity. He pursues us like a husband pursues his wife. He sent Yeshua, His own right arm, to die for us so that we could be saved from the consequences of our sins. To come back to God, Hosea says that we will bring the "fruit of our lips." We will confess our sins and ask forgiveness from Yeshua, who died in place of us for those sins. Yeshua will forgive us and cleanse us, and we will be saved. To be saved today, ask Yeshua to forgive you of your sins and to save you, to make you a new creation in Him. Pray and discuss with your parents.

LESSON 31
AMOS AND OBADIAH

Lesson Objective: Students will understand tikkun olam, the concept of leaving this world better than we found it, and have some real life application ideas on how to do that.

Memory Verse: Amos 5:24 But let justice roll on like a river, righteousness like a never-failing stream!

Hebrew Word: תיקון עולם tikkun olam – repair of the world

Lesson Summary:

Amos and Obadiah are two of the Minor Prophets. Obadiah wrote after the fall of Jerusalem (586 BC). Amos wrote to Israel in the 8th century BC. Both prophets address the same issue we have been discussing: cycles of disobedience bring judgment.

There are two kinds of evil:

1) The evil that is obvious. Murder is obviously wrong. Hurting someone's feelings is obviously wrong. Not cleaning your room when your parents ask you to is obviously wrong.

2) The evil that is not obvious. Sometimes it can be disguised by religious behavior - going through the motions of being religious while inside we are counting the minutes until lunch. (Amos 8:5)

The consequences of evil are that the world itself and the people in it suffer. Sin leads to death, spiritual and physical.

The concept of tikkun olam is that we leave the world a better place than we found it. For example, who picks up litter they see on the ground? When someone notices, picks it up, and throws it in the trash can, they are practicing tikkun olam, leaving the world better than they found it.

What are some other examples of tikkum olam you can think of?

Practicing tikkun olam *correctly* comes from the heart. We do not make the world a better place to gain glory for ourselves, or to check a box off a "Righteousness" list showing that we did our good deed for the day, but we do it so that we can bring glory to Adonai and to be good stewards of this earth that He put us in charge of caring for.

If we are true Yeshua followers, we live our lives walking as He walked. We make our world a better place because He, in the beginning, made this world very good, and when sin entered and corrupted our world, He entered as well and gave Himself sacrificially to cover our sins and its consequences. Yeshua, on the cross, made a way for us to return to our Heavenly Father. This was the best act of tikkun olam ever!

To truly make this world a better place, we must operate under the power of the Ruach HaKodesh, which is

116

only available to us through Yeshua. To follow Yeshua, to accept His salvation and be saved, we only need to believe with our hearts and confess with our mouths that He is our Savior, He is our God, He died for us, and the fact that He rose again from the dead is the promise for us that we, too, will be resurrected and be together forever with Adonai.

Day 1:

1) Bible Memory: Memorize Amos 5:24.
2) Hebrew Word: תיקון עולם tikkun olam – repairing the world
3) Think about the lesson: Read Amos 5:10-15, Amos 8:4-6, and Obadiah 12. What were the people doing that Adonai was not pleased with?

_____

_____

_____

_____

_____

Day 2:

1) Bible Memory: Review Amos 5:24 and review three other verses.
2) Hebrew Word: תיקון עולם tikkun olam – repairing the world
3) Think about the lesson: Read the list you made yesterday from the verses you read above. How do these sins affect our world in a negative way?

_____

_____

How does obeying God affect our world in a positive way?

_____

_____

Day 3:

1) Bible Memory: Review Amos 5:24 and review three other verses.
2) Hebrew Word: תיקון עולם tikkun olam – repairing the world
3) Think about the lesson: List some ways you can practice tikkun olam on a daily basis. Pray about this and discuss with your parents.

_____

_____

_____

_____

Day 4:

1) Bible Memory: Review Amos 5:24 and review three other verses.

2) Hebrew Word: עולם תיקון tikkun olam – repairing the world

3) Think about the lesson: As part of your Bar or Bat Mitzvah journey, you will be performing a service project. It should be something you enjoy doing, and it should be something that makes life better for someone else. Pray about this, and discuss with your parents. List some ideas you have of some service project possibilities:

_____

_____

_____

_____

Day 5:

1) Bible Memory: Review Amos 5:24 and review three other verses.

2) Hebrew Word: עולם תיקון tikkun olam – repairing the world

3) Think about the lesson: Read Amos 9:11-15. Who is performing tikkun olam in this passage? What acts of tikkun olam are being performed?

_____

_____

_____

_____

Day 6:

1) Bible Memory: Review Amos 5:24 and review three other verses.

2) Hebrew Word: עולם תיקון tikkun olam – repairing the world

3) Think about the lesson: Our righteous acts are nothing compared to the goodness of God. Pray and discuss with your parents.

LESSON 32
JONAH

Lesson Objective: God wants all people throughout the world to come to repentance and salvation through Messiah Yeshua, not just Jews. Jews have a special calling to be priests to the world.

Memory Verse: (same as last week) Amos 5:24 But let justice roll on like a river, righteousness like a never-failing stream!

Hebrew Word: (same as last week) תִּיקוּן עוֹלם tikkun olam – repairing the world

Lesson Summary:

Unlike the prophets we've studied so far, Jonah was called to be a prophet to the Ninevites rather than to the Jewish people. He was a Jewish prophet who was told by God to go call the Ninevites to repentance. Jonah didn't want to go. He knew that God would forgive the Ninevites, and since the Ninevites had done evil things to Jonah's people, Jonah didn't want to see their forgiveness; he wanted to see their judgment. Jonah tried to run away from his calling, but God brought him back in a miraculous way. When Jonah preached, the Ninevites repented, and when Jonah sulked about that, God showed him the wickedness of his own heart.

This is the main idea in Jonah: God wants everyone to obey Him, to follow His word, because He loves the entire world He created. When Yeshua came, we know that He offered salvation to the whole world, not just to the Jews, and we know from Exodus 19:5-6 that God calls the Jews to be priests to the nations, and from Isaiah 49:6, a light to the world. This book of Jonah opens our eyes to part of God's bigger picture. He loves us, and He loves everyone else, too! He doesn't want us to be destroyed by the consequences of our sins.

God wants all people to come to repentance and salvation. God does not have different paths of salvation for different people. He gave everyone in the world the same laws, through the Jewish people as priests to the nations, and He wants us to follow them in order to live a good and blessed life.

Day 1:

1) Bible Memory: Review Amos 5:24 and review four other verses.
2) Hebrew Word: תִּיקוּן עוֹלם tikkun olam – repairing the world
3) Think about the lesson: Read Jonah 1. What do you notice?

_____

_____

Day 2:

1) Bible Memory: Review Amos 5:24 and review four other verses.
2) Hebrew Word: תִּיקוּן עוֹלם tikkun olam – repairing the world
3) Think about the lesson: Read Jonah 2. What do you notice?

_____

_____

Day 3:

1) Bible Memory: Review Amos 5:24 and review four other verses.
2) Hebrew Word: תיקון עולם tikkun olam – repairing the world
3) Think about the lesson: Read Jonah 3. What do you notice?

_____

_____

Day 4:

1) Bible Memory: Review Amos 5:24 and review four other verses.
2) Hebrew Word: תיקון עולם tikkun olam – repairing the world
3) Think about the lesson: Read Jonah 4. What do you notice?

_____

_____

Day 5:

1) Bible Memory: Review Amos 5:24 and review four other verses.
2) Hebrew Word: תיקון עולם tikkun olam – repairing the world
3) Think about the lesson: Why didn't Jonah want to go to Ninevah?

_____

Do you think he was afraid of getting killed? Or do you think he wanted them to suffer the consequences of their sins?

_____

Note that Yeshua referenced Jonah's three days and nights inside the belly of the whale to illustrate that He would be three days and nights inside the grave and then He would resurrect.

Day 6:

1) Bible Memory: Review Amos 5:24 and review four other verses.
2) Hebrew Word: תיקון עולם tikkun olam – repairing the world
3) Think about the lesson: After Jonah preached to the Ninevites, was he happy that they listened to him and repented? Why or why not?

_____

What was the point that God was making to Jonah at the end of the story? What did God teach him with the plant that gave him shade and then withered and died?

_____

_____

Discuss the last verse of the book of Jonah with your parents.

LESSON 33
MICAH AND NAHUM

Lesson Objective: See the prophecies of Yeshua HaMashiach in Micah 5. Recognize that His story has been told from the beginning, and that He is eternal.

Memory Verse: Micah 6:8 He has shown you, O man, what is good. And what does the LORD require of you? To act justly and to love mercy and to walk humbly with your God.

Hebrew Word: מֶלֶךְ melek - king

Lesson Summary:

We have seen over and over again the cycles of repentance, obedience, blessing, drifting, sinning, rebellion, and judgment both in Israel and in Judah, and also in other nations like Ninevah and even here in America. The wages of sin is death. Throughout history and across the globe, we have all sinned and fallen short. The Assyrians in Ninevah knew this, and they repented once, but then they continued to sin. Because of this, they were destroyed. We should not fear those who can kill our bodies, but we should fear Adonai, who will allow us to go to hell if that's what we choose. But if we choose today to repent of our sins and follow Adonai, Yeshua will forgive us; He is Adonai; He is our Savior. He loves us, and He is not willing that any should perish.

Micah contains prophecy about the coming of the Messiah and future times; we'll read some of these prophecies this week.

Nahum's message was for Ninevah. The Ninevites during Jonah' time were Assyrians. They repented after Jonah's visit to them, but later they fell back into their old sinful ways, bringing God's judgment upon them. They were conquered by the Babylonians.

Day 1:

1) Bible Memory: Memorize Micah 6:8.

2) Hebrew Word: מֶלֶךְ melek - king

3) Think about the lesson: Read Nahum 3:1-5. Why was Adonai against them?

_____

_____

Day 2:

1) Bible Memory: Review Micah 6:8 and review three other verses.

2) Hebrew Word: מֶלֶךְ melek - king

3) Think about the lesson: Read Nahum 1:14-15. What does Adonai promise to Judah?

_____

_____

Day 3:

1) Bible Memory: Review Micah 6:8 and review three other verses.

2) Hebrew Word: מלך melek - king

3) Think about the lesson: Read Micah 2:12. What does Adonai promise to do?

_____

_____

Day 4:

1) Bible Memory: Review Micah 6:8 and review three other verses.

2) Hebrew Word: מלך melek - king

3) Think about the lesson: Read Micah 4:10b. This is a prophecy that they will be conquered by the Babylonians and deported to Babylon, but Adonai promises to

_____.

Day 5:

1) Bible Memory: Review Micah 6:8 and review three other verses.

2) Hebrew Word: מלך melek - king

3) Think about the lesson: Read Micah 2:13 "Their King will pass before them; the LORD as their leader." This is set up grammatically as Hebrew poetry, and the parallelism between the lines equates the King as the LORD. The Messiah is the LORD. This is an evidence of Yeshua's deity. Read Micah 5:1-2 – this is a prophecy of the coming of Messiah. They will strike Him on the rod with a cheek – does this sound like Isaiah 53? Read Isaiah 53 and compare. And note also in verse 2 – His origin is from antiquity, from eternity – again, equating Yeshua the Messiah with Adonai. Only Adonai is from eternity past (everyone else He created is eternal moving forward into the future, whether our future be in heaven or hell after our physical deaths). Discuss all these verses with your parents.

Day 6:

1) Bible Memory: Review Micah 6:8 and review three other verses.

2) Hebrew Word: מלך melek - king

3) Think about the lesson: Read Micah 4:2. Do you recognize this verse as a song? If you have family worship time tonight (erev Shabbat) you might all consider singing this song together.

LESSON 34
HABAKKUK AND ZEPHANIAH

Lesson Objectives: Adonai defines right from wrong. Adonai separates the holy from the unholy. He wants us to worship Him and not any idols. He does not want our worship tainted by syncretism (a mixing of the holy with the unholy). He saves us by faith (yes, we see this in the "old" testament!).

Memory Verse: Habakkuk 2:4b The righteous will live by his faith.

Hebrew Word: **אֱמוּנָה** emunah - faith

Lesson Summary:

We live in a land where many cultures are practiced. This was the same for the prophets Habakkuk and Zephaniah. God's word for the people was to worship Him the way he said to worship Him, not to do it the way the other people around them worshipped their gods. Any worship that is not of the God of the Bible is pagan worship. There are often demonic entities behind pagan practices. God does not want his holiness mixed up with unholiness.

Historically, missionaries have understood that basic principle, but they haven't necessarily worked it out in a way that separated acceptable cultural differences from unacceptable pagan practices. As a result, many missionaries focused on changing cultures instead of changing hearts. As you read the following verses throughout this week, discuss each one with your parents. Draw connections to what you see happening in our culture today. Practice discerning the holy from the unholy. Discuss which practices are acceptable cultural differences versus which practices are pagan and ungodly in nature.

Adonai gives us one way to return to Him, and that way is Yeshua, Adonai's right arm of salvation.

Day 1:

1) Bible Memory: Memorize Habakkuk 2:4b.

2) Hebrew Word: **אֱמוּנָה** emunah - faith

3) Think about the lesson: Read Habakkuk 1:2-3. What is Habakkuk upset about?

_____

_____

Are there similar problems in our culture today? List them:

_____

_____

Day 2:

1) Bible Memory: Review Habakkuk 2:4b and review three other verses.

2) Hebrew Word: אמונה emunah - faith

3) Think about the lesson: Read Habakkuk 1:6-7, 11. God will send the Babylonians as judgment against the unrighteousness in Judah. However, the Babylonians are also unrighteous. (God will judge them later.) Describe what these verses say about the Babylonians. Who is their god?

_____

_____

Who is the god of most of the people we see in our culture today?

_____

_____

Day 3:

1) Bible Memory: Review Habakkuk 2:4b and review three other verses.

2) Hebrew Word: אמונה emunah - faith

3) Think about the lesson: Read Habakkuk 2:4. Contrast the righteous versus the unrighteous in this verse.

_____

_____

Are these characteristics the same in our culture today?

_____

_____

Day 4:

1) Bible Memory: Review Habakkuk 2:4b and review three other verses.

2) Hebrew Word: אמונה emunah - faith

3) Think about the lesson: Read Habakkuk 2:5. Can sin ever truly satisfy?_____

Day 5:

1) Bible Memory: Review Habakkuk 2:4b and review three other verses.

2) Hebrew Word: אמונה emunah - faith

3) Think about the lesson: Read Habakkuk 3:17-19. Even if circumstances aren't the greatest, what will Habakkuk do? In whom will he rejoice?

_____

_____

What can we learn from his example?

_____

_____

124

Day 6:

1) Bible Memory: Review Habakkuk 2:4b and review three other verses.

2) Hebrew Word: אמונה emunah - faith

3) Think about the lesson: Read Zephaniah 1:4-6. God tolerates paganism for a time. He gives people every chance to repent, but if people do not repent, what will He do?

_____

_____

What pagan practices and forms of idolatry do you see in our culture today?

_____

_____

What practices are syncretic (a mixture of the holy with the unholy)?

_____

_____

LESSON 35
HAGGAI, ZECHARIAH, AND MALACHI

Lesson Objectives:

Haggai – the people are more focused on their own homes than on restoring the Temple of Adonai.

Zechariah – rebuilding the Temple and the coming of Messiah.

Malachi – many of the people thought it was "useless to serve God (3:14)" but Adonai remembers those who continue to follow Him (3:16-18).

Memory Verse: Zechariah 12:10 And I will pour out on the house of David and the inhabitants of Jerusalem a spirit grace and supplication. They will look on me, the one they have pierced, and they will mourn for him as one mourns for an only child, and grieve bitterly for him as one grieves for a firstborn son.

Hebrew Word: יהושוע Yehoshua – YHWH is salvation – Yeshua's full name; Translated Joshua – see Zechariah 3

Lesson Summary:

Over time, Adonai's presence has dwelt in different temples. He was present in the tabernacle, He was present in the 1st and 2nd Temples, and today, He is present in the midst of the Body of Messiah (all the people in the world who follow Yeshua), and, after salvation through Yeshua, He is present within our individual bodies, in which the Ruach HaKodesh (Holy Spirit) comes to dwell.

This is why it's good to take care of ourselves and each other. However, we need to make sure we are taking care of ourselves and our bodies in a way that glorifies Yeshua and makes our bodies a fitting temple for His dwelling. Our bodies are not our own. He purchased us with a price, the price of His life.

Day 1:

1) Bible Memory: Memorize Zechariah 12:10.
2) Hebrew Word: יהושוע Yehoshua – YHWH is salvation
3) Think about the lesson: Read Haggai 1:2-4. The people were investing all their interest in building their own lives while Adonai's Temple lay in ruins. Read Matthew 6:33. If we put _____ first, He will align everything else in our lives. How do we put God first?

   _____

   _____

Day 2:

1) Bible Memory: Review Zechariah 12:10 and review three other verses.
2) Hebrew Word: יהושע Yehoshua – YHWH is salvation
3) Think about the lesson: Read Zechariah 3:1-10. This is a beautiful picture of Yeshua. Discuss the parallels between this priest, Joshua, and our ultimate high priest Yeshua, with your parents. Record your observations here:

_____

_____

_____

Day 3:

1) Bible Memory: Review Zechariah 12:10 and review three other verses.
2) Hebrew Word: יהושע Yehoshua – YHWH is salvation
3) Think about the lesson: Read Zechariah 11:7-14. Adonai is the Good Shepherd. Note that His wages are 30 pieces of silver. Read Matthew 26:15. What parallels do you see?

_____

_____

_____

Day 4:

1) Bible Memory: Review Zechariah 12:10 and review three other verses.
2) Hebrew Word: יהושע Yehoshua – YHWH is salvation
3) Think about the lesson: Read Zechariah 12:10. Read Isaiah 53. Compare these prophecies of Yeshua:

_____

_____

_____

_____

Read Zechariah 14:16. Who will celebrate Sukkot?

_____

Day 5:

1) Bible Memory: Review Zechariah 12:10 and review three other verses.
2) Hebrew Word: יהושע Yehoshua – YHWH is salvation
3) Think about the lesson: Read Zechariah 7:5-6 and 7:8-10. Consider: is your faith for real? How? Where does your faith need strengthening?

_____

_____

_____

Day 6:

1) Bible Memory: Review Zechariah 12:10 and review three other verses.

2) Hebrew Word: יהושׁוע Yehoshua – YHWH is salvation

3) Think about the lesson: Read Malachi 3:14 and 3:16-18. When the people felt like it was useless to follow God, why did they think that? And how did God respond?

_____

_____

_____

SECTION 3 – BRIT CHADASHAH

LESSON 36
COMPARING MATTHEW, MARK, LUKE, AND JOHN

Lesson Objective: See that each one of the synoptic gospels tell the story of Yeshua from each writer's individual perspective.

Memory Verse: John 14:6 Yeshua answered, "I am the way and the truth and the life. No one comes to the Father except through me."

Hebrew Word: יְהוָה the Name of God

Lesson Summary:

The four gospels tell one story of Yeshua from four different perspectives. Each of the writers focused on areas that they felt were most important or affected them the most or were most important for others to hear and understand. That's why they're not all exactly the same. Any crime detective knows that this is one way to prove the veracity (the truth) of the Bible, because this is how they know they have true and honest witnesses – their stories will be generally the same but will differ in areas that are important to each individual's unique focus.

Getting to know Matthew, Mark, Luke, and John:

Matthew – a Jewish tax collector who became a follower of Yeshua. He was one of the Twelve disciples. He recorded Yeshua's genealogy. Yeshua's stories and teachings were important to him.

Mark – probably wrote his gospel first. The book is shorter than the others. He liked getting to the point quickly. He was a Yeshua follower, even if not one of the Twelve disciples. The miracles of Yeshua were important to Mark.

Luke – a gentile doctor who became a follower of Yeshua. He traveled with Paul on missionary journeys after Yeshua's death and resurrection. He was a historian, and he tended to focus on the "outcasts" – lost things, a thief, a tax collector (Zaccheus), and women (who were considered second class citizens in this culture).

John – the one who was not like the others! John was a close friend and disciple of Yeshua. His focus was definitely spiritual. He understood Yeshua's divine nature.

Day 1:

1) Bible Memory: Memorize John 14:6.
2) Hebrew Word: יְהוָה the Name of God
3) Think about the lesson: Read Matthew 1, Mark 1, Luke 1, and John 1. Compare. What do you notice?

_____

_____

_____

_____

_____

Day 2:

    1)   Bible Memory: Review John 14:6 and review three other verses.

    2)   Hebrew Word: יהוה the Name of God

    3)   Think about the lesson: Read Matthew 3:13-17, Mark 1:9-11, and Luke 3:21-23. What do you notice?

    _____

    _____

    _____

Day 3:

    1)   Bible Memory: Review John 14:6 and review three other verses.

    2)   Hebrew Word: יהוה the Name of God

    3)   Think about the lesson: Read Matthew 4:1-11, Mark 1:12-13, and Luke 4:1-13. What do you notice?

    _____

    _____

    _____

Day 4:

    1)   Bible Memory: Review John 14:6 and review three other verses.

    2)   Hebrew Word: יהוה the Name of God

    3)   Think about the lesson: Read Mark 1:21-28 and Luke 4:31-37. What do you notice?

    _____

    _____

Day 5:

    1)   Bible Memory: Review John 14:6 and review three other verses.

    2)   Hebrew Word: יהוה the Name of God

    3)   Think about the lesson: Read Mark 3:13-19 and Luke 6:12-16. What do you notice?

    _____

    _____

Day 6:

    1)   Bible Memory: Review John 14:6 and review three other verses.

    2)   Hebrew Word: יהוה the Name of God

3) Think about the lesson: How do we know that each of these accounts is true?

_____

_____

_____

LESSON 37
GETTING TO KNOW THE DISCIPLES

Lesson Objective: Be familiar with the twelve disciples, know what a disciple is, and realize that God is calling us to discipleship.

Memory Verse: Matthew 4:19 "Come, follow me," Yeshua said, "and I will make you fishers of men."

Hebrew Word: תלמיד talmeed – student/disciple

Lesson Summary:

The twelve disciples were chosen by Yeshua not on the basis of their own merits but on the purpose that Yeshua had for each of them. We'll look at each of them individually throughout this week.

Like the disciples, we all come from different backgrounds and we have different callings, gifts, and talents.

Being a disciple involves studying and learning the Word of God and then serving by going into the world and training new disciples.

Day 1:

1) Bible Memory: Memorize Matthew 4:19.

2) Hebrew Word: תלמיד talmeed – student/disciple

3) Think about the lesson: Read about Peter and Andrew.

Peter	Andrew
Brother to Andrew	Brother to Peter
Luke 4:38	John 1:35
1 Cor 9:5	
Gal 2:7 John 1:40-42	

Day 2:

1) Bible Memory: Review Matthew 4:19 and review three other verses.

2) Hebrew Word: תלמיד talmeed – student/disciple

3) Think about the lesson: Read about James and John.

James	John
Brother to John	John 3:23
Mark 5:37	Brother to James
Matt 17:1	Wrote 1 John, 2 John, 3 John, Revelation
Mark 14:33	
Acts 12:1-3	

Day 3:

1) Bible Memory: Review Matthew 4:19 and review three other verses.
2) Hebrew Word: תלמיד talmeed – student/disciple
3) Think about the lesson: Read about Philip and Bartholomew.

Philip	Bartholomew
John 1:43, 45	Also called Nathanael
	John 21:2
	John 1:46, 47

Day 4:

1) Bible Memory: Review Matthew 4:19 and review three other verses.
2) Hebrew Word: תלמיד talmeed – student/disciple
3) Think about the lesson: Read about Matthew and Thomas.

Matthew	Thomas
Matt 9:9	John 11:16
Mark 2:16	John 14:4-5
	John 20:28

133

Day 5:

1) Bible Memory: Review Matthew 4:19 and review three other verses.
2) Hebrew Word: תלמיד talmeed – student/disciple
3) Think about the lesson: Read about James and Simon.

James son of Alphaeus	Simon the Zealot
Also called James the Lesser	"mystery man in the scriptures"
Luke 6:14	Mentioned only in the lists of the disciples, but little else is known
Mark 15:40	Acts 1:13
Matt 27:56	

Day 6:

1) Bible Memory: Review Matthew 4:19 and review three other verses.
2) Hebrew Word: תלמיד talmeed – student/disciple
3) Think about the lesson: Read about Judas, son of James, and Judas Iscariot.

Judas, the son of James	Judas Iscariot
John 14:22	John 6:70-71
	Matt 26:15

LESSON 38
CULTURAL CONTEXT OF THE 1ST CENTURY

Lesson Objective: Understand the cultural context and historical background that existed before and during Yeshua's life.

Memory Verse: Galatians 4:4-5 But when the time had fully come, God sent his Son, born of a woman, born under law, to redeem those under law, that we might receive the full rights of sons.

Hebrew Word: עלם - olam - world, eternity, or forever (especially when used with "vaed"), universe

Lesson Summary:

Can you imagine a world without cell phones? Without the internet?
How about cars? What if you had to get everywhere you needed to go on foot?
How different would your life be?

Mentally, we think in our own world, our own culture. It can be tough to really understand another culture.

Yeshua was born, lived, died, and resurrected in the 1st century, about 2000 years ago. Paul called this the "fullness of time." We'll see why he called it the fullness of time and what he meant by that in this lesson; and we'll see how the 1st century culture and historical context enabled the spread of the gospel worldwide.

There were two major factors important for the spread of the gospel in the 1st century: a common language spoken worldwide, and relative ease and safety of travel.

Alexander the Great conquered the entire known world by 323BC, and with his conquering armies, he spread the Koine Greek, or Common Greek language.

He also spread Greek religion, which we know caused a problem for the Jews, especially during the time leading up to the Maccabean revolt in 165BC.

Following on the heels of the Greeks were the Romans, and they were the ones in charge when Yeshua was born. The Roman religion was similar in many ways to the Greek religion, with many of the same gods and goddesses who were simply called by different names. People at this time still spoke the Common Greek.

In addition to a common language that enabled the gospel to be spread quickly, travel throughout the Roman Empire at this time was fairly safe (with a few major exceptions) and travel was fairly quick and easy (although it was nowhere near as quick and easy as today!).

In addition to a common language and ease of travel, this was also "the fullness of time" in God's plan. God tells us the end from the beginning, and this is the prophesied time for the Messiah to have come.

Day 1:

1) Bible Memory: Memorize Galatians 4:4-5.

2) Hebrew Word: עלם - olam - world, eternity, or forever (especially when used with "vaed"), universe

3) Think about the lesson: *Greek language and the Septuagint*: Read Daniel 2:31-35. Remember Nebuchadnezzar's dream that Daniel interpreted? Babylon was the head of gold; the Medes and Persians (Esther's time), were the arms of silver. Greece would be the belly and thighs of bronze. Led by Alexander the Great, the Greek armies conquered the known world of that time. Greek rule for over 100 years (332BC – 170ish BC) was fairly kind to the Jewish people. This changed under the rule of Antiochus Epiphanes, and his harsh treatment of Jews and outlawing of Jewish tradition sparked the Maccabean revolt, which we'll learn more about during Chanukah. There were Jews living in Alexandria, Egypt, who by that time had adopted Greek language and culture; they assembled 72 scribes to translate the Tanach (the Hebrew Bible or "Old Testament") into Greek. This translation became known as the Septuagint (which means 70 in Greek). This translation was the copy of the Bible that was the most well-known and the most commonly read version of the Bible throughout the known world at that time. During the 1st century, when Yeshua and others quoted from the scriptures, this translation is often the one that is quoted. Jews that adopted Greek ways were called Hellenized Jews. They represented most of the Jewish people, especially those living outside Israel.

Day 2:

1) Bible Memory: Memorize Galatians 4:4-5.

2) Hebrew Word: עלם - olam - world, eternity, or forever (especially when used with "vaed"), universe

3) Think about the lesson: *Travel in the 1st century and life under Roman rule*: Not too long after the Maccabean revolt (165 BC), the Romans conquered Greece (146 BC). Greek gods and goddesses adopted Roman names. Romans began building roads. By 300AD, they had built over 50,000 roads. Most of these were built for military purposes, but citizens could use them for transportation as well. The primary mode of transportation was walking. People walked in sandals and carried their supplies. Transportation was similar to a backpacking trip. Miles were slightly shorter than the miles we measure today, and they were marked with stone mile markers along the roads, which were about 12 feet wide and paved with stones. Periodically, there were inns along the roads for travelers to stop and sleep for the night; however, many people accepted the hospitality of others and stayed with others in their homes rather than staying in inns if that was at all an option for them. People with more money at their disposal could ride horses or ride in carriages. The carriages did not have springs, so the ride was very bumpy and probably uncomfortable. Sailing was an option as well, if waterways connected people to the places they wanted to go. The boats at that time did not have large sails or multiple sails, so tacking in a fierce wind was difficult and dangerous. The apostle Paul shares some of his experiences in 2 Corinthians 11:26. You can read about other trips he took in Acts 10:23-24 and Acts 20:13-14. Emperor Augustus (27BC – 14AD) established the Pax Romana, which enabled people to travel safely in the 1st century. This assisted Paul greatly as he carried the

message of Yeshua throughout the known world by land and by sea.

Day 3:

1) Bible Memory: Review Galatians 4:4-5 and review three other verses.

2) Hebrew Word: עלם - olam - world, eternity, or forever (especially when used with "vaed"), universe

3) Think about the lesson: *Prophecies about this time*: Prophecies throughout the Tanach had foretold the arrival of the Messiah during this period of time in the 1st century. There was some confusion as to whether there would be one Messiah or two. There was the idea of the Messiah ben Joseph, or Suffering Servant, and the Messiah ben David, who would be the King. The religious leaders during the 1st century were looking for a King Messiah who would come and defeat the Romans, kick them out of the land, and set up his reign from Jerusalem. Yet before we can acknowledge Yeshua as our King, our sin must be dealt with. So Yeshua came first as the Suffering Servant of Isaiah 53. When He returns, He will reign as King from Jerusalem. Read Genesis 3:15 and Galatians 4:4. Read Isaiah 52:13-53:12 and Luke 22-24. Read Psalm 2:6-9 and Revelation 19:15-16. A lesson for us in this is that during our time, we look eagerly for Yeshua's return. There are different ideas about how that will look. We must remember that the educated religious folk of the 1st century did not recognize Him because He didn't look like what they were expecting; however, the lay people who were not necessarily part of the academic controversies just knew the scriptures, and they recognized Him from the simplicity of the prophecies. If we want to recognize Him when He returns, we need to know the scriptures.

Day 4:

1) Bible Memory: Review Galatians 4:4-5 and review three other verses.

2) Hebrew Word: עלם - olam - world, eternity, or forever (especially when used with "vaed"), universe

3) Think about the lesson: *The groups: Scribes and Pharisees, Sadducees, Essenes, Zealots.*

Not all Jews during the 1st century (or any century) believed exactly the same things. They understood scripture differently and had different ideas about key cultural debates. The scribes knew the scriptures well, because that was their job to copy them. There were no printing presses at that time to make copies of books; scrolls were written carefully and painstakingly by hand by scribes. Scribes are called "teachers of the law" in some translations because they taught the people about what they knew of the scriptures. The scribes and Pharisees are often mentioned together in the scriptures.

The Pharisees are sometimes portrayed as legalistic hypocrites in the scriptures. They were very religious. Read Matthew 23. Discuss this passage with you parents. What were Yeshua's concerns?

The Pharisees reigned in the synagogues; the Sadducees reigned in the Temple. Sadducees were the upper class, the appointed priests, and they had vastly different views on scripture than the scribes and Pharisees. They trusted the Torah only and viewed the writings of the prophets and later writings with suspicion. They did not believe in the resurrection, nor did they believe in the existence of angels or demons. Read Matthew 22:23-33 and discuss the passage with your parents. What are the Sadducees trying to do? How does Yeshua answer them?

There were two other main Jewish groups in the 1ˢᵗ century: the Essenes, and the Zealots. Not much is known of the Essenes. Some say they were the people who lived along the Dead Sea and preserved the Dead Sea scrolls in caves. It is surmised that they died off because they were a group of men who did not marry or have children. The Zealots were young Jewish men who were zealous for the Jewish people and ready to fight the Romans and kick them out of Israel. Simon, one of Yeshua's twelve disciples, was called Simon the Zealot (Matthew 10:4).

Day 5:

1) Bible Memory: Review Galatians 4:4-5 and review three other verses.

2) Hebrew Word: עלם - olam - world, eternity, or forever (especially when used with "vaed"), universe

3) Think about the lesson: *Daily life in the 1ˢᵗ century*. The family was the basic social unit and included the extended family members with the oldest patriarch (father) in charge. Fathers taught their children Torah and also a trade. For example, Yeshua learned carpentry because his earthly father was a carpenter (Mark 6:3). Workers were paid daily. Land belonged to families within their tribal areas, and any time they sold it, the land returned to them at the Jubilee year. During the day, people took care of their land, their homes, and their animals, which sometimes lived inside the courtyard of the home, and any other business dealings they had. Business in the city was done in the city courtyard. Men and women had defined roles; men were to take care of their families by providing for them, while women were to take care of their families by managing the home. Some women worked and earned money, but many did not and needed to be cared for. This is why the Bible emphasizes care for the orphans and widows. The first century culture was heavily based on concepts of honor and shame. Each member of a family was to act in such a way that he or she would bring honor to the family and not in such a way that the family would be shamed. Meals included bread, fish, cakes made of dates and figs, milk, cheese, and, on special occasions, meat, usually lamb or goat.

Day 6:

1) Bible Memory: Review Galatians 4:4-5 and review three other verses.

2) Hebrew Word: עלם - olam - world, eternity, or forever (especially when used with "vaed"), universe

3) Think about the lesson: *Our cultural context today*. Consider all that you have learned this week about the cultural context and historical background of the 1ˢᵗ century. How does it compare to your cultural context and historical background now in the 21ˢᵗ century? What is the same? What is different? Do the differences make it easier or harder to share the gospel? How? Discuss with your parents.

LESSON 39
YESHUA FULFILLED PROPHECIES

Lesson Objective: We can know that Yeshua is the Messiah based on the prophecies given before His birth that He fulfilled during His life.

Memory Verse: Proverbs 30:4 Who has gone up to heaven and come down? Who has gathered up the wind in the hollow of his hands? Who has wrapped up the waters in his cloak? Who has established all the ends of the earth? What is his name, and the name of his son? Tell me, for you know.

Hebrew Word: נבואה nevuah - prophecy

Lesson Summary:

Yeshua is the Messiah that Adonai promised from the beginning.

We are separated from God because of our sins. No matter how good we think we are, one sin in an entire lifetime is enough to separate us from God. We cannot make up for it. There is not enough good in the world to erase one bad thing that we've done. Think about it this way: imagine a flock of whit sheep on a green, grassy hill. The sheep look quite clean against the backdrop of green. Yet, look again after it has snowed. When the hill is covered in pure white snow, the sheep no longer look as white as they did the day before when contrasted against the green grass. They look dirty and dingy in contrast with the pure white snow. We are like the sheep; the snow is like the righteousness of God. We do not measure up. We cannot ever be that clean, that pure, that unblemished. Yeshua did all the work for us that we could not do. We have sinned, but He paid the price for our sins, and He offers us forgiveness. Accept His forgiveness today. Yeshua provided the only way back to God.

We know from the scriptures that He fulfilled all of the prophecies that foretold His coming and we can be sure that He is the Messiah.

We are to have a ready answer for everyone who asks about the hope within us. Knowing some of the many prophetic fulfillments can help us show our friends who are not yet believers in Yeshua that He is the Messiah.

Day 1:

1) Bible Memory: Memorize Proverbs 30:4.

2) Hebrew Word: נבואה nevuah - prophecy

3) Think about the lesson: Read the verses and place them in the appropriate places in the chart:

Genesis 3:15	Genesis 12:3, 18:18	Deuteronomy 18:15, 19	Genesis 49:10
Psalm 132:11	Numbers 24:17-19	Galatians 4:4	Matthew 1:2
Luke 3:33	Matthew 21:11	Romans 1:3	Luke 3:34

Topic	Hebrew Scriptures Prophecy	Yeshua's Fulfillment
Seed of a woman		
Seed of Abraham		
Seed of Judah		
Seed of Jacob		
Seed of David		
Prophet like Moses		

Day 2:

1) Bible Memory: Review Proverbs 30:4 and review three other verses.

2) Hebrew Word: נבואה nevuah - prophecy

3) Think about the lesson: Read the verses and place them in the appropriate places in the chart:

Psalm 110:1	Hebrews 5:5-6	Matthew 27:64	Psalm 110:4
Psalm 68:18	Luke 24:51	John 13:18, 21	Psalm 41:9
Psalm 22	Psalm 16:10	John 19:28-30	Proverbs 30:4
Matthew 3:17	Acts 13:35-37		

Topic	Hebrew Scriptures Prophecy	Yeshua's Fulfillment
The Son of God		
A priest like Melchizedek		
Betrayed by a friend		
Crucified		
Raised from the dead		
Ascended to heaven		
Sits at the right hand of God the Father		

Day 3:

1) Bible Memory: Review Proverbs 30:4 and review three other verses.

2) Hebrew Word: נבואה nevuah - prophecy

3) Think about the lesson: Read the verses and place them in the appropriate places in the chart:

Isaiah 7:14   Psalm 118:22-23   Isaiah 52:13-53:12   Psalm 2:6-9
Isaiah 53:1   Jeremiah 23:5-6   Acts 2:36   John 12:38
Revelation 19:15-16   Acts 4:11   Luke 1:26-35
Matthew 20:28

Topic	Hebrew Scriptures Prophecy	Yeshua's Fulfillment
Born of a virgin		
Rejected stone becomes head cornerstone		
Suffering Messiah		
King Messiah		
Right arm of God		
Called "the Lord"		

Day 4:

1) Bible Memory: Review Proverbs 30:4 and review three other verses.

2) Hebrew Word: נבואה nevuah - prophecy

3) Think about the lesson: Read the verses and place them in the appropriate places in the chart:

Isaiah 59:16
Hebrew 9:15
Isaiah 61:1-11
Luke 4:16-21
Micah 5:2
Luke 2:4-6
Daniel 9:24-26
Ephesians 1:10
Matthew 21:12
Malachi 3:1

Topic	Hebrew Scriptures Prophecy	Yeshua's Fulfillment
Two comings of the Messiah		
Our intercessor		
Born in Bethlehem		
Time of His coming prophesied		
Enters the Temple with authority		

Day 5:

1) Bible Memory: Review Proverbs 30:4 and review three other verses.

2) Hebrew Word: נבואה nevuah - prophecy

3) Think about the lesson: Read the verses and place them in the appropriate places in the chart:

Jeremiah 31:31-33
Hebrews 8:6-13
Isaiah 25:8
1 Corinthians 15:54
Zechariah 9:9
Matthew 21:1-10
Zechariah 13:7
Matthew 26:31, 56
Zechariah 12:10
John 19:34, 37

Topic	Hebrew Scriptures Prophecy	Yeshua's Fulfillment
The new covenant		
Enters Jerusalem on a donkey		
Pierced		
Forsaken by disciples		
Victory over death		

Day 6:

1) Bible Memory: Review Proverbs 30:4 and review three other verses.

2) Hebrew Word: נבואה nevuah - prophecy

3) Think about the lesson: Read the verses and place them in the appropriate places in the chart:

Micah 4:1-4
Revelation 12:5
Isaiah 11:10
Romans 11:2
Psalm 2:2
Revelation 19:19
Matthew 12:21
Isaiah 42:1
Isaiah 9:1-8
Matthew 4:12-16

Topic	Hebrew Scriptures Prophecy	Yeshua's Fulfillment
Ministers in Galilee first		
Ministers to the Gentiles		
Opposition of the nations		
Gentiles seek the Messiah of Israel		
All nations submit to Messiah's rule		

LESSON 40
PARABLES OF YESHUA

Lesson Objective: Students will know that Yeshua taught using stories.

Memory Verse: Luke 18:14b "For everyone who exalts himself will be humbled, and he who humbles himself will be exalted."

Hebrew Word: מָשָׁל mashal – a short story that teaches a lesson

Lesson Summary:

Last week we examined many prophecies about the Messiah that Yeshua fulfilled. Another prophecy is that He would come speaking in parables. A parable is a short story that teaches a lesson. This prophecy is found in Psalm 78, and we see Yeshua fulfilling it in Matthew 13:35.

When Yeshua was teaching, sometimes He spoke clearly and plainly. However, other times, He taught in parables. Why do you think He did this?

Day 1:

1) Bible Memory: Memorize Luke 18:14b.

2) Hebrew Word: מָשָׁל mashal – a short story that teaches a lesson

3) Think about the lesson: Read Psalm 78 and discuss it with your parents. What do you notice?

_____

_____

_____

Day 2:

1) Bible Memory: Review Luke 18:14b and review three other verses.

2) Hebrew Word: מָשָׁל mashal – a short story that teaches a lesson

3) Think about the lesson: Read Matthew 13 and discuss it with your parents. What do you notice?

_____

_____

_____

Day 3:

1) Bible Memory: Review Luke 18:14b and review three other verses.

2) Hebrew Word: מָשָׁל mashal – a short story that teaches a lesson

3) Think about the lesson: Consider the parables in Matthew 13 that you read yesterday. What is the lesson in each of the stories?

Parable	Reference	Lesson
Sower and seeds	Matthew 13:3-8	
Weeds (tares)	Matthew 13:24-30	
Mustard seed	Matthew 13:31-32	
Yeast	Matthew 13:33	
Hidden treasure	Matthew 13:44	
Pearl of great price	Matthew 13:45-46	
Net	Matthew 13:47-50	

Day 4:

1) Bible Memory: Review Luke 18:14b and review three other verses.
2) Hebrew Word: מָשָׁל mashal – a short story that teaches a lesson
3) Think about the lesson: Read Matthew 18:23-35. What is the lesson?

_____

_____

Day 5:

    1) Bible Memory: Review Luke 18:14b and review three other verses.

    2) Hebrew Word: מָשָׁל mashal – a short story that teaches a lesson

    3) Think about the lesson: Read Matthew 20:1-16. What is the lesson?

_____

_____

_____

Day 6:

    1) Bible Memory: Review Luke 18:14b and review three other verses.

    2) Hebrew Word: מָשָׁל mashal – a short story that teaches a lesson

    3) Think about the lesson: Read Luke 10:25-37. What is the lesson?

_____

_____

_____

146

LESSON 41
MIRACLES OF YESHUA

Lesson Objective: Yeshua performed miracles to show that He loves us and that He is sovereign over all that He created. Because of this, we can have faith that He can and save us.

Memory Verse: John 11:25-26 Yeshua said to her, "I am the resurrection and the life. He who believes in me will live, even though he dies; and whoever lives and believes in me will never die. Do you believe this?"

Hebrew Word: **נס** nes - miracle

Lesson Summary:

Why does Yeshua perform miracles?

- Miracles offer proof of who He is – they are a testimony.
- Miracles are proof that He loves us. (However, this does not mean that He does not love us if we pray for a miracle and He doesn't answer that prayer the way we want Him to. He sees the bigger picture and sometimes, He doesn't answer our prayers for reasons that He understands.)

Miracles offer us an opportunity to show faith, and faith is a crucial part of a miracle.

Day 1:

1) Bible Memory: Memorize John 11:25-26.

2) Hebrew Word: **נס** nes - miracle

3) Think about the lesson: Read John 2:1-11. What was Yeshua's first miracle?

   _____

   We learn that Yeshua is sovereign over _____ and that He wants us to enjoy life – especially eternal life!

Day 2:

1) Bible Memory: Review John 11:25-26 and review three other verses.

2) Hebrew Word: **נס** nes - miracle

3) Think about the lesson: Read Luke 7:11-15. What did Yeshua do?

   _____

   We learn that Yeshua is sovereign over _____ and we see that he comforts the mother.

Day 3:

1) Bible Memory: Review John 11:25-26 and review three other verses.

2) Hebrew Word: נס nes - miracle

3) Think about the lesson: Read Matthew 8:23-27. What did Yeshua do?

_____

We learn that Yeshua is sovereign over _____ and He calls His disciples to have faith.

Day 4:

1) Bible Memory: Review John 11:25-26 and review three other verses.

2) Hebrew Word: נס nes - miracle

3) Think about the lesson: Read Matthew 9:27-31. What did Yeshua do?

_____

We learn that Yeshua is sovereign over _____ and we see that the measure of our faith plays a part in whether or not we will see miracles.

Day 5:

1) Bible Memory: Review John 11:25-26 and review three other verses.

2) Hebrew Word: נס nes - miracle

3) Think about the lesson: Read John 6:16-21. What did Yeshua do?

_____

We learn that Yeshua is sovereign over _____ and He calls us to be courageous.

Day 6:

1) Bible Memory: Review John 11:25-26 and review three other verses.

2) Hebrew Word: נס nes - miracle

3) Think about the lesson: Read Luke 9:12-17. What did Yeshua do?

_____

We learn that Yeshua is the eternal source of all _____ and that He calls us to be active participants.

LESSON 42
THE REAL YESHUA

Lesson Objectives: Since Yeshua's historical existence cannot be denied, all major religions of the world have had to create an explanation for who He was: A teacher? A prophet? A good man? The first angel? God Himself? Understand that the defining characteristic (His Deity) proves He is who He is and that's how He can be our Savior.

Memory Verse: John 1:14 "And the Word became flesh and dwelt among us, and we beheld His glory, glory as of the only begotten from the Father, full of grace and truth."

Hebrew Word: יֵשׁוּעַ – Yeshua – Salvation

Note: Some Jews who do not believe He is the Messiah will call him Yeshu – without the ayin – which stands for "may his name be blotted out" – may we have eyes (the ayin) to see the real Yeshua!

Lesson Summary:

Yeshua's existence is historically recorded, and not just in the Bible. There are many external sources written during that time that attest to His existence here on earth. He was a person who was born, had a family and friends, walked this earth teaching, healing, and performing miracles, was killed on a cross by the Romans, and somehow disappeared from an impenetrable, guarded tomb. These are facts recorded in many sources. Therefore, every other religion recognizes that He existed. However, other religions cannot and do not accept His deity (which means that they do not believe that He is God.) This is the one major difference between how different people and religions see Yeshua.

The Hebrew Scriptures prophesied that the Savior was God, and only God has the power to forgive sins.

When Yeshua stated the truth of Who He was, many wanted to kill him. Claiming to be God if you're not God is blasphemy.

Read the scriptures this week and discuss them with your parents. Who do you say that Yeshua is?

Day 1:

1) Bible Memory: Memorize John 1:14.
2) Hebrew Word: יֵשׁוּעַ – Yeshua – Salvation
3) Think about the lesson: Read Isaiah 43:11 and 25, and Isaiah 44:6. Who is the Savior, the Redeemer, and the One who can blot out sins?

_____

   Read Joel 2:32 and Acts 2:21. By which Name can we be saved?

_____

Day 2:

1) Bible Memory: Review John 1:14 and review three other verses.

2) Hebrew Word: יֵשׁוּעַ – Yeshua – Salvation

3) Think about the lesson: Read John 1:1, John 10:30-33, and John 9:35-38. What do you notice?

_____

_____

_____

Day 3:

1) Bible Memory: Review John 1:14 and review three other verses.

2) Hebrew Word: יֵשׁוּעַ – Yeshua – Salvation

3) Think about the lesson: Read Colossians 2:9, John 8:58, John 1:14 and John 20:28. What do you notice?

_____

_____

_____

Day 4:

1) Bible Memory: Review John 1:14 and review three other verses.

2) Hebrew Word: יֵשׁוּעַ – Yeshua – Salvation

3) Think about the lesson: Read Matthew 9:1-7, Matthew 12:8 and 14, and Matthew 14:32. What do you notice?

_____

_____

_____

Day 5:

1) Bible Memory: Review John 1:14 and review three other verses.

2) Hebrew Word: יֵשׁוּעַ – Yeshua – Salvation

3) Think about the lesson: Read Matthew 17:5, Matthew 12:23, Matthew 21:9, and Matthew 22:41-45. What do you notice?

_____

_____

Read John 10:22-42. What do you notice?

_____

_____

_____

Day 6:

1) Bible Memory: Review John 1:14 and review three other verses.

2) Hebrew Word: יֵשׁוּעַ – Yeshua – Salvation

3) Think about the lesson:
   Think about the relationship between the Father, Son, and Spirit. We can see the relationship between father and son in the Hebrew word for stone.

   אבן

   Even = stone
   First two letters – aleph and bet = av = father
   Last two letters – ben and nun = ben = son
   Father and son in one = the stone that causes men to stumble, the cornerstone/capstone, the rock in the wilderness that followed them through the desert providing water

LESSON 43
FRUITS OF THE SPIRIT

Lesson Objective: Godly character attributes grow naturally out of a close relationship with God and are indicative of spiritual growth.

Memory Verse: Galatians 5:22-23 But the fruit of the Spirit is love, joy, peace, patience, kindness, goodness, gentleness, faithfulness, and self-control. Against these things there is no law.

Hebrew Word: רוח Ruach – Spirit (literally means wind or breath) The Ruach is the breath of God.

Lesson Summary:

Many people believe that we can make the decision to be kind or to be patient or to be self-controlled, and that we will be able to be kind, patient, or self-controlled.

However, sometimes we realize we really can't. Someone hurts us and the last thing we want to do is be kind in response. Or we've been patient as long as we can stand it and we just can't stop being impatient. Or we're trying to be self-controlled, and yet inside we just really want to yell or hit something. It happens! We are human and we have a sinful nature.

Sin is the natural fruit of our lives. We can try to produce good fruit all we want, but if our nature is sinful, we will produce sin. It's like asking a bramble bush to produce grapes instead of thorns. A bramble bush cannot produce grapes. It can only produce thorns.

To produce grapes, it has to become a grapevine. How does a bramble bush become a grapevine?

How do we, as sinful people, become holy? How can we produce Godly fruit?

It's impossible. A plant can't make itself into a different plant any more than we can make ourselves holy by trying. (Works righteousness doesn't work)

Only God can do the impossible.

And He did the impossible for us! We are like seeds. When we are planted in the earth and watered, it's like being planted in God and being fed by his Holy Spirit, the Ruach. Our growth will not happen overnight! It will take a long time, but if we stay rooted in Him and stay close to his Word, walk in His ways, pray continuously, then we will experience spiritual growth, and one day we will wake up to realize that the fruits of the Spirit describe us! And we didn't even have to try! Growth happened because God planted us in Him, fed us with His Word, and we stayed close to Him through prayer☺

Summary of how to grow:

1) Stay close to God
2) Stay in consistent communication with God
3) Pray
4) Read your Bible
5) Be in Godly community with others
6) Be obedient to God's leading

Day 1:

1) Bible Memory: Memorize Galatians 5:22-23.

2) Hebrew Word: רוח Ruach – Spirit (literally means wind or breath)

3) Think about the lesson: Stay close to God. How can you stay close to God this week? Pray about this and discuss with your parents. Read John 15:4. What do you notice?

_____

_____

Day 2:

1) Bible Memory: Review Galatians 5:22-23 and review three other verses.

2) Hebrew Word: רוח Ruach – Spirit (literally means wind or breath)

3) Think about the lesson: Stay in consistent communication with God. How can you stay in consistent communication with God this week? Pray about this and discuss with your parents.

Day 3:

1) Bible Memory: Review Galatians 5:22-23 and review three other verses.

2) Hebrew Word: רוח Ruach – Spirit (literally means wind or breath)

3) Think about the lesson: Pray. Review the types of prayer: acclamation (God, you are awesome!), confession (asking for forgiveness of specific sins), thanksgiving (continuous thankfulness for everything), supplication (asking God for help, either for yourself or for someone else). Read how Yeshua taught us to pray in Matthew 6:9-13. If you don't already, begin praying every day.

Day 4:

1) Bible Memory: Review Galatians 5:22-23 and review three other verses.

2) Hebrew Word: רוח Ruach – Spirit (literally means wind or breath)

3) Think about the lesson: Read your Bible. Are you reading your Bible a little bit every day? Remember that you need to eat the Word just like you need to eat food every day in order to grow. If you haven't already established a time during the day that you set aside for reading the Bible, do that now. And do it consistently all this week. Read Galatians 5:16-23. What do you notice?

_____

_____

_____

Day 5:

1) Bible Memory: Review Galatians 5:22-23 and review three other verses.

2) Hebrew Word: רוח Ruach – Spirit (literally means wind or breath)

3) Think about the lesson: Are you in Godly community with others? Are you regularly attending a congregation? When you are there, are you focused on God and what He is doing in your midst? How does being in community with like-minded believers boost your own faith and prepare you for your next week? Discuss with your parents.

Day 6:

1) Bible Memory: Review Galatians 5:22-23 and review three other verses.

2) Hebrew Word: רוח Ruach – Spirit (literally means wind or breath)

3) Think about the lesson: Be obedient to God's leading. How can you recognize God's voice? How can you tell when, where, and how He leads you? Are you obedient? Pray and discuss with your parents.

LESSON 44
RELATIONSHIP VS. RELIGION

Lesson Objective: See the difference between following the stipulations of a religious in order to seek God versus developing a relationship with God through Yeshua.

Memory Verse: Proverbs 18:24 One who has unreliable friends soon comes to ruin, but there is a friend who sticks closer than a brother.

Hebrew Word: אהבה Ahavah – love; from the root word ahav which means give – true love is more interested in giving than receiving

Lesson Summary:

Religion is humanity's attempt to either seek God's favor or reach some sort of higher plane. We cannot, by our own efforts, attain the position with God that we want. We are sinful. He is not.

Relationship, on the other hand, is a loving and close friendship. This is what we seek. We can only achieve relationship with God through Yeshua, who is the only way to God because He conquered sin and defeated its consequences, and we stay in relationship with Him and deepen and cultivate that relationship through prayer, time in His Word, abiding in His Spirit, and doing the things that He enjoys, which will also give us joy if we are walking in the Spirit with Him.

In a marriage, we seek to please our spouse. So, if a spouse hates it when we squeeze toothpaste from the center of the tube instead of the rolling it up from the bottom, we change our habits and begin rolling the toothpaste up from the bottom so that we will stay in a loving relationship with our spouse. That's one reason why we obey God's Torah – it pleases Him. And since we love Him (because He loves us) we want to please Him (relationship). We don't follow the Torah because we can be saved by doing so (religion).

Day 1:

1) Bible Memory: Memorize Proverbs 18:24.
2) Hebrew Word: אהבה Ahavah – love
3) Think about the lesson: Read Proverbs 18:24. Who do you think is the friend who sticks closer than a brother?

_____

Day 2:

1) Bible Memory: Review Proverbs 18:24 and review three other verses.
2) Hebrew Word: אהבה Ahavah – love
3) Think about the lesson: Read Proverbs 19:3. Who's heart rages against the Lord, and what is the solution?

_____

155

Day 3:

1) Bible Memory: Review Proverbs 18:24 and review three other verses.
2) Hebrew Word: אהבה Ahavah – love
3) Think about the lesson: Read Psalm 51:17. What are the sacrifices that God seeks?

_____

_____

Day 4:

1) Bible Memory: Review Proverbs 18:24 and review three other verses.
2) Hebrew Word: אהבה Ahavah – love
3) Think about the lesson: Read Romans 5:1-5. What do you notice?

_____

_____

Day 5:

1) Bible Memory: Review Proverbs 18:24 and review three other verses.
2) Hebrew Word: אהבה Ahavah – love
3) Think about the lesson: Read Psalm 23. How does this psalm describe the relationship between the shepherd and his sheep? How does it describe a believer's relationship with God?

_____

_____

_____

Day 6:

1) Bible Memory: Review Proverbs 18:24 and review three other verses.
2) Hebrew Word: אהבה Ahavah – love
3) Think about the lesson: As a family, during Erev Shabbat dinner, prepare two slices of challah bread. Put one in the refrigerator and the other in the toaster. Place a pat of cold butter on the cold piece. Spread melted butter on the toasted piece. As a family, examine each option. Discuss: Which is more appetizing? Which do you think looks better? Smells better? Tastes better? Discuss: The butter is like our hearts, and the bread is like Yeshua, the bread of life. On the first plate, the bread and butter are distinct. They are separate and can be easily separated. The butter (our cold, hard hearts) can easily be lifted off of the bread (Yeshua). It is like religion. One the second plate, the butter (a softened heart) is melted into the bread of life, Yeshua, and the two have become one. The butter cannot be removed from the bread. It looks inviting, and it smells great. This is a relationship with Yeshua. Both plates contain the same ingredients – i.e. adherence to Torah may be the same in both religion and relationship, but the relationship includes a total heart change while religion is just an outward act.

156

LESSON 45
LAW AND GRACE

Lesson Objective: See that grace does not negate the law; neither can law do what God designed grace to do; but the two, law and grace, are designed by God to work in balance with each other.

Memory Verse: Galatians 5:16 So I say, live by the Spirit, and you will not gratify the desires of the sinful flesh.

Hebrew Words: תורה Torah – instructions, law

רוח Ruach – Spirit, breath, wind

Lesson Summary:

Law and grace are designed by God to be in balance with each other.

Law without grace results in fruitless religious adherence.

Grace without law results in antinomianism, which Yeshua rejects.

God intends for law and grace to be in balance with each other. First, we believe in Yeshua; then, we are saved; after that, we obey His law because we want to deepen our relationship with Him (NOT the reverse – which would be obeying His law so that we can be saved, which does not work).

Day 1:

1) Bible Memory: Memorize Galatians 5:16.

2) Hebrew Words: תורה Torah – instructions, law

רוח Ruach – Spirit, breath, wind

3) Think about the lesson: Discuss with your parents the concepts of law and grace. How do you understand each? What is commonly understood in your culture? How are law and grace balanced?

_____

_____

_____

_____

Day 2:

1) Bible Memory: Review Galatians 5:16 and review three other verses.

2) Hebrew Words: תורה Torah – instructions, law

157

רוח Ruach – Spirit, breath, wind

3) Think about the lesson: Read Galatians 5:4-5. What do you notice?

_____

_____

_____

Day 3:

1) Bible Memory: Review Galatians 5:16 and review three other verses.

2) Hebrew Words: תורה Torah – instructions, law

   רוח Ruach – Spirit, breath, wind

3) Think about the lesson: Read Jonah 2:8. What do you notice?

_____

_____

Day 4:

1) Bible Memory: Review Galatians 5:16 and review three other verses.

2) Hebrew Words: תורה Torah – instructions, law

   רוח Ruach – Spirit, breath, wind

3) Think about the lesson: Read John 1:17. What do you notice?

_____

_____

_____

Day 5:

1) Bible Memory: Review Galatians 5:16 and review three other verses.

2) Hebrew Words: תורה Torah – instructions, law

   רוח Ruach – Spirit, breath, wind

3) Think about the lesson: Read Romans 5:20-6:18. In the letter to the Romans, the phrase "being under the law" is understood to mean being a "slave to sin." Why? What does that mean? Does grace "free" us from following God's laws? Is this how some people interpret these passages? Discuss with your parents.

Day 6:

1) Bible Memory: Review Galatians 5:16 and review three other verses.

2) Hebrew Words: תורה Torah – instructions, law

   רוח Ruach – Spirit, breath, wind

3) Think about the lesson: Read Galatians 5 and continue your family discussions of law and grace.

158

LESSON 46
SERMON ON THE MOUNT

Lesson Objective: Students will glimpse the richness, depth, and purity of Yeshua's teachings, see how He loves us, and see how He wants us to live so that we might enjoy the blessings of His Kingdom.

Memory Verses: Matthew chapters 5-7 are scriptures full of pure gold! This week's memory verses are your choice. Here is a list to choose from. Memorize your favorite one or choose several if you are quick at memorization.

Matthew 5:8 "Blessed are the pure in heart, for they will see God."
Matthew 5:13 "You are the salt of the earth. But if the salt loses its saltiness, how can it be made salty again? It is no longer good for anything, except to be thrown out and trampled by men."
Matthew 5:14 "You are the light of the world. A city on a hill cannot be hidden."
Matthew 5:17-18 Do not think that I have come to abolish the Law or the Prophets; I have not come to abolish them but to fulfill them. I tell you the truth, until heaven and earth disappear, not the smallest letter, not the least stroke of a pen, will by any means disappear from the Law until everything is accomplished."
Matthew 5:19 "Anyone who breaks one of the least of these commandments and teaches others to do the same will be called least in the kingdom of heaven, but whoever practices and teaches these commands will be called great in the kingdom of heaven."
Matthew 5:43-44 "You have heard that is was said, 'Love your neighbor and hate your enemy,' but I tell you: Love your enemies and pray for those who persecute you."
Matthew 6:9-13 "This, then, is how you should pray: Our Father in heaven, hallowed by your name, your kingdom come, your will be done on earth as it is in heaven. Give us today our daily bread. Forgive us our debts, as we have also forgiven our debtors. And lead us not into temptation, but deliver us from the evil one."
Matthew 7:7-8 "Ask and it will be given to you; seek and you will find; knock and the door will be opened to you. For everyone who asks receives; he who seeks finds; and to him who knocks, the door will be opened."
Matthew 7:12 "So in everything, do to others what you would have them do to you, for this sums up the Law and the Prophets."
Matthew 7:13-14 "Enter through the narrow gate. For wide is the gate and broad is the road that leads to destruction, and many enter through it. But small is the gate and narrow the road that leads to life, and only a few find it."

Hebrew Word: בָּרוּךְ baruch - blessed

Lesson Summary:

Yeshua taught as one who had authority because He is the authority. He is the Word made flesh. His teachings brought both comfort and conviction. In many ways He confirmed and strengthened the Torah. Yeshua taught His disciples how to live in His Kingdom, and these teachings turned the world upside down! He is the way, the truth, and the life. No one comes to the Father but through Yeshua.

Yeshua teaches us how to live in these chapters (5-7) in the book of Matthew. He starts with telling us how to be blessed! His kingdom is not about being a slave or a servant – it's about being a blessed child of God who gets to invite others to join him or her as brothers and sisters in the kingdom! Some teachings are hard – for example, we don't get to take revenge when someone hurts our feelings – but when we follow Yeshua's teachings, we show the world who He is through our unusual actions. It's normal for someone to be mean back, but it really makes us stand out as different and holy when we follow Yeshua's teachings. He calls us salt and light, He confirms His Torah, He talks about how we love others - for example, we don't murder, even by thinking hateful thoughts – we love our enemies and we even pray for them! That's a teaching that rocks the world! We give, we pray, we fast, and we don't worry because we trust that Yeshua will provide for us. If we follow these instructions today, we will be powerfully fruitful for His glory!

Day 1:

1) Bible Memory: Memorize the verse or verses you chose.

2) Hebrew Word: בָּרוּךְ baruch - blessed

3) Think about the lesson: Read Matthew 5:1-26. What do you notice?

_____

_____

_____

_____

Day 2:

1) Bible Memory: Review verses of your choosing.

2) Hebrew Word: בָּרוּךְ baruch - blessed

3) Think about the lesson: Read Matthew 5:27-48. What is surprising about Yeshua's approach to his listeners? To us?

_____

_____

_____

_____

Day 3:

1) Bible Memory: Review verses of your choosing.

2) Hebrew Word: בָּרוּךְ baruch - blessed

3) Think about the lesson: Read Matthew 6:1-15. What do you notice?

_____

_____

_____

Day 4:

1) Bible Memory: Review verses of your choosing.

2) Hebrew Word: בָּרוּךְ baruch - blessed

3) Think about the lesson: Read Matthew 6:16-34. Where does Yeshua want us to focus? Why?

_____

_____

_____

Day 5:

1) Bible Memory: Review verses of your choosing.

2) Hebrew Word: בָּרוּךְ baruch - blessed

3) Think about the lesson: Read Matthew 7:1-12. Discuss judging with your parents. When is it appropriate to make good judgment calls? When is judgment wrong? How does our culture view judging? What is sometimes hypocritical about our culture's views on judging?

Day 6:

1) Bible Memory: Review verses of your choosing.

2) Hebrew Word: בָּרוּךְ baruch - blessed

3) Think about the lesson: Read Matthew 7:13-28. How does Yeshua say we will recognize His followers from those who say they are following Him but are not?

_____

_____

_____

LESSON 47
ACTS

Lesson Objective: See the first fulfilling of the Great Commission in Acts and recognize your part in the plan of God today.

Memory Verse: Acts 4:12 Salvation is found in no one else, for there is no other name under heaven given to men by which we must be saved.

Hebrew Word: שֶׁלַח Shelach – sent one (apostle)

The "apostles" were people sent out to preach the gospel. We are sent out as well! Matthew 28:19-20

Lesson Summary:

At the end of the book of Matthew, Yeshua leaves us with these words: "All authority on heaven and on earth has been given to me. Therefore, go and make disciples of all nations, baptizing them in the name of the Father and of the Son and of the Holy Spirit, and teaching them to obey everything I have commanded you. And surely I am with you always, to the very end of the age." (Matthew 28:18-20)

In the book of Acts, we see the apostles obeying this commission (these last words are called the Great Commission of Yeshua). At the beginning of the book, we see that the Ruach HaKodesh, the Holy Spirit, comes to all believers, and through the Ruach, believers have the ability to carry the message of salvation through Yeshua to the world.

As were the apostles in the first century, so we believers in the 21st century must be about the business of making disciples through the power of the Ruach in obedience to Yeshua.

Day 1:

1) Bible Memory: Memorize Acts 4:12.
2) Hebrew Word: שֶׁלַח Shelach – sent one (apostle)
3) Think about the lesson: Read Acts 1:8. What will empower the apostles to be Yeshua's witnesses?

   _____

   Read Acts 2:1-4. What do you notice?

   _____

   Read Acts 2:17-21. What do you notice?

   _____

   _____

Day 2:

1) Bible Memory: Review Acts 4:12 and review three other verses.
2) Hebrew Word: שֶׁלַח Shelach – sent one (apostle)

3) Think about the lesson: Read Acts 2:38. What was Peter's message to the people?

_____

_____

_____

Read Acts 26:22-23. What was Paul's message to King Agrippa?

_____

_____

_____

_____

Day 3:

1) Bible Memory: Review Acts 4:12 and review three other verses.

2) Hebrew Word: שָׁלִיחַ Shelach – sent one (apostle)

3) Think about the lesson: Read Acts 7 and discuss the sermon and martyrdom of Stephen with your parents.

Day 4:

1) Bible Memory: Review Acts 4:12 and review three other verses.

2) Hebrew Word: שָׁלִיחַ Shelach – sent one (apostle)

3) Think about the lesson: Read Acts 9:1-31. Discuss the conversion of Paul with your parents.

Day 5:

1) Bible Memory: Review Acts 4:12 and review three other verses.

2) Hebrew Word: שָׁלִיחַ Shelach – sent one (apostle)

3) Think about the lesson: Read Acts 9:32 – Acts 11:18 and discuss with your parents how God prepared Peter to take the message of Yeshua's salvation to the Gentiles. What does the vision of the sheet with unclean animals on it represent?

_____

_____

_____

Day 6:

1) Bible Memory: Review Acts 4:12 and review three other verses.

2) Hebrew Word: שָׁלִיחַ Shelach – sent one (apostle)

3) Think about the lesson: Read Acts 8:26-39. Discuss with your parents how Philip was fulfilling the Great Commission of Yeshua with the Ethiopian eunuch.

LESSON 48
ROMANS

Lesson Objective: God has not rejected His people, the Jewish people. He is making a way to bring in the Gentiles along with the Jews.

Memory Verse: Romans 11:13-16 "I am talking to you Gentiles. Inasmuch as I am the apostle to the Gentiles, I make much of my ministry in the hope that I may somehow arouse my own people to envy and save some of them. For if their rejection is the reconciliation of the world, what will their acceptance be but life from the dead? If the part of the dough offered as firstfruits is holy, then the whole batch is holy; if the root is holy, so are the branches."

Hebrew Word: גויים goyim – nations. Goy is also term used to identify a person who is not Jewish.

Lesson Summary:

God used the Jewish people to bring His Word to the world. Exodus 19:5-6 says He sets Jews apart to be priests to the nations, and He entrusts them with His Word, the scriptures, in Romans 3:1-2. Yeshua is Jewish; therefore, "salvation comes from the Jews." The rejection of Yeshua by His own people opens the doors for the Gentiles to be grafted in, which in turn will cause a jealousy among the Jewish people. When all the "fullness of the nations" comes into the Body of Messiah, then the Jewish people as a community will also have "eyes to see and ears to hear." They will recognize Yeshua, turn to Him, and be healed.

God wants all of us to be saved. He gives us many chances, over and over again. One day, our chances will run out. We will die in our sins if we do not accept Yeshua as our Savior. Whether Jew or Gentile, accept Yeshua's free gift of salvation today, while you still have a chance!

Day 1:

1) Bible Memory: Memorize Romans 11:13-16.
2) Hebrew Word: גויים goyim – nations
3) Think about the lesson: Read Romans 3:1-2. What advantage is there in being Jewish?

_____

_____

Day 2:

1) Bible Memory: Memorize Romans 11:13-16.
2) Hebrew Word: גויים goyim – nations
3) Think about the lesson: Read Romans 3:20. What are the benefits of the Torah? What can the Torah not do?

_____

_____

Day 3:

1) Bible Memory: Memorize Romans 11:13-16.

2) Hebrew Word: גויים goyim – nations

3) Think about the lesson: Romans 3:23. What have we all done?
_____

Day 4:

1) Bible Memory: Memorize Romans 11:13-16.

2) Hebrew Word: גויים goyim – nations

3) Think about the lesson: Read Romans 6:22-23. What are the wages of sin? _____
What is the gift of God? _____

Day 5:

1) Bible Memory: Memorize Romans 11:13-16 and review three other verses.

2) Hebrew Word: גויים goyim – nations

3) Think about the lesson: Read Romans 11:11-32. What is God's plan for the Jewish people?
_____
_____
_____

What is important for Gentiles to know?
_____
_____
_____

Day 6:

1) Bible Memory: Memorize Romans 11:13-16 and review three other verses.

2) Hebrew Word: גויים goyim – nations

3) Think about the lesson: Discuss Romans 11:11-32 as a family.

165

LESSON 49
JAMES AND 1 JOHN

Lesson Objective: True faith = acting upon the Word of God – living it out day by day with clear spiritual discernment.

Memory Verses: James 1:22 Do not merely listen to the word and so deceive yourselves; do what it says.
1 John 1:9 If we confess our sins to God, He is faithful and just to forgive us our sins and to cleanse us from all unrighteousness.

Hebrew Word: אהבה ahavah – love (yes, this is a review word)

Lesson Summary:

Today's lesson is all about how to live once we are saved. When we read our Bibles, we see how we fall short and how we are to imitate Yeshua now instead of doing the things we used to do before we knew Him. We see that we can love God and others because God loved us first. We see that we need to be in daily prayer for the forgiveness of our sins, for our needs, and for the needs of others.

Day 1:

1) Bible Memory: Memorize James 1:22.

2) Hebrew Word: אהבה ahavah – love

3) Think about the lesson: Read James 1:22-25. Discuss with your parents how the Torah is like a mirror. What do you notice?

_____

_____

_____

Day 2:

1) Bible Memory: Memorize 1 John 1:9 and review James 1:22.

2) Hebrew Word: אהבה ahavah – love

3) Think about the lesson: Read James 2:18-26. Our actions show what we really believe. Pray about this. What do you notice in the passage? In your own experience? In the world around you?

_____

_____

_____

Day 3:

1) Bible Memory: Review James 1:22 and 1 John 1:9.

2) Hebrew Word: אהבה ahavah – love

3) Think about the lesson: Read James 5:13-16. Consider the effectiveness and importance of prayer. What do you notice in the passage? In your own experience? In the world around you?

_____

_____

_____

Day 4:

1) Bible Memory: Review James 1:22, 1 John 1:9, and three other verses.

2) Hebrew Word: אהבה ahavah – love

3) Think about the lesson: Recite 1 John 1:9. This verse is a daily practice for believers in order to be clean and holy as God desires us to be. If you haven't already, let this practice become a new daily habit.

Day 5:

1) Bible Memory: Review James 1:22, 1 John 1:9, and three other verses.

2) Hebrew Word: אהבה ahavah – love

3) Think about the lesson: Read 1 John 2:3-5. God's love is made complete in us when we live as Yeshua lived. Read 1 John 5:1-2. Yeshua is the Messiah, and we show love for God by keeping His commands. Discuss these verses with your parents. What do you notice in the passage? In your own experience? In the world around you? How do these verses describe the relationship between God and His children?

_____

_____

_____

_____

Day 6:

1) Bible Memory: Review James 1:22, 1 John 1:9, and three other verses.

2) Hebrew Word: אהבה ahavah – love

3) Think about the lesson: Read 1 John 4:1-10. This is an excellent passage about testing the spirits. There are many unseen spirits in the world; they are not all Godly! Many imitate God's Spirit, but they are not the Ruach HaKodesh, and they will lead us astray if we listen to them and follow their deceptions. Based on what we have studied this week, what are some ways we can test the spirits? Discuss real life examples with your parents.

_____

_____

_____

_____

SECTION 4 – HOLY DAYS AND DAILY LIFE

LESSON 50
FOOD LAWS AND TODAY

Lesson Objective: Students will understand the importance of keeping God's food laws in the 21st century.

Memory Verse: Matthew 15:11 "What goes into a man's mouth does not make him unclean, but what comes out of his mouth, that is what makes him unclean."

Hebrew Word: טהורה tahora – clean (ritutally)

Lesson Summary:

Food is necessary to sustain life. Eating what is not food can hurt us. Adonai gives us food laws so that we can exercise making right choices - choices that glorify Him as the creator, sovereign God - and so that we can take the best care of our temporal bodies.

The first sin involved eating a food that God said not to eat. Because of that choice, sin entered the world, and without God's help, we cannot escape it. We all sin. We all fall short. The wisdom that the serpent promised Eve did nothing to help her. Spiritually, her eyes were opened to evil.

Yeshua is the only reversal of this. When we choose Him we choose life! We can show through every action of every day, even the simple things like choosing what to eat, that we choose Him – we choose Life!

Day 1:

1) Bible Memory: Memorize Matthew 15:11.

2) Hebrew Word: טהורה tahora – clean (ritutally)

3) Think about the lesson: Read Genesis 3. Notice that in Genesis 3:22, we see that eating from the tree of life grants eternal life. Its fruit was blocked to humanity after Adam and Eve sinned so that we would not live eternally in a sinful state. Adonai's plan is for us to be restored so that we can live with Him eternally in a clean state. If the first sin involved food, how important do you think our food choices are today? Discuss your thoughts with your parents. What do you think? Why?

_____
_____
_____
_____

Day 2:

1) Bible Memory: Review Matthew 15:11 and review three others verses.

2) Hebrew Word: טהורה tahora – clean (ritutally)

3) Think about the lesson: Read Leviticus 11 and Deuteronomy 14. These are the food law passages. What do you notice?

_____

_____

_____

_____

Day 3:

1) Bible Memory: Review Matthew 15:11 and review three others verses.

2) Hebrew Word: טהורה tahora – clean (ritutally)

3) Think about the lesson: Read Isaiah 66:17. How are the enemies of God described? They are those who_____.

Day 4:

1) Bible Memory: Review Matthew 15:11 and review three others verses.

2) Hebrew Word: טהורה tahora – clean (ritutally)

3) Think about the lesson: Read Matthew 15:1-20. Yeshua focused on the heart (not the handwashing tradition). Discuss this passage with your parents. What do you notice?

_____

_____

_____

_____

Day 5:

1) Bible Memory: Review Matthew 15:11 and review three others verses.

2) Hebrew Word: טהורה tahora – clean (ritutally)

3) Think about the lesson: Read Acts chapter 10. What is God's message to Peter? Is the message about food? Or is the food symbolic? If so, what does it symbolize? Does Peter ever eat any of the unclean animals he sees on the sheet in the vision? Discuss with your parents.

_____

_____

_____

_____

Day 6:

1) Bible Memory: Review Matthew 15:11 and review three others verses.

2) Hebrew Word: טהורה tahora – clean (ritutally)

3) Think about the lesson: Read Romans 14:2, 1 Corinthians 8:13, and 1 Corinthians 10:25-31. These are passages that are focused on being considerate of others (no food sacrificed to idols/meat or

wine debates with those who abstained). Discuss with your parents. How were these laws worked out in the 1st century between the Jewish believers who were witnessing to the Gentiles who wanted to become believers? What considerations do we have in the 21st century? How can we live as the best witnesses in our culture?

_____
_____
_____
_____
_____
_____

LESSON 51
SABBATH

Lesson Objective: Understand that Adonai gave us Shabbat so that we might rest and enjoy the work of His creation; observance of Shabbat is a distinct marker of the people of God.

Memory Verse: Exodus 20:8 Remember the Sabbath day by keeping it holy.

Hebrew Word: שַׁבָּת Shabbat – cease/stop – the Sabbath (Saturday)

Lesson Summary:

Shabbat is a delight! Established by God at creation, observance of the Shabbat is the fourth of the Ten Commandments.

As you study the Shabbat through your readings and discussions this week, consider the difference between religion and relationship. How does our observance of Shabbat reflect our relationship with God? What are our family Shabbat traditions? How did Yeshua observe Shabbat?

In Hebrews chapters 3-4, Paul equates entering God's rest with entering eternal life, and he urges his readers not to harden their hearts towards God. The end of chapter 4 reminds us that Yeshua was tempted in all ways just as we are, but He never sinned. Because of this, His sacrifice on our behalf is acceptable to God, satisfying the wages of sin. Because of Yeshua, we can have eternal life; we can enter His eternal rest.

Day 1:

1) Bible Memory: Memorize Exodus 20:8.
2) Hebrew Word: שַׁבָּת Shabbat – cease/stop – the Sabbath (Saturday)
3) Think about the lesson: Consider Genesis 2:2-3, which you have already memorized. What does it mean for the world that God established the Shabbat at the beginning of creation?

_____

_____

_____

Day 2:

1) Bible Memory: Review Exodus 20:8 and review three other verses.
2) Hebrew Word: שַׁבָּת Shabbat – cease/stop – the Sabbath (Saturday)
3) Think about the lesson: This week, you are memorizing Exodus 20:8. Observance of the Shabbat is the fourth of the Ten Commandments. How important do you think observing Shabbat is?

_____

_____

_____

Day 3:

1) Bible Memory: Review Exodus 20:8 and review three other verses.

2) Hebrew Word: שַׁבָּת Shabbat – cease/stop – the Sabbath (Saturday)

3) Think about the lesson: Read Exodus 31:16-17. What does God say the Shabbat is?

_____

_____

_____

Day 4:

1) Bible Memory: Review Exodus 20:8 and review three other verses.

2) Hebrew Word: שַׁבָּת Shabbat – cease/stop – the Sabbath (Saturday)

3) Think about the lesson: Read Isaiah 58:13-14. What do you notice?

_____

_____

_____

Day 5:

1) Bible Memory: Review Exodus 20:8 and review three other verses.

2) Hebrew Word: שַׁבָּת Shabbat – cease/stop – the Sabbath (Saturday)

3) Think about the lesson: Read Mark 2:21-3:6. What does Yeshua say about the Sabbath? About humanity? About Himself? What does He do on the Sabbath? Why does it upset the Pharisees?

_____

_____

_____

Day 6:

1) Bible Memory: Review Exodus 20:8 and review three other verses.

2) Hebrew Word: שַׁבָּת Shabbat – cease/stop – the Sabbath (Saturday)

3) Think about the lesson: Read Hebrews 4:1-9. Discuss this passage with your parents over Erev Shabbat dinner.

LESSON 52
OVERVIEW OF THE FESTIVALS

Lesson Objective: See the big picture of the holidays that God gave us and understand why we celebrate them.

Memory Verse: Leviticus 23:2 Speak to the Israelites and say to them, "These are my feasts, the appointed feasts of the LORD, which you are to proclaim and sacred assemblies."

Hebrew Word: מוֹעֵד moed – festival, appointed time

Lesson Summary:

Holidays are times that we gather together as a family and faith community to worship God together and to meet with Him. Holidays are holy days, days that are specially set apart to meet with Adonai and enjoy His presence within our community. These times are special appointments!

Leviticus chapter 23 lists all of the holidays that God gave us. On our calendar, we do have additional holidays that were added later. The main additional holidays include Chanukah, which was added after the Maccabean revolt, Purim, which was added during the time of Esther, and the 9th of Av, which commemorates the destruction of the 1st and 2nd Temples.

Each of God's holy days shows us how much He cares for us and how He provides for us. He has provided a way for us to return to Him through Yeshua. All of the holy days teach us something about Yeshua and how Yeshua came to save us.

Here is a chart that outlines the holy day with what it meant historically and prophetically. Use this chart as you complete this week's readings.

Holy Day	Literal Ancient Meaning	Prophetic Meaning
Sabbath	God rested	Sabbath observance is a sign that we belong to the one true God
Pesach	Exodus from Egypt – freedom from slavery	Freedom from slavery to sin and death
Unleavened Bread	Hebrews left in a hurry	Living a life without sin
First Fruits	We offer God our first and best – because He is the one who gave us everything!	Promise of the resurrection
Shavuot	Giving of the Torah	Giving of the Spirit
Yom Teruah	Day of Trumpets; books are opened for judgment, memorial of entrance into the promised land	Yeshua's return
Yom Kippur	Day of Atonement; books are closed – judgments sealed, names are inscribed in the Book of Life	Yeshua's future restoration of Israel
Sukkot	Memorial of the desert wanderings	Yeshua tabernacle among us in a human body; He will return to dwell with us as King

Day 1:

1) Bible Memory: Memorize Leviticus 23:2.
2) Hebrew Word: מוֹעֵד moed – festival, appointed time
3) **Think about the lesson:** Read the verses and then write them in the appropriate boxes in the chart above: Sabbath – Leviticus 23:2-3; Hebrews 4:9; Exodus 31:17

Day 2:

1) Bible Memory: Review Leviticus 23:2 and review three other verses.
2) Hebrew Word: מוֹעֵד moed – festival, appointed time
3) Think about the lesson: Read the verses and then write them in the appropriate boxes in the chart

above:
Passover/Pesach – Leviticus 23:4-5; 1 Corinthians 5:7
Unleavened Bread – Leviticus 23:6-8; Exodus 13:6-9
First Fruits – Leviticus 23:10-11; 1 Corinthians 15:20

Day 3:

1) Bible Memory: Review Leviticus 23:2 and review three other verses.

2) Hebrew Word: מוֹעֵד moed – festival, appointed time

3) Think about the lesson: Read the verses and then write them in the appropriate boxes in the chart above:
Shavuot – Leviticus 23:15-21; Exodus 19:4-6 and 16-19; Acts 2:1-4

Day 4:

1) Bible Memory: Review Leviticus 23:2 and review three other verses.

2) Hebrew Word: מוֹעֵד moed – festival, appointed time

3) Think about the lesson: Read the verses and then write them in the appropriate boxes in the chart above:
Yom Teruah (Rosh HaShanah) – Leviticus 23:24-25; 1 Corinthians 15:52, 1 Thessalonians 4:16

Day 5:

1) Bible Memory: Review Leviticus 23:2 and review three other verses.

2) Hebrew Word: מוֹעֵד moed – festival, appointed time

3) Think about the lesson: Read the verses and then write them in the appropriate boxes in the chart above:
Yom Kippur – Leviticus 23:27-32; Revelation 20:11-15

Day 6:

1) Bible Memory: Review Leviticus 23:2 and review three other verses.

2) Hebrew Word: מוֹעֵד moed – festival, appointed time

3) Think about the lesson: Read the verses and then write them in the appropriate boxes in the chart above:
Sukkot – Leviticus 23:34-36; John 1:14; Revelation 7:15

LESSON 53
PASSOVER AND UNLEAVENED BREAD

Lesson Objective: Understand the historical Exodus.

Memory Verse: Exodus 12:13 The blood will be a sign for you on the houses where you are; and when I see the blood, I will pass over you. No destructive plague will touch you when I strike Egypt.

Hebrew Word: מצה matzah – unleavened bread

Lesson Summary:

At the close of Genesis, we see that Joseph brought all his family, all twelve tribes to join him in Egypt. They were fruitful and protected for many years. However, after staying in Egypt for 400 years, times had changed. Exodus opens with mention of the new leadership, the new Pharaoh in Egypt, who had no idea about his history. He didn't know that the Israelites were descended from Joseph, the man who followed God and, through God's revelation and guidance had saved Egypt and the rest of the world from starving to death in a famine. He didn't know about Joseph at all. He saw that the Israelites were numerous, and he feared that they might one day challenge his rule, so he enslaved them and killed their male babies. The Hebrews cried out to God for salvation from this horrible predicament, and God answered by sending Moshe (Moses).

Moshe was born, and his mother hid him as long as she could so that he would not be drowned by the Egyptians in the Nile River. When she could not hide him any longer, she built a boat for him and set him on the Nile River, with his sister Miriam watching. Miriam followed little Moshe in the boat until it floated past the palace. The princess found the baby (in the river in which he was supposed to be drowned!) and decided to keep him. Miriam burst out of the bushes and suggested she find a Hebrew nurse to feed the baby. The princess agreed, and so Miriam brought her mother to the palace to nurse him. In this way, Moshe was raise by his own mother in the palace of the Pharaoh who had wanted to kill him along with all the Hebrew baby boys!

When Moshe grew up, he saw an Egyptian beating a Hebrew slave, and he killed him. When he realized that his sin was known, he ran away. Moshe ran to the land of Midian. He stayed there for 40 years. While he was there, he got married and had two sons.

One day, he was tending his flocks in the wilderness and passed by a bush that was burning but did not burn up. Adonai was waiting to meet with him in that bush. Adonai told Moshe to return to Egypt to free his people.

Moshe was nervous about that, so Adonai sent his brother Aaron with him, and he returned to Egypt. Over the course of 10 different plagues, Adonai displayed His power over the false gods of the Egyptians. We'll read about those in this week's readings.

The tenth and final plague was the death of the firstborn. Within every household throughout Egypt, the firstborn male would die when the angel of the Lord passed through the land, unless the inhabitants of the household had killed a lamb and placed its blood across the top and down the sides of their doors. Those who did this were saved; the angel of death passed over their homes, and everyone inside was safe.

176

When the Hebrews finally left Egypt, they left so quickly that they did not allow their bread to rise. The tenth plague, the death of the firstborn, and the unleavened bread, are key components to remember in our celebration of Pesach/Passover.

Day 1:

1) Bible Memory: Memorize Exodus 12:13.

2) Hebrew Word: מַצָּה matzah – unleavened bread

3) Think about the lesson: Read Exodus 7:14-24 and 7:25-8:15. What are the first two plagues?

_____
_____

What do you notice?

_____
_____
_____

Day 2:

1) Bible Memory: Review Exodus 12:13 and review three other verses.

2) Hebrew Word: מַצָּה matzah – unleavened bread

3) Think about the lesson: Read Exodus 8:16-19 and Exodus 8:20-32. What are the third and fourth plagues?

_____
_____

What do you notice?

_____
_____
_____

Day 3:

1) Bible Memory: Review Exodus 12:13 and review three other verses.

2) Hebrew Word: מַצָּה matzah – unleavened bread

3) Think about the lesson: Read Exodus 9:1-7 and Exodus 9:8-12. What are the fifth and sixth plagues?

_____
_____

What do you notice?

_____
_____
_____

Day 4:

1) Bible Memory: Review Exodus 12:13 and review three other verses.

177

2) Hebrew Word: מַצָּה matzah – unleavened bread

3) Think about the lesson: Read Exodus 9:13-35 and Exodus 10:1-20. What are the seventh and eighth plagues?

_____

_____

What do you notice?

_____

_____

_____

Day 5:

1) Bible Memory: Review Exodus 12:13 and review three other verses.

2) Hebrew Word: מַצָּה matzah – unleavened bread

3) Think about the lesson: Read Exodus 10:21-29 and Exodus 11:1-12:36. What are the ninth and tenth plagues?

_____

_____

What do you notice?

_____

_____

_____

Day 6:

1) Bible Memory: Review Exodus 12:13 and review three other verses.

2) Hebrew Word: מַצָּה matzah – unleavened bread

3) Think about the lesson: As a family, read and discuss Exodus chapter 12.

LESSON 54
YESHUA AS THE PASSOVER LAMB

Lesson Objective: See that Yeshua is the Passover Lamb.

Memory Verse: 1 Corinthians 5:7 Get rid of the old yeast that you may be a new batch without yeast – as you really are. For Messiah, our Passover Lamb, has been sacrificed.

Hebrew Word: פֶּסַח Pesach - Passover

Lesson Summary:

The tenth plague was the death of the firstborn. Through Moshe, God told the Hebrews to slaughter a lamb and place its blood across the top and down the sides of their doorways. Whoever obeyed and did this protected their homes from the angel of death. When the angel of death passed through Egypt, he saw the blood and passed over that house. Any door not covered by the blood of an innocent lamb, the angel of death would enter and take the life of the firstborn male within the home.

This was not the first time God had asked His people to do something a little strange. Remember in Genesis 22 when God told Abraham to take his son Isaac and sacrifice him? And then when Abraham obeys, God stops his hand and says He will provide the lamb. After that, Abraham sees a ram caught in a thicket and that becomes their sacrifice offering instead of Isaac.

God does not want the death of humans; He wants the restoration of humans.

Sin causes death.

Sin affects and changes our minds, bodies, and the world around us. We are tainted. We cannot bring righteousness out of our sinful being. Neither can the blood of an animal bring righteousness, but the blood of an animal can be symbolic of the substitutionary death that is needed for our restoration.

God speaks in symbols sometimes so that we can understand a little bit. The blood of the innocent lamb symbolizes the substitutionary sacrifice that takes away the sins of the entire world and enables us to be back in right relationship with God.

Yeshua offered Himself as our substitute. He is our Passover Lamb.

Day 1:

1) Bible Memory: Memorize 1 Corinthians 5:7.
2) Hebrew Word: פֶּסַח Pesach - Passover
3) Think about the lesson: Read Genesis 22:8 and Exodus 12:21. What do you notice?

_____

_____

179

Day 2:

    1)   Bible Memory: Review 1 Corinthians 5:7 and review three other verses.

    2)   Hebrew Word: פֶּסַח Pesach - Passover

    3)   Think about the lesson: Read Isaiah 53:7, Mark 14:12, and John 1:29. What do you notice?

    _____

    _____

    _____

Day 3:

    1)   Bible Memory: Review 1 Corinthians 5:7 and review three other verses.

    2)   Hebrew Word: פֶּסַח Pesach - Passover

    3)   Think about the lesson: Read Acts 8:32 and 1 Peter 1:19. What do you notice?

    _____

    _____

    _____

Day 4:

    1)   Bible Memory: Review 1 Corinthians 5:7 and review three other verses.

    2)   Hebrew Word: פֶּסַח Pesach - Passover

    3)   Think about the lesson: Read Revelation 5:6 and 5:12. Read Revelation 7:14. What do you notice?

    _____

    _____

    _____

Day 5:

    1)   Bible Memory: Review 1 Corinthians 5:7 and review three other verses.

    2)   Hebrew Word: פֶּסַח Pesach - Passover

    3)   Think about the lesson: Read Revelation 14:4, 15:3, and 17:14. What do you notice?

    _____

    _____

    _____

Day 6:

    1)   Bible Memory: Review 1 Corinthians 5:7 and review three other verses.

    2)   Hebrew Word: פֶּסַח Pesach - Passover

    3)   Think about the lesson: Read Revelation 19:9, 21:23, and 21:27. What do you notice?

_____

_____

Pray and discuss these passages with your parents over Erev Shabbat dinner.

LESSON 55
FIRST FRUITS AND THE RESURRECTION

Lesson Objective: See that Yeshua is the first fruits of the resurrection, and that since He resurrected, we can be assured that He will resurrect us as well.

Memory Verse: 1 Corinthians 15:20 But Messiah has indeed been raised from the dead, the firstfruits of those who have fallen asleep.

Hebrew Word: בכורים bikkurim – first fruits

Lesson Summary:

First Fruits is on Nisan 17. Some amazing events occurred on that day in history.

Anciently, this was the day during the week of Passover/Unleavened Bread when the Israelites would bring the first of their harvest to offer to the Lord.

During the Exodus, which occurred the night of Nisan 14, the people left Egypt and followed Adonai in the pillar of cloud and fire into the wilderness. By Nisan 17, they had come to the Sea of Reeds and Pharaoh's army was in hot pursuit. The Lord in the pillar positioned Himself between Pharaoh's army and the Israelites, while Moshe stood between the Israelites and the Sea. Moshe raised his staff and the waters miraculously parted. The Israelites passed through the sea on dry ground on Nisan 17. When Pharaoh's army tried to follow, the waters closed in over them and they drowned. Adonai saved the Israelites on this day.

Because of the Exodus, we celebrate Passover on Nisan 14 today, as Yeshua did in the 1st century. On the night that He was betrayed, He ate his last meal with his disciples. The following day, He gave his life for us as our Passover Lamb. Three days later, He rose from the dead. This was Nisan 17.

Nisan 17 is a day of salvation from death. For the ancient Israelites, the first fruit of the new crop was an assurance that they would not starve that season. They thanked God for the food that would sustain them. For the Hebrews leaving Egypt, they were saved from sure death at either the hands of Pharaoh's army on one side or from drowning in the sea on the other. On Nisan 17, Miriam led a celebration praising God for His deliverance after they passed through the sea on dry ground and then witnessed the death of their enemies. And on Nisan 17, when Yeshua rose from the dead, His disciples stood in awe, wrapping their minds around what this meant for them – physical death is not the end. The fact that Yeshua resurrected was a promise that He could and would raise them as well! Nisan 17 is a day to celebrate salvation and look forward to future eternal life with Adonai!

Day 1:

1) Bible Memory: Memorize 1 Corinthians 15:20.

2) Hebrew Word: בכורים bikkurim – first fruits

3) Think about the lesson: Read Deuteronomy 26:1-11. What do you notice?

_____
_____

Day 2:

1) Bible Memory: Review 1 Corinthians 15:20 and review three other verses.

2) Hebrew Word: בכורים bikkurim – first fruits

3) Think about the lesson: Read 1 Corinthians 15:12-58. Discuss this passage with your parents. What do you notice?

_____
_____
_____
_____
_____

Day 3:

1) Bible Memory: Review 1 Corinthians 15:20 and review three other verses.

2) Hebrew Word: בכורים bikkurim – first fruits

3) Think about the lesson: Read Romans 8:18-25. Discuss the first fruits of the Spirit, the redemption of our bodies, and groaning of creation with your parents. How does Yeshua's resurrection change us? Change the world?

_____
_____
_____
_____

Day 4:

1) Bible Memory: Review 1 Corinthians 15:20 and review three other verses.

2) Hebrew Word: בכורים bikkurim – first fruits

3) Think about the lesson: Read Revelation 14:1-5. Discuss with your parents. What do you notice?

_____
_____
_____

Day 5:

1) Bible Memory: Review 1 Corinthians 15:20 and review three other verses.

2) Hebrew Word: בכורים bikkurim – first fruits

3) Think about the lesson: Read Revelation 20:4-6. What do you notice?

_____
_____
_____

Day 6:

1) Bible Memory: Review 1 Corinthians 15:20 and review three other verses.

2) Hebrew Word: בכורים bikkurim – first fruits

3) Think about the lesson: Read Romans 1:1-6. Discuss with your parents. What does this passage affirm (looking for multiple answers)?

_____

_____

_____

_____

LESSON 56
SHAVUOT

Lesson Objective: Know that Shavuot commemorates the giving of the Torah and the giving of the Ruach.

Memory Passage: The Ten Commandments.
And God spoke all these words: I am the LORD your God, who brought you out of Egypt, out of the land of slavery. You shall have no other gods before me. You shall not make for yourself an idol in the form of anything in heaven above or on the earth beneath or in the waters below. You shall not bow down to them or worship them; for I, the LORD your God, am a jealous God, punishing the children for the sin of the fathers to the third and fourth generation of those who hate me, but showing love to a thousand generations of those who love me and keep my commandments. You shall not misuse the name of the LORD your God, for the LORD will not hold anyone guiltless who misuses his name. Remember the Sabbath day by keeping it holy. Six days you shall labor and do all your work, but the seventh day is a Sabbath to the LORD your God. On it you shall not do any work, neither you, nor your son or daughter, nor your manservant or maidservant, nor your animals, nor the alien within your gates. For in six days the LORD made the heavens and the earth, the sea, and all that is in them, but he rested on the seventh day. Therefore the LORD blessed the Sabbath day and made it holy. Honor your father and your mother, so that you may live long in the land that the LORD your God is giving you. You shall not murder. You shall not commit adultery. You shall not steal. You shall not give false testimony against your neighbor. You shall not cover your neighbor's house. You shall not covet your neighbor's wife, or his manservant or maidservant, his ox or donkey, or anything that belongs to your neighbor.

Hebrew Word: שבועות Shavuot - weeks

Lesson Summary:

From the miraculous victory at the Sea of Reeds, Moshe and the Israelites followed the Lord in the pillar of cloud through the wilderness until they arrived at Mount Sinai. 50 days elapsed from First Fruits to Shavuot. This counting of days is very important. The name of this holiday means weeks, and the count is 7 weeks plus one day. That's 7 days x 7 weeks = 49 days +1 more day = 50 days. Counting the days is called counting the omer (an omer is a measurement of grain).

After the Exodus, Adonai met with His people at Mt. Sinai. He gave them the Ten Commandments. This holiday celebrates the giving of the Torah.

After Yeshua's resurrection, He appeared to many; He walked, talked, and ate with His disciples, and then He ascended to heaven with the promise that He would send a Helper. The Helper came in the form of the Holy Spirit, or Ruach HaKodesh, on Shavuot, 50 days after Yeshu's resurrection.

Do you see how Adonai consistently honors His pattern of days? His holy days are days that He meets with us! These are days that great things happen!

Day 1:

1) Bible Memory: Memorize Exodus 20:1-3.

2) Hebrew Word: שָׁבוּעוֹת Shavuot - weeks

3) Think about the lesson: Read Exodus chapter 19. What do you notice?

_____

_____

_____

Day 2:

1) Bible Memory: Memorize Exodus 20:4-6. Review Exodus 20:1-3.

2) Hebrew Word: שָׁבוּעוֹת Shavuot - weeks

3) Think about the lesson: Read Acts chapter 2. What do you notice?

_____

_____

_____

Day 3:

1) Bible Memory: Memorize Exodus 20:7-11. Review Exodus 20:1-6.

2) Hebrew Word: שָׁבוּעוֹת Shavuot - weeks

3) Think about the lesson: Read John 16:5-15. What do you notice?

_____

_____

_____

Day 4:

1) Bible Memory: Memorize Exodus 20:12-15. Review Exodus 20:1-11.

2) Hebrew Word: שָׁבוּעוֹת Shavuot - weeks

3) Think about the lesson: Discuss with your parents: Why do you think the giving of the Torah and the giving of the Spirit are on the same day? Why do you think Adonai did that? What parallels might you draw between the two major events that Shavuot commemorates?

_____

_____

_____

Day 5:

1) Bible Memory: Memorize Exodus 20:16-17. Review Exodus 20:1-15.

2) Hebrew Word: שָׁבוּעוֹת Shavuot - weeks

3) Think about the lesson: Exodus 19:5-6 says that we are a kingdom of priests, a holy nation. What does this mean? How does this call you to personal responsibility spiritually? Discuss with your

parents. Record your thoughts:

_____

_____

_____

Day 6:

1) Bible Memory: Review Exodus 20:1-17.

2) Hebrew Word: שבועות Shavuot - weeks

3) Think about the lesson: Read Matthew 5:14-16. In light of Exodus 19:5-6, what does Matthew 5:14-16 call you to do with your life?

_____

_____

_____

LESSON 57
9TH OF AV

Lesson Objective: Know all the events that occurred on this historic and tragic date.

Memory Verse: Lamentations 3:40 Let us examine our ways and test them, and let us return to the LORD.

Hebrew Word: באב תשעה Tisha b'av – 9th of Av

Lesson Summary:

The book of Lamentations is the book that is read on the 9th of Av. The 9th of Av is a fast day, a day of mourning.

Lamentations is a lament (a poem that expresses grief or pain) over the judgment that befell Jerusalem when the Babylonians invaded and conquered the city in 586 BC. The first Temple was destroyed at this time on the 9th of Av. God works according to His calendar, and this day, the 9th of Av, is infamous for defeats. Other tragic occurrences on the 9th of Av throughout history include 1) the day the 10 spies came back with a bad report (Numbers 13), 2) the day the Second Temple was destroyed, 3) the day the Bar Kochba revolt was smashed by the Romans, 4) the day Jews were expelled from England, 5) the day Jews were expelled from Spain, and 5) the day the first world war started when Germany declared war on Russia. Why is this a day of defeats? Some believe that it is because the Israelites did not trust God to take them in to the Promised Land, to fight for them against the "giants." When we lose our trust in God, we forfeit our victories.

Something cool about the format of the laments in Hebrew is that the book is written as an acrostic with each section beginning with a subsequent letter of the Hebrew aleph-bet. If you have a Hebrew Tanach, take a look! See how if you can identify the letters of the acrostic.

Day 1:

1) Bible Memory: Memorize Lamentations 3:40.
2) Hebrew Word: באב תשעה Tisha b'av – 9th of Av
3) Think about the lesson: Read Lamentations 1. What do you notice?

   _____

   _____

Day 2:

1) Bible Memory: Review Lamentations 3:40 and review three other verses.
2) Hebrew Word: באב תשעה Tisha b'av – 9th of Av
3) Think about the lesson: Read Lamentations 2. Pay close attention to Lamentations 2:7 and 2:14. What do you notice?

   _____

188

Day 3:

1) Bible Memory: Review Lamentations 3:40 and review three other verses.
2) Hebrew Word: בְּאָב תִּשְׁעָה Tisha b'av – 9th of Av
3) Think about the lesson: Read Lamentations 3. What do you notice? What hope do we find in Lamentations 3:22-31?

Day 4:

1) Bible Memory: Review Lamentations 3:40 and review three other verses.
2) Hebrew Word: בְּאָב תִּשְׁעָה Tisha b'av – 9th of Av
3) Think about the lesson: Read Lamentations 4. What do you notice?

Day 5:

1) Bible Memory: Review Lamentations 3:40 and review three other verses.
2) Hebrew Word: בְּאָב תִּשְׁעָה Tisha b'av – 9th of Av
3) Think about the lesson: Read Lamentations 5. What do you notice?

Day 6:

1) Bible Memory: Review Lamentations 3:40 and review three other verses.
2) Hebrew Word: בְּאָב תִּשְׁעָה Tisha b'av – 9th of Av
3) Think about the lesson: If you have a Hebrew Tanach, look up Lamentations and identify as many letters of the aleph-bet as you can as part of the acrostic structure.

LESSON 58
ROSH HASHANAH

Lesson Objectives: Know that this holy day is called Yom Teruah, the day of trumpets; see the significance of trumpets in God's Word and in the Israelites' history. This is also the day that marks the beginning of the civil Jewish year and also the day of the High Holy days that Adonai's books are opened to judge the people of the world.

Memory Verse: Leviticus 23:24 Say to the Israelites, "On the first day of the seventh month, you are to have a day of rest, a sacred assembly commemorated with trumpet blasts."

Hebrew Words: יום תרוה - Yom Teruah – Day of Trumpets

ראש השנה - Rosh HaShanah – head of the year (New Year)

Lesson Summary:

In Jewish tradition, this is the day that God created the world. Therefore, this is our New Year. It is traditional to eat apples and honey as a way to invite a sweet new year. After the Exodus, when God established Passover, He told us this would be the beginning of our year. Hence we have two calendars – the civil and the religious. Rosh HaShanah is the Jewish New Year on the civil calendar.

In the Bible, this day has another name – Yom Teruah, which means Day of Trumpets. In your readings this week, you'll see some reasons why we blow the trumpets. There are different kinds of trumpets. In some of the readings, you will read about blowing a shofar. A shofar is a trumpet made of a ram's horn.

Rosh HaShanah and Yom Kippur are called the High Holy Days. These holy days are ten days apart, and the days in between them are called the Days of Awe. This is a time of year for personal and national repentance. The Bible and Jewish tradition say that on Yom Teruah/Rosh HaShanah, God's books are open, and on Yom Kippur, the books are closed. This period of time is a time of judgment. We'll read about God's judgement day, His books of works, and the Lamb's Book of Life this week.

Day 1:

1) Bible Memory: Memorize Leviticus 23:24.

2) Hebrew Words: יום תרוה - Yom Teruah – Day of Trumpets

ראש השנה - Rosh HaShanah – head of the year (New Year)

3) Think about the lesson: Read Psalm 98:6, Exodus 19:18-19, and Ezekiel 33:4. What reasons do you see for blowing the shofar?

_____

_____

_____

190

Day 2:

1) Bible Memory: Review Leviticus 23:24 and review three other verses.

2) Hebrew Words: יום תרוה - Yom Teruah – Day of Trumpets

   ראש השנה - Rosh HaShanah – head of the year (New Year)

3) Think about the lesson: Read Zephaniah 1:14-18, Jeremiah 4:5-6, and Isaiah 27:13. What does the shofar blast mean in these verses?

   _____

   _____

   _____

Day 3:

1) Bible Memory: Review Leviticus 23:24 and review three other verses.

2) Hebrew Words: יום תרוה - Yom Teruah – Day of Trumpets

   ראש השנה - Rosh HaShanah – head of the year (New Year)

3) Think about the lesson: Read Jeremiah 4:19, 1 Thessalonians 4:14-17, and Revelation 20:11-15. What do each of these shofar blasts signal?

   _____

   _____

   _____

Day 4:

1) Bible Memory: Review Leviticus 23:24 and review three other verses.

2) Hebrew Words: יום תרוה - Yom Teruah – Day of Trumpets

   ראש השנה - Rosh HaShanah – head of the year (New Year)

3) Think about the lesson: Read Exodus 32:31-33 and Daniel 12:1. What do you notice about the Book of Life?

   _____

   _____

Day 5:

1) Bible Memory: Review Leviticus 23:24 and review three other verses.

2) Hebrew Words: יום תרוה - Yom Teruah – Day of Trumpets

   ראש השנה - Rosh HaShanah – head of the year (New Year)

3) Think about the lesson: Read Psalm 69:27-28 and Malachi 3:16. What do you notice about the Book of Life?

   _____

Day 6:

1) Bible Memory: Review Leviticus 23:24 and review three other verses.

2) Hebrew Words: יום תרוה - Yom Teruah – Day of Trumpets

   ראש השׁנה - Rosh HaShanah – head of the year (New Year)

3) Think about the lesson: Read Philippians 4:3 and Revelation 21:27. What do you notice about the Book of Life?

LESSON 59
YOM KIPPUR

Lesson Objective: Yom Kippur is the Day of Atonement. Understand what that means with the work of Yeshua. Know that this holy day signifies the closing of the Book on Adonai's Day of Judgment.

Memory Passage: Revelation 20:11-15 Then I saw a great white throne and Him who was seated on it. Earth and sky fled from his presence, and there was no place for them. And I saw the dead, great and small, standing before the throne, and books were opened. Another book was opened, which is the Book of Life. The dead were judged according to what they had done as recorded in the books. The sea gave up the dead that were in it, and death and Hades gave up the dead that were in them, and each person was judged according to what he had done. Then death and Hades were thrown into the lake of fire. The lake of fire is the second death. If anyone's name was not found written in the Book of Life, he was thrown into the lake of fire.

Hebrew Word: כפר יום Yom Kippur – Day of Atonement

Lesson Summary:

On Rosh HaShanah, the books are opened, and on Yom Kippur, they are closed. Many Jewish New Year greeting cards will bless the recipient with "May you be inscribed for a good new year." Inscribed means written, so this conveys the idea that being written in the books is for one year at a time. We have seen in our scripture readings that the Book of Life on Judgment Day is for eternity. Why the difference?

Yom Kippur is the one and only day of the year that the High Priest could enter the Holy of Holies. We know that Yeshua is our eternal High Priest. The book of Hebrews shows us the difference between the human high priests and Yeshua as our divine High Priest. It is a difference between a yearly repetition vs. once for all eternity.

On Yom Kippur, we fast. We do not eat. We spend the day in community with our congregation, praying together for the forgiveness of our sins. This is the highest holy day of the year.

Day 1:

1) Bible Memory: Memorize Revelation 20:11.

2) Hebrew Word: כפר יום Yom Kippur – Day of Atonement

3) Think about the lesson: Read Leviticus 23:26-32. What do you notice?

_____

_____

Day 2:

1) Bible Memory: Memorize Revelation 20:12 and review Revelation 20:11.

2) Hebrew Word: כפר יום Yom Kippur – Day of Atonement

193

3) Think about the lesson: Read Leviticus chapter 16 and discuss it with your parents. This chapter is about what happened in the Temple times on Yom Kippur. What do you notice?

_____

_____

Day 3:

1) Bible Memory: Memorize Revelation 20:13 and review Revelation 20:11-12.

2) Hebrew Word: יוֹם כִּפֻּר Yom Kippur – Day of Atonement

3) Think about the lesson: Read Hebrews chapter 5 and discuss it with your parents. What do you notice?

_____

_____

Day 4:

1) Bible Memory: Memorize Revelation 20:14 and review Revelation 20:11-13.

2) Hebrew Word: יוֹם כִּפֻּר Yom Kippur – Day of Atonement

3) Think about the lesson: Read Hebrews chapter 6 and discuss it with your parents. What do you notice?

_____

_____

Day 5:

1) Bible Memory: Memorize Revelation 20:15 and review Revelation 20:11-14.

2) Hebrew Word: יוֹם כִּפֻּר Yom Kippur – Day of Atonement

3) Think about the lesson: Read Hebrews chapters 7-8 and discuss it with your parents. What do you notice?

_____

_____

Day 6:

1) Bible Memory: Review Revelation 20:11-15.

2) Hebrew Word: יוֹם כִּפֻּר Yom Kippur – Day of Atonement

3) Think about the lesson: Read Hebrews chapter 9 and discuss it with your parents. What do you notice?

_____

_____

LESSON 60
SUKKOT

Lesson Objective: Sukkot is a special week that commemorates the Israelites' time following Adonai in the wilderness and also looks forward to the time when all nations will worship the one true God together with all Israel.

Memory Verse: Zechariah 14:16 Then the survivors from all the nations that have attacked Jerusalem will go up year after year to worship the King, the LORD Almighty, and to celebrate the Feast of Sukkot.

Hebrew Word: סֻכּוֹת Sukkot - Tabernacles

Lesson Summary:

In contrast with the solemnness of Yom Kippur, Sukkot is a time of great celebration! The Torah commands us to build a sukkah and live in it for a week so that we remember the special time in the wilderness led by Adonai. Many Jews today will build a sukkah on their porches or in their backyards and enjoy meals together inside the sukkah. Some Messianic Jewish groups today will take the week to go camping, building their sukkot at their campsites.

Another commandment is to rejoice before the Lord with leafy fronds. The lulav is made of three different species of trees. Trees are symbolic representations of people.

One of the three species is the date palm. When the date palm was cultivated for harvest in ancient Israel, the workers would climb up the tree and bind the branches together on the sides and top. This made the tree look like a cross. There are engravings on archeological artifacts that predate Yeshua's death on the cross that appear to be decorated with a cross, but these engravings are actually representations of the date palm. Yeshua's death on the cross means life for us.

The rabbis say that the three species represent three parts of the human body: the eyes, the mouth, and the spine. The date palm branches, which are straight, represent the spine. The willow represents the mouth, and the myrtle leaves represent our eyes. When we add the Etrog to the mix, this fruit represents our heart. When we wave it all before Adonai, we are offering ourselves to Him and rejoicing in His presence.

In Temple times, there was also a water libation ceremony during Sukkot. The water libation involved pouring water and wine on the altar. Light is also a major theme of Sukkot. We'll read about the light of the world this week.

Day 1:

1) Bible Memory: Memorize Zechariah 14:16.

2) Hebrew Word: סֻכּוֹת Sukkot - Tabernacles

3) Think about the lesson:

Read Leviticus 23:33-43. Why do we live in booths (sukkot) for seven days? Which choice fruits do we rejoice with?

_____

_____

Read Acts 7:44-47. What is a tabernacle? _____

Day 2:

1) Bible Memory: Review Zechariah 14:16 and review three other verses.

2) Hebrew Word: סֻכּוֹת Sukkot - Tabernacles

3) Think about the lesson: Read John 1:14. Who made His dwelling among us?

_____

Read Revelation 21:1-4. The dwelling of God is with _____.
Read Zechariah 14:16. Sukkot is for _____
(Jews? Gentiles? Everyone?)

Day 3:

1) Bible Memory: Review Zechariah 14:16 and review three other verses.

2) Hebrew Word: סֻכּוֹת Sukkot - Tabernacles

3) Think about the lesson: Read John 8:12. Who is the light of the world? _____
Read Isaiah 12:1-3 and John 7:37-39. Who provides living waters?

_____

Day 4:

1) Bible Memory: Review Zechariah 14:16 and review three other verses.

2) Hebrew Word: סֻכּוֹת Sukkot - Tabernacles

3) Think about the lesson: Read Mark 8:24. What do trees symbolize?

_____

Day 5:

1) Bible Memory: Review Zechariah 14:16 and review three other verses.

2) Hebrew Word: סֻכּוֹת Sukkot - Tabernacles

3) Think about the lesson: Read Proverbs 3:18 and Proverbs 11:30. What do you notice?

_____

_____

Day 6:

1) Bible Memory: Review Zechariah 14:16 and review three other verses.

2) Hebrew Word: סֻכּוֹת Sukkot - Tabernacles

3) Think about the lesson: Read John 19:34, John 4:14, 1 Corinthians 11:23-25, and Mark 14:22-24. What do you notice?

_____

_____

_____

_____

LESSON 61
CHANUKAH

Lesson Objective: Understand the historical background of this time period, see where it falls on the historical timeline, and understand the importance of rededicating not only the Temple but also our very selves – the temples of our bodies – to Adonai.

Memory Verse: John 10:22-30 Then came the Feast of Dedication (Chanukah) at Jerusalem. It was winter, and Yeshua was in the temple area walking in Solomon's Colonnade. The Jews gathered around him, saying, "How long will you keep us in suspense? If you are the Messiah, tell us plainly." Yeshua answered, "I did tell you, but you do not believe. The miracles I do in my Father's name speak for me, but you do not believe because you are not my sheep. My sheep listen to my voice; I know them, and they follow me. I give them eternal life, and they shall never perish; no one can snatch them out of my hand. My Father, who has given them to me, is greater than all; no one can snatch them out of my Father's hand. I and the Father are one."

Hebrew Word: חנוכה Chanukah - dedication

Lesson Summary:

After Alexander the Great conquered the known world (323 BC), he died. His empire was divided between his generals. Different generals treated the Jewish people differently.

(As you already know, this is when Greek culture, language, and religion spread across the world, and roads were built to connect areas and make travel easier.)

Eventually, a Greek ruler named Antiochus Ephinanes came to power, and he ruled over Judah and Jerusalem. He was not kind to the Jewish people and did not allow them to practice their own religion. He outlawed observance of Shabbat, circumcision of baby boys, Torah study, and everything else that specifically identified the Jewish people and set them apart. He wanted everyone to look, act, walk, talk, eat, and worship like the Greeks. He took over the Temple and set up pagan practices in it. He sent soldiers from town to town to enforce Greek-style worship, which at that time involved sacrificing a pig and then eating it. This, of course, was not an appropriate sacrifice and was absolutely not kosher to eat. Many of the Hellenized (remember that word? it means Greek-like) Jews complied. They did what they were told.

Others, however, did not. There is a story of a mother named Hannah and her seven sons who all died holding strong in their faith in the one true God. They refused to compromise their faith even in the face of torture and death.

When the soldiers came to the town of Modin, they met the Maccabees. The father and all the sons refused to worship in the Greek way. After killing the Jewish priest who stepped forward to comply with the Greek orders, they then called for a revolt.

From 165-162 BC, the Maccabees led a successful revolt, kicking the Greeks out of their towns and Temple. They cleaned up and rededicated the Temple to Adonai. Chanukah, which means "dedication," is the holiday born from this event.

We don't see the history of this time in the Bibles we have now, but the history is recorded in the books that were written between the end of the Hebrew Bible and the beginning of the Brit Chadashah, and we know that Yeshua observed this holiday based on what we read in this week's memory passage.

Chanukah is celebrated by lighting one additional light each night on the special nine-branched menorah for Chanukah. The lights are lit with the center candle, the shamash, or servant-candle, and thus the light increases each night.

There is a story that this is done to commemorate the rededication of the Temple when they discovered there was only enough oil left for one night, but the candles miraculously burned for eight nights.

Day 1:

1) Bible Memory: Memorize John 10:22-25.

2) Hebrew Word: חנוכה Chanukah - dedication

3) Think about the lesson: Read 1 Maccabees 1. It's ok if it's not in your Bible. You can find it online☺ Read it together with your parents and discuss what you read.

Day 2:

1) Bible Memory: Memorize John 10:26-28 and review John 10:22-25.

2) Hebrew Word: חנוכה Chanukah - dedication

3) Think about the lesson: Read 1 Maccabees 2 together with your parents and discuss what you read.

Day 3:

1) Bible Memory: Memorize John 10:29-30 and review John 10:22-28.

2) Hebrew Word: חנוכה Chanukah - dedication

3) Think about the lesson: Read 1 Maccabees 3 together with your parents and discuss what you read.

Day 4:

1) Bible Memory: Review John 10:22-30.

2) Hebrew Word: חנוכה Chanukah - dedication

3) Think about the lesson: Read 1 Maccabees 4 together with your parents and discuss what you read.

Day 5:

1) Bible Memory: Review John 10:22-30.

2) Hebrew Word: חנוכה Chanukah - dedication

3) Think about the lesson: Yeshua is the light of the world. He IS the ultimate servant-leader, shamash candle, who give light to us – He is the vine; we are the branches. Read Isaiah 60:1, 19-20, Isaiah 49:6, Psalm 119:105, Romans 13:12, John 1:9, and Matthew 5:14-16. You thoughts:

199

_____

_____

_____

_____

_____

Day 6:

1) Bible Memory: Review John 10:22-30.

2) Hebrew Word: חנוכה Chanukah - dedication

3) Think about the lesson: Read Psalm 27:1. Your thoughts:

_____

_____

_____

LESSON 62
PURIM

Lesson Objective: Sometimes we need bravery and boldness to accomplish the good works that He has given us to do – other people's lives, temporal and eternal, rest on our willingness to speak out, even when it may be dangerous.

Memory Verse: Esther 4:14 For if you remain silent at this time, relief and deliverance for the Jews will arise from another place, but you and your father's family will perish.

Hebrew Word: פוּרִים Purim - lots

Lesson Summary:

If you've studied dramatic irony in English class, you will enjoy the irony in the book of Esther! If not, here is your introduction.

Purim is a holiday that was established during the reign of the Persians when the Hebrews were living there after the Babylonian dispersion. Many Jews were living in Persia, including Esther and her cousin Mordecai. You will read this week about how Haman, second in command to the King, desired to kill Modecai and all the Jews, yet Esther's actions saved her people, and Haman was hung on the very gallows he built for Mordecai!

Purim is a fun holiday that often includes a Purim play acting out the events recorded in the book of Esther. Observers will loudly boo and cheer for Haman, Esther, and Mordecai, respectively, Enjoy!

Day 1:

1) Bible Memory: Memorize Esther 4:14.
2) Hebrew Word: פוּרִים Purim - lots
3) Think about the lesson: Read and/or act out Esther 1-2 with your family. Include discussion afterwards.

Day 2:

1) Bible Memory: Review Esther 4:14 and review three other verses.
2) Hebrew Word: פוּרִים Purim - lots
3) Think about the lesson: Read and/or act out Esther 3-4 with your family. Include discussion afterwards.

Day 3:

1) Bible Memory: Review Esther 4:14 and review three other verses.

2) Hebrew Word: פורים Purim - lots

3) Think about the lesson: Read and/or act out Esther 5-6 with your family. Include discussion afterwards.

Day 4:

1) Bible Memory: Review Esther 4:14 and review three other verses.

2) Hebrew Word: פורים Purim - lots

3) Think about the lesson: Read and/or act out Esther 7-8 with your family. Include discussion afterwards.

Day 5:

1) Bible Memory: Review Esther 4:14 and review three other verses.

2) Hebrew Word: פורים Purim - lots

3) Think about the lesson: Read and/or act out Esther 9-10 with your family. Include discussion afterwards.

Day 6:

1) Bible Memory: Review Esther 4:14 and review three other verses.

2) Hebrew Word: פורים Purim - lots

3) Think about the lesson: Present a family play of Esther, bake hamentaschen cookies, discuss forms of irony in Esther, and/or discuss Esther as a family. Some ideas for discussion might include the role of prayer combined with fasting in our lives, the authority of the king, our responsibility to our brothers and sisters, etc.

LESSON 63
WORLD VIEWS VS. A BIBLICAL WORLD VIEW

Lesson Objective: Contrast the outcomes of a godless world view versus a Godly world view.

Memory Verse: Psalm 14:1 The fool says in his heart, "There is no God." They are corrupt, their deeds are vile; there is no one who does good.

Hebrew Word: טוב tov - good

Lesson Summary:

A world view is a particular philosophy of life or conception of the world. Godly vs ungodly world views are fueled by either daily immersion in scripture or fueled by daily immersion in secular culture. Our world views begin to be shaped in early, early childhood, often with cartoons and television shows geared for babies, and are heavily influenced by schooling as we grow.

A conflicting world view can prevent us from clearly seeing what is presented. We can look at the exact same thing and see something totally different. For example, creationists and evolutionists look at the same evidence and come to opposite conclusions. Other examples include all the various world religions and the way people view God and each other through the lens of their particular religious view.

How do we avoid confusion, develop a Biblical world view and avoid other world views that are in contrast to the one true God? Develop and maintain a firm foundation in the Bible, stay close to God in prayer, trust in Yeshua for salvation, and ask the Ruach Hakodesh for spiritual discernment.

Watch the movie *God's Not Dead* if you can. If you've already watched it, watch it again. Pay close attention to the arguments that are presented. Basically, if there is no God, then there is no right and wrong. Yet, we all innately know that there is a right and a wrong. If there is no great Lawgiver, then how do we know what is right and what is wrong? How do we define right and wrong? We can't. If I believe that it is right to take what you have (steal), how can you tell me it's wrong? Modern culture says that what is right and what is wrong is defined by what the society accepts as right and wrong. But then, right and wrong would be subjective and would change over the years. Was it right for the Nazis to murder Jews? They as a group decided it was. Culture cannot define right and wrong.

Science also claims to have knowledge of the way the world works. Is what science teaches true? Well, that depends. Sometimes, the scientists get it right, and sometimes they don't. Scientists used to think the world was flat (some people still teach that today, too, believe it or not). The problem with relying on science is that our understanding of it is still very limited, so as new discoveries are made, our understanding of "truth" changes. Science cannot define truth.

The problem with understanding the world through culture, through science, or through any means other than God is that all of these are part of the creation. We are inside the box. To understand the laws of the

203

universe, one must understand the Lawgiver – the One who made the universe.

Why do people deny the existence of God? At the heart of the matter is a rejection of responsibility. We are engaged in a spiritual battle – whether we acknowledge it or not. If we deny that there is a God, then we also deny any need for responding to Him. If there is no God, then anything is permissible. If there is no God, then there is no punishment for wrongdoing, because there is no right or wrong.

What are the consequences of this kind of thinking? We fail to see that we are created in God's image for a purpose and that we have hope. Rather, a godless world view leads to hopelessness and a view that does not value human life. After all, the human is simply a complex organism evolved from monkeys, crystals, primordial ooze, whatever.

We, of course, know this is not true. There is a God, and He made us fearfully and wonderfully in His image. He is involved in our daily lives. We have hope and purpose, life with meaning, and eternal life through Yeshua.

Day 1:

1) Bible Memory: Memorize Psalm 14:1.

2) Hebrew Word: טוֹב tov - good

3) Think about the lesson: If your parents permit, watch *God's Not Dead* with them and then discuss. Feel free to pause the movie frequently and discuss as you watch. Spend as any days this week as you need to. Your thought:

_____

_____

_____

_____

Day 2:

1) Bible Memory: Review Psalm 14:1 and review three other verses.

2) Hebrew Word: טוֹב tov - good

3) Think about the lesson: With your parents, discuss some of the false philosophies present in this world. Which ones do you see as pervasive in our culture?

_____

_____

_____

_____

Day 3:

1) Bible Memory: Review Psalm 14:1 and review three other verses.

2) Hebrew Word: טוֹב tov - good

204

3) Think about the lesson: Look up the full title of Darwin's book *Origin of the Species*. What is the full title?

_____

How does this title lessen the value of human life? How does it perpetuate racism?

_____

_____

_____

Day 4:

1) Bible Memory: Review Psalm 14:1 and review three other verses.

2) Hebrew Word: טוֹב tov - good

3) Think about the lesson: Read Colossians 2:8. What do you notice?

_____

_____

_____

Day 5:

1) Bible Memory: Review Psalm 14:1 and review three other verses.

2) Hebrew Word: טוֹב tov - good

3) Think about the lesson: Are there areas where your own faith falters? Carefully consider where you may have accepted false philosophies. Discuss with your parents. Record your thoughts:

_____

_____

_____

Day 6:

1) Bible Memory: Review Psalm 14:1 and review three other verses.

2) Hebrew Word: טוֹב tov - good

3) Think about the lesson: Define your world view:

_____

_____

_____

_____

LESSON 64
BASIC LIFE QUESTIONS:
WHO AM I?
WHY AM I HERE?
WHERE DID I COME FROM?
WHERE AM I GOING?

Lesson Objective: Consider the identity, origins, purpose, and destiny of our lives.

Memory Verse: Jeremiah 29:11 For I know the plans I have for you, declares the LORD, plans to prosper you and not to harm you, plans to give you hope and a future.

Hebrew Word: תִקְוָה tikvah - hope

Lesson Summary:

How would you answer these questions?

Who am I?

Where did I come from?

Why am I here?

Where am I going?

The answers to these questions form our basic world view, which we then act upon as we live out our lives. We want our lives to be fruitful and productive, so that we might stand before our Maker one day and hear Him say, "Well done, good and faithful servant." There is comfort in knowing the answers to these questions, and we need to know the answers to these questions in order to accomplish the works the Lord has set before each of us and to find peace, joy, and fulfillment in our lives.

How does the world answer these questions? Are we nothing but a "mass of tissue?" An evolved animal? Did we evolve from goo? Or crystals? Or amoeba? Or . . . fill in the blank with whatever "scientific" theory is the popular one today. If any of these are true, then there is no purpose to our lives, and there is nothing after death.

There is no hope in these answers.

There is no responsibility in these answers.

Atheists cannot answer these questions, and wrong answers or no answers lead to depression and anxiety. Additionally, if there are no answers to these questions, then what we do doesn't matter, so this thinking leads to immoral and ungodly behavior. This is not the plan that God has for you. God has plans for your future, and they are good. Yeshua died to save us from the consequences of an ungodly life so that we can have eternal life, purpose, and destiny in Him.

To really know who you are and to live a life that changes others for the better, get to know Yeshua. Accept Him as your Savior today and commit your life to fulfilling the good plans He has for you.

We'll see these answers in our readings this week:

Who am I? A child of God

Where did I come from? God made me

Why am I here? To make disciples of Yeshua

Where am I going? To live with Yeshua in heaven

Day 1:

1) Bible Memory: Memorize Jeremiah 29:11.
2) Hebrew Word: תִּקְוָה tikvah - hope
3) Think about the lesson: Read John 1:12 and 1 Corinthians 12:27. Who am I?

_____

_____

Day 2:

1) Bible Memory: Review Jeremiah 29:11 and review three other verses.
2) Hebrew Word: תִּקְוָה tikvah - hope
3) Think about the lesson: Read Genesis 1:27, Jeremiah 1:5, and Psalm 139:13. Where did I come from?

_____

_____

Day 3:

1) Bible Memory: Review Jeremiah 29:11 and review three other verses.
2) Hebrew Word: תִּקְוָה tikvah - hope
3) Think about the lesson: Read Exodus 19:6, 1 Peter 2:9, and Matthew 28:19-20. Why am I here?

_____

_____

Day 4:

1) Bible Memory: Review Jeremiah 29:11 and review three other verses.

2) Hebrew Word: תִקְוָה tikvah - hope

3) Think about the lesson: Read Genesis 3:19 and Hebrews 9:27. Where am I going?

_____

_____

Day 5:

1) Bible Memory: Review Jeremiah 29:11 and review three other verses.

2) Hebrew Word: תִקְוָה tikvah - hope

3) Think about the lesson: Read Revelation 20:12-15. Where am I going?

_____

_____

Day 6:

1) Bible Memory: Review Jeremiah 29:11 and review three other verses.

2) Hebrew Word: תִקְוָה tikvah - hope

3) Think about the lesson: Read 1 Thessalonians 5:9-10. Where am I going?

_____

_____

LESSON 65
WHY TO MEMORIZE SCRIPTURE AND HOW TO USE IT

Lesson Objectives: We memorize scripture because it protects us, conforms our minds with God's (Romans 12:2), leads us into His paths, comforts us, reminds us of His promises, and provides us with tools against the false philosophies of this world (i.e. the lies of the enemy).

Memory Verses:
Isaiah 41:10 So do not fear, for I am with you; do not be dismayed, for I am your God. I will strengthen you and help you; I will uphold you with my righteous right hand.
1 Peter 5:7 Cast all your anxiety on Him because He cares for you.

Hebrew Word: כִּי־אֲנִי ki-ani – because I

Lesson Summary:

Did you ever have a bad dream and wake up scared? Alone in the dark at night, remembering Isaiah 41:10 can remind you that God is with you. He will comfort you and protect you. When God makes a promise to us, we can claim that promise by reciting His words out loud in prayer.

When we call on the name of Yeshua, He will be there with us. He is the good shepherd of Psalm 23. He will walk through any valley of the shadow of death with us.

The more we know of His Word, the more we see of His plans, the big picture, and the plans He has for us. Storing up God's words in our hearts helps us to discern right from wrong so that we can make good decisions.

Every Bible verse we memorize is like adding a new tool to our spiritual tool belt. In our readings this week, we will see how Yeshua used scripture to stop Satan from leading Him astray.

Notice also that Satan used scripture to try to lead Yeshua astray. Satan knows the scriptures very well. We need to sharpen our spiritual swords by learning God's Word better so that we will not be led astray.

Day 1:

1) Bible Memory: Memorize Isaiah 41:10.

2) Hebrew Word: כִּי־אֲנִי ki-ani – because I

3) Think about the lesson: Read Romans 12:2. What do you notice?

_____

_____

Day 2:

1) Bible Memory: Memorize 1 Peter 5:7. Review Isaiah 41:10.

2) Hebrew Word: כִּי־אָנִי ki-ani – because I

3) Think about the lesson: Read Matthew 4:1-11. How and when did Satan attack? How did Yeshua respond?

_____

_____

_____

Day 3:

1) Bible Memory: Review Isaiah 41:10 and 1 Peter 5:7. Review two other verses.

2) Hebrew Word: כִּי־אָנִי ki-ani – because I

3) Think about the lesson: Read Ephesians 6:10-20. How do we prepare for spiritual battle?

_____

_____

_____

_____

Day 4:

1) Bible Memory: Review Isaiah 41:10 and 1 Peter 5:7. Review two other verses.

2) Hebrew Word: כִּי־אָנִי ki-ani – because I

3) Think about the lesson: Re-read Ephesians 6:12. What do you notice?

_____

_____

Day 5:

1) Bible Memory: Review Isaiah 41:10 and 1 Peter 5:7. Review two other verses.

2) Hebrew Word: כִּי־אָנִי ki-ani – because I

3) Think about the lesson: Read Psalm 119:9-11. What do you notice?

_____

_____

Day 6:

1) Bible Memory: Review Isaiah 41:10 and 1 Peter 5:7. Review two other verses.

2) Hebrew Word: כִּי־אָנִי ki-ani – because I

3) Think about the lesson: Read Colossians 3:16. What do you notice?

_____

_____

LESSON 66
BOOKS OF THE BIBLE

Lesson Objective: Be able to locate a book, chapter, and verse in the Bible.

Bible Memory: This week, we are memorizing the order of the books of the Bible.

Hebrew Word: תַּנַךְ tanakh – Torah, Neviim, Ketuvim (Torah , Prophets, Writings)

Lesson Summary:

It is good to know the order of the books of the Bible so that we can look up Bible verses quickly and easily. Similar to learning the alphabet, using a song to help learn the books of the Bible can make memorizing them easier.

It's important to know that not all Bibles have the same books in the same order.

Hebrew Bibles are called Tanakh, which is an acronym that tells us the three parts of the Bible. The Torah includes the first five books: Genesis, Exodus, Leviticus, Numbers, and Deuteronomy; the Neviim are all the writings of the prophets, and the Ketuvim are all the other writings.

Christian Bibles have the books in the same order for the Torah, but then the prophets and the writings are not in the same order as the Hebrew Tanakh. The Christian Bible somewhat assembles the writings and the prophets in more of an historically chronological way. Christian Bibles will also have the Brit Chadashah, or writings of the New Testament, which are not included in the Hebrew Bible (even though they were written by Jews, for Jews, about the greatest Jew who ever walked the face of this earth!)

Catholic Bibles will have extra books (including the Maccabees) in between their old and new testaments. These books were written during that time period between the prophets and the first century, but they are not universally recognized as scripturally authoritative.

So before you begin memorizing the order of the books of the Bible, choose the Bible you plan to use the most, and then memorize that order specifically!

Day 1:

1) Bible Memory: Look at the front pages of your Bible and find the list of the books in order. Memorize the order.
2) Hebrew Word: תַּנַךְ tanakh – Torah, Neviim, Ketuvim (Torah , Prophets, Writings)
3) Think about the lesson: Discuss with your parents the different ways that Bibles are organized. Understand the differences between the organization of the Hebrew Bible and the Christian Bible.

Day 2:

1) Bible Memory: Memorize the order of the books of the Bible.

2) Hebrew Word: תַּנַךְ tanakh – Torah, Neviim, Ketuvim (Torah , Prophets, Writings)

3) Think about the lesson: Practice finding verses of your choice in the Bible. One idea might be to look up a list of verses you would like to memorize, in the interest of storing God's Word in your heart. Then, time yourself to see how quickly you can find those verses using the locations of the books of the Bible from memory.

Day 3:

1) Bible Memory: Memorize the order of the books of the Bible.

2) Hebrew Word: תַּנַךְ tanakh – Torah, Neviim, Ketuvim (Torah , Prophets, Writings)

3) Think about the lesson: Practice finding verses of your choice in the Bible. One idea might be to look up a list of verses you would like to memorize, in the interest of storing God's Word in your heart. Then, time yourself to see how quickly you can find those verses using the locations of the books of the Bible from memory. Can you beat yesterday's times?

Day 4:

1) Bible Memory: Memorize the order of the books of the Bible.

2) Hebrew Word: תַּנַךְ tanakh – Torah, Neviim, Ketuvim (Torah , Prophets, Writings)

3) Think about the lesson: Practice finding verses of your choice in the Bible. One idea might be to look up a list of verses you would like to memorize, in the interest of storing God's Word in your heart. Then, time yourself to see how quickly you can find those verses using the locations of the books of the Bible from memory. Can you beat yesterday's times?

Day 5:

1) Bible Memory: Memorize the order of the books of the Bible.

2) Hebrew Word: תַּנַךְ tanakh – Torah, Neviim, Ketuvim (Torah , Prophets, Writings)

3) Think about the lesson: Practice finding verses of your choice in the Bible. One idea might be to look up a list of verses you would like to memorize, in the interest of storing God's Word in your heart. Then, time yourself to see how quickly you can find those verses using the locations of the books of the Bible from memory. Can you beat yesterday's times?

Day 6:

1) Bible Memory: Memorize the order of the books of the Bible.

2) Hebrew Word: תַּנַךְ tanakh – Torah, Neviim, Ketuvim (Torah , Prophets, Writings)

3) Think about the lesson: Practice finding verses of your choice in the Bible. One idea might be to look up a list of verses you would like to memorize, in the interest of storing God's Word in your heart. Then, time yourself to see how quickly you can find those verses using the locations of the books of the Bible from memory. Can you beat yesterday's times?

LESSON 67
DINOSAURS, SCIENCE, AND THE BIBLE

Lesson Objective: Know that science confirms the Bible.

Memory Verse: Job 40:15 Look at the behemoth which I made along with you and which feeds on grass like an ox.

Hebrew Word: הִנֵּה hineh - behold

Lesson Summary:

Science can tell us a lot about the earth and everything in it. Many people believe that science supports the theory of evolution, but many people believe this because they are told this. They haven't necessarily looked at the scientific evidence for themselves. What we know of science changes and develops over the centuries.

God created science, and He knows all the rules which we are continuously "discovering."

There are some major problems with the theory of evolution. Scientific discoveries are consistently pointing towards an intelligent designer of the universe. Even in evolutionist textbooks, writers cannot get away from writing as if evolution has an intelligence behind it. Watch the sentence construction. You will see that the sentences state "evolution chose" or "natural selection decided." How do random occurrences make choices or decisions? Why do random occurrences care if the fittest survive? Only something with intelligence and emotions can make choices and care about something.

Intelligence and emotions are immaterial and cannot be explained in purely natural ways.

DNA contains information. Information is also immaterial and cannot be explained in purely natural ways.

We could go on, but we digress. Let's get back to dinosaurs.

Evolution says that dinosaurs came before humans. God says He created land animals and humans on the 6th day. According to God, dinosaurs and humans would have therefore coexisted at the same time.

What does the scientific record show?

The scientific record shows us fossils. Think for a minute: what typically happens to an animal that dies? Other animals or insects eat it, it decays, and it returns to dust. For a fossil to be formed, an animal must be buried quickly in wet dirt. The wet dirt will cut off oxygen that can cause decay and will also prevent access for other animals to eat it. Being buried quickly in wet dirt can logically happen in a flood. This is not likely to happen outside of a flood situation. The Bible records a global flood; secular scientists deny a global flood.

What do we see in the fossil record? We see marine life, animals, dinosaurs, and plants.

The evolutionists believe that the fossil record shows a progression from simpler marine life to more complex land dwelling life occurring over millions and millions of years. Evolution teaches that the simpler life forms

213

evolved into more complex life forms as the millennia passed. Yet there are no transitional forms in the fossil record.

Creationists see that the marine life in the simplest forms are at the base layers because they lived at the bottom of the seas, hence were buried and fossilized first in the global flood. Land dwelling animals were at the top layers because the water was rising and they were running from it.

Fossil evidence includes polystrate fossils, which are fossils that protrude through multiple layers of rock. These are usually trees. How could these trees survive for millions of years as the rock layers were gradually formed around them? Evolutionists cannot explain polystrate fossils.

Fossil graveyards have a mixture of animals and dinosaurs buried together, indicating that they died together and were all mixed up with marine and land animals. This is what we would expect if there were a global flood with powerful surges of water washing and sifting back and forth over the earth.

Dinosaur fossils have been found that contain soft tissue and blood vessels inside them. How could that have lasted millions of years? It couldn't. This is evidence that the earth and the dinosaurs were not as old as the evolutionists believe.

When scientists are trying to figure out what a dinosaur looked like from examining the fossils, they are often guessing. Most of the time, the fossils are not complete. Much or even most of an animal's remains might be missing. This means that much of what we know about dinosaurs is from a scientist's imagination as he or she tries to piece it together and figure it out. This means that sometimes, they get it wrong!

The book of Job records creatures that coexisted with Job; God tells him to "behold" or to look at them as God teaches Job a lesson using these creatures as props for His lesson. These creatures fit the description of dinosaurs. Evolutionists say dinosaurs and humans did not coexist; the Bible says they did.

There is also evidence outside the Bible that prove that dinosaurs and humans coexisted. These include drawings on cave walls or rocks that show humans hunting dinosaurs and other animals. There are stories of knights fighting dragons. The Chinese have a year named after the dragon. These are just a few examples.

So what happened to the dinosaurs?

They are mostly extinct today, dying the same way many other extinct species died out: they were either killed off by humans or their preferred habitat or food sources were depleted.

Day 1:

1) Bible Memory: Memorize Job 40:15.

2) Hebrew Word: הִנֵּה hineh - behold

3) Think about the lesson: Read Job 40:15-24. What do you notice?

_____

_____

_____

Day 2:

1) Bible Memory: Review Job 40:15 and review three other verses.

2) Hebrew Word: הִנֵּה hineh - behold

3) Think about the lesson: Read Job 41:1-34. What do you notice?

_____

_____

_____

Day 3:

1) Bible Memory: Review Job 40:15 and review three other verses.

2) Hebrew Word: הִנֵּה hineh - behold

3) Think about the lesson: With your parents, discuss and research fossils and fossil layers.

Day 4:

1) Bible Memory: Review Job 40:15 and review three other verses.

2) Hebrew Word: הִנֵּה hineh - behold

3) Think about the lesson: With your parents, discuss and research evidence of humans and dinosaurs coexisting.

Day 5:

1) Bible Memory: Review Job 40:15 and review three other verses.

2) Hebrew Word: הִנֵּה hineh - behold

3) Think about the lesson: With your parents, discuss and research the claims that early hominid or neaderthal fossils have been found. Are they human? What are they?

Day 6:

1) Bible Memory: Review Job 40:15 and review three other verses.

2) Hebrew Word: הִנֵּה hineh - behold

3) Think about the lesson: Record your findings from the week of research and discussion:

_____

_____

_____

_____

_____

_____

_____

SECTION 5 – HISTORY

LESSON 68
HISTORY OF THE 1ST AND 2ND CENTURIES

Lesson Objective: See how Judaism and Christianity split.

Memory Verse: Isaiah 46:10 I make known the end from the beginning, from ancient times what is still to come. I say: My purpose will stand, and I will do all that I please.

Hebrew Word: אחרית acharit – end, after

Lesson Summary:

The first and second centuries witnessed Yeshua's death and resurrection, the destruction of the 2nd Temple, and the momentous Battle of Bar Kochba. All of these events changed the course of Jewish History, and indeed of the history of the world.

Here is a brief outline of the events of this time:

30 AD – Yeshua died and resurrected. A few strange occurrences happened in the Temple after this. First, the veil was torn, top to bottom. This is recorded in the Brit Chadashah. The ner tamid kept going out. The red thread tied around the Azazel goat stopped turning white. The doors of the Temple kept opening by themselves. These are recorded in the Talmud (Soncino version, Yoma 39b).

70 AD – Romans destroyed the 2nd Temple on the 9th of Av; just before this happened, Rabbi Yochanan ben Zakkai had himself smuggled out of Jerusalem in a coffin. He then established a house of Torah study in Yavneh, and thus Rabbinic Judaism was born.

132-135 AD – Battle of Bar Kochba. Of Simon Bar Kochba, Rabbi Akiva says "He is the king messiah" while another rabbi says "grass will be growing from your cheeks and the son of David still will not have come" in Midrash Rabba Eicha 2:2.4. In other words, some Jews in the second century thought he was the Messiah and others did not. Letters from Simon Bar Kochba himself claim that he is the "prince of Israel," indicating that he thought he was the Messiah. Historian Eusibius says in *History of the Church* 4:6.2 that Bar Kochba was "murderous and a bandit, but claimed to be a luminary come from heaven and was magically enlightening those who were in misery."

Simon Bar Kochba was a false Messiah. Rabbi Akiva and almost all of the Jewish people had supported him.

The Romans destroyed Jerusalem and it became Rome's Aelia Capitolina. Any Jews left living after the battle were cast out from the city, and very few Jews lived there until the return in 1948.

216

This marks the final split between Judaism and Christianity – aside from those followers of Yeshua who did not follow Simon Bar Kochba as the Messiah, all the other Jews worked together in support of Bar Kochba against the Romans. After they were defeated, the survivors were angry with the Yeshua followers for not lending their support, and they told the Yeshua followers that they were no longer Jewish.

Jewish believers in Yeshua were at a crossroads: deny their Jewishness, or deny Yeshua. This attitude continues today, but it is entirely unnecessary. It is the most natural thing in the world to be both Jewish and a Yeshua follower! Yeshua is Jewish!! Part of the goal of a Messianic congregation is to bring this realization to pass for both Jews and Gentiles and to provide a place for Jews to worship and follow Yeshua as Jews.

Day 1:

1) Bible Memory: Memorize Isaiah 46:10.

2) Hebrew Word: אחרית acharit – end, after

3) Think about the lesson: Read Matthew 27:45-54. Reflect on the importance of Yeshua's death. What is the significance of the veil of the Temple being torn in two from top to bottom? What else happened? Do you see prophecy fulfilled? Where?

_____

_____

_____

_____

_____

Day 2:

1) Bible Memory: Review Isaiah 46:10 and review three other verses.

2) Hebrew Word: אחרית acharit – end, after

3) Think about the lesson: Read Leviticus 16:20-22. This is the Azazel goat, the one that was released into the wilderness (driven off a cliff) on Yom Kippur. What is the significance that the red cord stopped turning white after Yeshua's death? Discuss with your parents.

Day 3:

1) Bible Memory: Review Isaiah 46:10 and review three other verses.

2) Hebrew Word: אחרית acharit – end, after

3) Think about the lesson: Read John 9:13-41. What do you notice?

_____

_____

_____

Day 4:

1) Bible Memory: Review Isaiah 46:10 and review three other verses.

2) Hebrew Word: אחרית acharit – end, after

3) Think about the lesson: Read Psalm 141:2. After the destruction of the Temple, prayer replaced sacrifices. How does this Psalm, written by King David centuries earlier, support this replacement?

_____

_____

_____

Day 5:

1) Bible Memory: Review Isaiah 46:10 and review three other verses.

2) Hebrew Word: אחרית acharit – end, after

3) Think about the lesson: Read Psalm 51:16-17. Although it is sad that the Temple is gone, what is God really after?

_____

_____

Day 6:

1) Bible Memory: Review Isaiah 46:10 and review three other verses.

2) Hebrew Word: אחרית acharit – end, after

3) Think about the lesson: Do you know Jewish believers whose families have disowned them because of their faith in Yeshua? Do you see the roots of this beginning in the 1st and 2nd centuries? As a family, pray for these believers and pray also for the salvation of their families. Pray for restoration of their relationships. If it is your family, pray, and know that Adonai answers prayer! Sometimes it takes a while. Be persistent.

LESSON 69
HISTORY OF THE 3RD THROUGH 6TH CENTURIES

Lesson Objective: Compare and contrast the development of the three monotheistic religions.

Memory Verse: Joshua 24:15b As for me and my house, we will serve the LORD.

Hebrew Word: הַיּוֹם hayom – today (literally, the day)

Lesson Summary:

The 3rd through 6th centuries witnessed the development of the Mishnah and Talmud, the founding of Islam, and the beginning of the Byzantine Empire.

We saw in last week's lesson the beginning of what we recognize today as rabbinic Judaism. In rabbinic Judaism, Yeshua is recognized as a prophet, but not as the Messiah and certainly not as God. Within rabbinic Judaism, the oral Torah continued to develop via commentaries of various rabbis. The oral Torah was eventually written down and recorded in the writings of the Mishnah and the Talmud. Much of rabbinic study today includes study of these commentaries.

The Byzantine Empire lasted from 330 AD, when Emperor Constantine relocated the capital of the Roman empire to Byzantium (later named Constantinople after Emperor Constantine and then Istanbul after the Muslims conquered it) to 1453 AD when the Muslims conquered it. This developed into a Christian empire in the East, while Roman Catholicism developed in the West.

Islam began about 600 years after Yeshua when Muhammed claimed to receive revelation from the angel Gabriel. He wrote the Koran, even though it is purported that he was illiterate. He had four wives, the youngest of which he married when she was only nine years old. He believed that his new religion was righting the wrong understandings of Judaism and Christianity. At first, he tried to convert Jews and Christians, but he later decided they needed to die. Islam spread by the sword, meaning that the religion was spread through war and conquest. It is the fastest growing religion in the world today.

Day 1:

1) Bible Memory: Memorize Joshua 24:15b.
2) Hebrew Word: הַיּוֹם hayom – today
3) Think about the lesson: Read Exodus 24:3-4. According to the Bible, was there an oral Torah that Moshe passed down?

_____

_____

Day 2:

1) Bible Memory: Review Joshua 24:15b and review three other verses.

219

2) Hebrew Word: הַיּוֹם hayom – today

3) Think about the lesson: Read Genesis 16:1-12. Discuss with your parents what this passage means for the modern conflict between descendants of Ishmael (Arabs) and descendants of Isaac (Jews).

Day 3:

1) Bible Memory: Review Joshua 24:15b and review three other verses.

2) Hebrew Word: הַיּוֹם hayom – today

3) Think about the lesson: Read Deuteronomy 30:10-20. What do you notice?

_____

_____

_____

Day 4:

1) Bible Memory: Review Joshua 24:15b and review three other verses.

2) Hebrew Word: הַיּוֹם hayom – today

3) Think about the lesson: Read Joshua 24:14-15. What do you notice?

_____

_____

Day 5:

1) Bible Memory: Review Joshua 24:15b and review three other verses.

2) Hebrew Word: הַיּוֹם hayom – today

3) Think about the lesson: Discuss with your parents the difference between how Islam views Yeshua and how the Bible presents Yeshua. Islam teaches that Yeshua is the Messiah (meaning that he is an important prophet, but not divine), and their concept of that is that he will support the Mahdi when he returns to set up Islam worldwide. The picture of the antichrist given in Revelation 13 fits the Muslim concept of who Yeshua is.

Day 6:

1) Bible Memory: Review Joshua 24:15b and review three other verses.

2) Hebrew Word: הַיּוֹם hayom – today

3) Think about the lesson: Read 1 John 2:22. Discuss this with your parents. What do you notice?

_____

_____

LESSON 70
HISTORY OF THE 7ᵀᴴ THROUGH 14ᵀᴴ CENTURIES

Lesson Objectives: Contrast the Golden Age of the Jews in Spain (until the Inquisition) with the Dark Ages of Europe. See why the Jews were blamed for the Black Plague.

Memory Verse: Ephesians 4:32 Be kind and compassionate to one another, forgiving each other, just as in Messiah, God forgave you.

Hebrew Word: אֲשֶׁר asher – relative pronoun meaning who, which, or that

Lesson Summary:

Relationships between Jews, Christians, and Muslims throughout Europe and the Middle East varied over the centuries. Sometimes, Jews were welcomed; other times, they were not. Over the next few weeks, we'll see the Jewish people pass from favor to disfavor and back again from place to place throughout Europe. Century after century of this, time and again, has understandably caused a build-up of distrust, specifically Jewish distrust of Christians, which has been passed down through the generations.

Recall that the eventual split between Judaism and Christianity took time. Here is a brief overview of events over centuries.

Roman Emperor Constantine at the Council of Nicea in 325 AD said that Christians must not "Judaize" by resting on the Sabbath. If he had to tell them to stop resting on the Sabbath, then we know they were resting on the Sabbath. This means that many Christians were in the habit of "Judaizing," or observing Jewish customs and traditions, especially those that were Bible-based like the Sabbath.

The 700's were considered the Golden age of the Jews in Spain under Muslim rule (because they were permitted to practice their religion in relative freedom for a time), while throughout the rest of Europe, Christians and Jews were experiencing the Middle Ages, a time characterized by superstition and distrust. The majority of Christians at that time were illiterate. They did not have their own Bibles and would not have been able to read them if they had them. They only knew what their clergy told them about God. The clergy was the class under Feudalism that led churches; the knights were the army; and the serfs did all the work. Many Jews found jobs as moneylenders. They charged interest on their loans, and Christians at that time did not believe that charging interest was acceptable.

In France, a Jewish man named Rabbi Shlomo Itzhaki was born in 1040 AD. He was called Rashi, which is an acronym of the first letters of his full name. His commentaries on the Tanach and Talmud are world famous and still in use today. He died in 1105.

Islam grew and advanced. When the caliphate that had permitted relative peace for Jews and Christians in Muslim Spain died, Islamic rule split and violence reigned. Muslims captured Jerusalem from the Byzantines (the Eastern Christians) in 1070, sparking a Christian response.

The Crusades were the Christian response to Islamic domination. The first crusade occurred in 1095, and Jews were caught in the middle. Christians targeted Jews along with Muslims; anyone who wasn't a professing Christian was suspect. Muslims fought against Christians and Jews.

Moses ben Maimon, also called Maimonides or Rambam (another famous Jewish scholar identified by acronym) was a medieval Sephardic Jewish philosopher, Torah scholar, astronomer, and physician. He was born in 1137 and was famous for writing the Mishneh Torah (written from 1168-1178), which is about Jewish law (halakha).

During the Middle Ages, some Christians accused Jews of killing Christian children and using their blood to make their Passover matzah; they also accused Jews of reenacting the crucifixion of Yeshua through this barbaric process, so some Christians used this as an excuse to kill Jews. Today, some Muslims accuse Jews of killing Muslim children, which is modern day blood libel.

In the 1300's, a plague swept Europe. It was the Bubonic plague, also called the Black Death. It was highly contagious, and many Europeans died. The plague entered Europe carried by rats on merchant ships. However, at that time, few understood where the plague came from. The Jewish people were blamed. Stories circulated that the Jews had poisoned the water wells of the Christians.

All of this disinformation led to distrust and sometimes violence between Christians and Jews.

Day 1:

1) Bible Memory: Memorize Ephesians 4:32.

2) Hebrew Word: אֲשֶׁר asher – who, which, or that

3) Think about the lesson: Read Exodus 20:10. Does God have different laws for different people?

   _____

   Read Exodus 31:12-18. What do you notice?

   _____
   _____
   _____

Day 2:

1) Bible Memory: Review Ephesians 4:32 and review three other verses.

2) Hebrew Word: אֲשֶׁר asher – who, which, or that

3) Think about the lesson: With your parents, read Deuteronomy 4:25, and then look up Rashi's commentary on it. His commentary may be an apologetic to prove that God's covenant with the Jews remains intact. He may have been countering Augustine's (34-430 AD) supersessionist view that the church replaced the Jewish people, a view that is still widely accepted today. Look up some of Augustine's writings on this topic, and then discuss the ideas of each Biblical scholar with your parents.

Day 3:

1) Bible Memory: Review Ephesians 4:32 and review three other verses.

2) Hebrew Word: אֲשֶׁר asher – who, which, or that

3) Think about the lesson: Read Deuteronomy 12:5. What do you notice? How might this verse have been used to propel Crusaders to Jerusalem?

_____

_____

_____

_____

Day 4:

1) Bible Memory: Review Ephesians 4:32 and review three other verses.

2) Hebrew Word: אֲשֶׁר asher – who, which, or that

3) Think about the lesson: Read Exodus 24:12. What do you notice?

_____

Read Acts 8:30-31. Consider how commentaries help us understand what we read in the Bible.

_____

Day 5:

1) Bible Memory: Review Ephesians 4:32 and review three other verses.

2) Hebrew Word: אֲשֶׁר asher – who, which, or that

3) Think about the lesson: With your parents, look up some of Rashi's writings and discuss what you find together.

Day 6:

1) Bible Memory: Review Ephesians 4:32 and review three other verses.

2) Hebrew Word: אֲשֶׁר asher – who, which, or that

3) Think about the lesson: With your parents, look up some of Rambam's writings and discuss what you find together.

LESSON 71
HISTORY: THE CRUSADES

Lesson Objective: See the reasons that led to the Crusades (re Islam, Christianity, Judaism, and the battle for Jerusalem) and how the Crusades and various pogroms increased tensions between Jews and Christians.

Memory Verse: Psalm 122:6 Pray for the peace of Jerusalem: "May those who love you be secure."

Hebrew Word: שָׁלוֹם shalom – peace, wholeness

Lesson Summary:

Last week's lesson was a pretty broad overview of history spanning many centuries. This week, we're going to focus on the 11th and 12th centuries, specifically the Crusades.

Many Christians – Roman Catholics in the West and Byzantines (who became the Greek Orthodox) in the East – made pilgrimage to the Holy Land, which was largely under Islamic rule for 400 years. However, the Turks from 1030 and on gradually began taking over more land and restricting Christian pilgrimage. The Byzantine Emperor requested assistance from the Pope, Urban II, in defeating the Turks. The Pope called for a Crusade. This was to be the first of several over the following years.

The original goal of the Crusades was to take back Jerusalem from the Muslims. That goal was accomplished.

However, another broader goal was to kill infidels, and this is where the Crusades turned evil. Many Jews and other groups who were not professing Christians were brutally murdered as the Crusaders rampaged.

The Crusades were named thus as a way of referencing the cross of Christ. This term even today connotes someone who is passionate about their life's mission. In the 11th and 12th centuries, it was easy for the populace of Europe to be caught up in the religious fervor that the Crusades promoted. What a blessing to march to Jerusalem! What a victory over non-Christians and the forces of evil!

Typically in a war, only the soldiers venture to battle; however, with the Crusades, people of all ages, gender, and walks of life joined the adventure, resulting in some devastating consequences. The Crusades were largely unsupported, which meant that participants were responsible to provide their own food, clothing, shelter, weapons, etc. Marching from Europe to the Middle East in the 11th century was no easy walk! Few had enough supplies or money to make the trip. Many died. Children who marched suffered sickness, starvation, abuse, capture, slavery, and death. Others pillaged the land and its inhabitants as they passed through. In other words, they killed and stole their way to Jerusalem.

One infamous Crusader, Count Emicho, led groups through the Rhineland, brutally murdering many Jews on the way and stealing all that had belonged to them.

The effects of this still linger today.

Jews who were attacked had few options. Some fought back. Some converted to Christianity. Some killed their families and themselves before the attackers could do it. Some ran to their Christian leaders for assistance.

Not all Christians supported the Crusades, and many denounced the brutal actions of Crusaders like Count Emicho.

There were nine Crusades in total from the 11th to the 13th centuries.

Day 1:

1) Bible Memory: Memorize Psalm 122:6.
2) Hebrew Word: שָׁלוֹם shalom – peace, wholeness
3) Think about the lesson: With your parents, research Count Emicho.

Day 2:

1) Bible Memory: Review Psalm 122:6 and review three other verses.
2) Hebrew Word: שָׁלוֹם shalom – peace, wholeness
3) Think about the lesson: With your parents, research the nine different Crusades. Make a list of the Crusades by dates.

Day 3:

1) Bible Memory: Review Psalm 122:6 and review three other verses.
2) Hebrew Word: שָׁלוֹם shalom – peace, wholeness
3) Think about the lesson: With your parents, research some of the Jewish responses to attacks.

Day 4:

1) Bible Memory: Review Psalm 122:6 and review three other verses.
2) Hebrew Word: שָׁלוֹם shalom – peace, wholeness
3) Think about the lesson: With your parents, discuss the effects of these attacks on the Jewish people.

Day 5:

1) Bible Memory: Review Psalm 122:6 and review three other verses.
2) Hebrew Word: שָׁלוֹם shalom – peace, wholeness
3) Think about the lesson: With your parents, research and take a closer look at the People's and Children's Crusade.

Day 6:

1) Bible Memory: Review Psalm 122:6 and review three other verses.

2) Hebrew Word: שָׁלֹם shalom – peace, wholeness

3) Think about the lesson: With your parents, discuss the different Christian responses to the Jewish plight during the Crusades.

LESSON 72
HISTORY: CAUGHT BETWEEN MUSLIM AND CHRISTIAN DOMINATION

Lesson Objective: Explore how Jews caught between Muslim and Christian domination survived. See the rise of Jewish teachers (Rashi, Rambam, Ramban) to help explain the Law.

Memory Verse: Acts 8:30-31 Then Philip ran up to the chariot and heard the man reading Isaiah the prophet. "Do you understand what you are reading?" Philip asked. "How can I," he said, "unless someone explains it to me?" So he invited Philip to come up and sit with him.

Hebrew Word: ויאמר vayomer – and he said

Lesson Summary:

Jews were dispersed across Europe, the Middle East, and Northern Africa. Distinct differences between groups began to emerge from the 700's on. The Northern European group developed into the Ashkenazi Jews, while the Southern group became the Sephardic Jews.

Each group had contact with Christians and Muslims at different times and to varying degrees. With both groups, Jews were treated like second-class citizens. Christians recognized the need for Jews to exist so that they could validate Jesus as the Messiah when Jesus came the 2nd time (an idea passed on from the early church father and theologian Augustine). Yet, they didn't want Jews to grow too large or powerful for fear that Christianity would appear diminished. Christians relegated Jews to the jobs that they didn't want for themselves. Muslim leaders treated Jews and Christians both as second-class citizens, which they called dhimmis, under the Pact of Omar, which stated that Jews and Christians living in Muslim lands would be safe if they paid their poll tax, exhibited humility towards Muslims, wore clothes that marked their identity, and didn't build new houses of worship.

In Spain, which was under Muslim rule from approximately the 700's to the 1100's, the Sephardic Jews experienced what some call the "Golden Age," mostly because they were permitted to practice their religion unhindered, as long as they abided by the statutes of the Pact of Omar. This changed when Islamic rulers changed.

Although outbreaks of violence against Jews occurred in both the southern and northern areas of Europe (as well as around the rest of the world), the Ashkenazic Jews even today bear a heavy burden of distrust towards ancestors of those goyim (non-Jews) who severely persecuted their ancestors. In Europe, as pogroms (attacks against Jews) flared, as leaders decreed Jewish expulsions (making Jews leave cities or areas), and as the Crusades swept through German cities, Jews gradually moved further east, many settling in Poland.

In the 14th century, Spain changed hands and became a Christian land. In 1380, Jews were forced to convert to Christianity. Sephardic Jews agreed to conversion more readily than Ashkenazic Jews, and they welcomed their Jewish brethren back into the fold after forced conversion more readily that the Ashkenazi. However, by the 15th century, it was clear that forced conversion was not accomplishing the goal intended, which was to Christianize Spain. Jews were still Jews, and thus they were expelled.

Whether their rulers were Christian or Muslim, Jews lived in lands that were not their own. This meant that they were ruled by leaders whose governments were following Christian or Muslim laws. Within Jewish communities, however, rabbis arose who taught their people how to understand and interpret Jewish laws, based on Talmud and Torah. We've already been introduced to Rashi and Rambam.

Rashi, who lived in France, studied in Germany, and returned to France, lived through the time period of the beginning of the Crusades. His entire family (including his daughters) became a family of scholars, rabbis, and revered teachers among the Ashkenazic tradition, and his writings are still widely read today.

On the Sephardic side, Rambam, Moses ben Maimon, or Maimonides, was born in Spain and lived under Muslim rule his entire life. When he was ten years old, he and his family were faced with a choice: convert, leave, or die. They chose to leave. They traveled to Morocco and from there to Israel (which was called Palestine at the time.) Later, he went to Egypt and spent the rest of his life there. He was a doctor, and in fact, he was the doctor to the Sultan Saladin, who took Jerusalem back from the Christians for Islam.

Not to be confused with Rambam is Ramban: Rabbi Moshe ben Nahman, or Nahmanides. He was also a Spaniard and thus in the Sephardic tradition. Like Rashi, Nahmanides wrote a commentary on the Bible. They both sought to interpret the text on a literal and practical level. However, Nahamnides also believed that the Bible contained deep and mystical wisdom. He became a leader in the Kabbalist movement.

Day 1:

1) Bible Memory: Memorize Acts 8:30-31.

2) Hebrew Word: וַיֹּאמֶר vayomer – and he said

3) Think about the lesson: With your parents, research Ashkenazi and Sephardi. What similarities do you see? What differences do you see?

_____

_____

_____

Day 2:

1) Bible Memory: Review Acts 8:30-31 and review three other verses.

2) Hebrew Word: וַיֹּאמֶר vayomer – and he said

3) Think about the lesson: With your parents, research the relations between Christians and Jews in the 11th through 15th centuries. What do you notice?

_____

_____

_____

Day 3:

1) Bible Memory: Review Acts 8:30-31 and review three other verses.

2) Hebrew Word: וַיֹּאמֶר vayomer – and he said

3) Think about the lesson: With your parents, research the relations between Muslims and Jews in the 11th through 15th centuries. What do you notice?

Day 4:

1) Bible Memory: Review Acts 8:30-31 and review three other verses.

2) Hebrew Word: וַיֹּאמֶר vayomer – and he said

3) Think about the lesson: With your parents, read and discuss what you can find about Rashi. Read some of his writings. What do you notice?

_____
_____
_____

Day 5:

1) Bible Memory: Review Acts 8:30-31 and review three other verses.

2) Hebrew Word: וַיֹּאמֶר vayomer – and he said

3) Think about the lesson: With your parents, read and discuss what you can find about Rambam. Read some of his writings. What do you notice?

_____
_____
_____

Day 6:

1) Bible Memory: Review Acts 8:30-31 and review three other verses.

2) Hebrew Word: וַיֹּאמֶר vayomer – and he said

3) Think about the lesson: With your parents, read and discuss what you can find about Ramban. Read some of his writings. What do you notice?

_____
_____
_____

LESSON 73
HISTORY: CHRISTIAN REFORMATION (16TH CENTURY)

Lesson Objective: Understand the Christian Reformation and how it changed the religious landscape. Investigate Martin Luther's view of the Jewish people.

Memory Verse: Hebrews 4:12 For the Word of God is living and active. Sharper than any double edged sword, it penetrates even to the dividing of soul and spirit, joints and marrow; it judges the thoughts and attitudes of the heart.

Hebrew Word: חרב־פיפיות   cherev pipiyot – double-edged sword

Lesson Summary:

As the centuries progressed, Christianity, which was Roman Catholic across Western Europe, grew larger. The leaders of the Church functioned as spiritual leaders for the people, many of whom could not read and did not own Bibles of their own. They did not know what God's Word actually said; they just trusted the instructions of their priests, bishops, and the Pope.

The Church began selling indulgences, and the money raised from this was used to build enormous, extravagant cathedrals all across Europe. Indulgences were grants from the Pope that excused parishioners (the church-going people) from the consequences of their sins, or at least reduced the consequences. Basically, when someone sinned, he or she could pay money to the Church and be granted forgiveness.

A young church leader named Martin Luther found this teaching and the abuses of the sale of indulgences repugnant. How could the church forgive sin? The Pope was rich, so why didn't he use his own money to build the cathedrals instead of taking money from the poor? Martin Luther believed that salvation was by grace through faith; he did not believe that paying money could buy forgiveness. He also believed that the central authority was the Word of God, not the Pope. He wrote down 95 Theses, most of them decrying the sale of indulgences, and nailed the document to the church doors in his hometown of Wittenburg, Germany, on October 31, 1517. This act sparked the Protestant Reformation.

With the invention of the printing press by Johannes Gutenburg around 1450, information could be shared widely and rapidly. Bibles were printed in the commonly spoken languages of the European countries, and people could read God's Word for themselves. Culturally, this lessened the role of the Pope, bishops, and priests as spiritual authorities.

With regards to the Jewish people, Martin Luther's attitude shifted from admiration and respect to one of hatred. His earlier writings express hope for the salvation of the Jewish people, and indeed, the Jewish people at that time respected his efforts to right the wrongs of the Catholic teachings. Yet, after seeing that the Jewish people were not interested in his teachings, Luther's attitude began to change. His later writings reflect intense anti-Semitism. His suggestions, recorded in writing and widely distributed, served as fuel for future attacks on the Jewish people.

Day 1:

1) Bible Memory: Memorize Hebrews 4:12.

2) Hebrew Word: חרב־פיפיות cherev pipiyot – double-edged sword

3) Think about the lesson: Discuss with your parents: how is the Word of God a double-edged sword? What does that mean? How could this verse apply to our lesson for this week?

_____
_____
_____

Day 2:

1) Bible Memory: Review Hebrews 4:12 and review three other verses.

2) Hebrew Word: חרב־פיפיות cherev pipiyot – double-edged sword

3) Think about the lesson: Read Ephesian 2:8-9 and discuss it with your parents. What do you notice?

_____
_____
_____

Day 3:

1) Bible Memory: Review Hebrews 4:12 and review three other verses.

2) Hebrew Word: חרב־פיפיות cherev pipiyot – double-edged sword

3) Think about the lesson: John Calvin was another Protestant Reformation era theologian whose writings and viewpoints are still valued by many today. With your parents, research Calvinism. What are the five points?

_____
_____
_____
_____

Day 4:

1) Bible Memory: Review Hebrews 4:12 and review three other verses.

2) Hebrew Word: חרב־פיפיות cherev pipiyot – double-edged sword

3) Think about the lesson: With your parents, discuss Calvinism with your parents. What Bible verses support it? What problems might you see with it? Discussion notes:

_____
_____
_____
_____

Day 5:

1) Bible Memory: Review Hebrews 4:12 and review three other verses.
2) Hebrew Word: חרב־פיפיות cherev pipiyot – double-edged sword
3) Think about the lesson: Look up and read Martin Luther's 95 Theses. What do you notice?

_____
_____
_____

Day 6:

1) Bible Memory: Review Hebrews 4:12 and review three other verses.
2) Hebrew Word: חרב־פיפיות cherev pipiyot – double-edged sword
3) Think about the lesson: Discuss with your parents: what is salvation?

_____
_____
_____
_____

LESSON 74
HISTORY: JUDAISM DEVELOPS (17TH-19TH CENTURIES)

Lesson Objective: See the development of Hasidic Judaism, Reform Judaism, and Conservative Judaism.

Memory Verse: Proverbs 9:10 The fear of the LORD is the beginning of wisdom, and knowledge of the Holy One is understanding.

Hebrew Word: זָכַר zachar – 1) remember, 2) male (two meanings)

Lesson Summary:

There are basically three major categories of Judaism today (Orthodox, Conservative, and Reform) that stem from the developments that began in 1700. In 1700, the Baal Shem Tov was born, and when he grew up, he started the Chasidic movement. The Chasidic movement is part of Orthodox Judaism. One focus of the Baal Shem Tov was connecting with Adonai through nature and through ecstatic experiences. At first, the Chasidic deemphasized Torah study, but as the years passed, the movement refocused and combined Torah study, Talmudic study, and ecstatic experiences. Ultra-Orthodox groups like this one are easily recognized by their special dress. The men often wear black pants and jackets with white shirts, they grow the hair above their ears long and let it hang in braids or curls, and different ultra-Orthodox groups wear hats that mark which group they belong to. Some hats are black, and others are lined with fur. Women wear long skirts, long sleeve shirts, and hair coverings. They do not sit together in the congregation. Men and women sit on opposite sides of the center aisle.

In the 1700's, the Enlightenment swept Europe, and people began focusing less on tradition and more on reason. The first Reform congregation opened in 1810 in Seesen, Germany, in direct response to the Enlightenment. Many Reform Jews at this time engaged with the world around them with as little distinction from the rest of the culture as possible, even to the point of forming choirs in their congregations just like the Christian churches and not keeping kosher. Men and women could sit together in services, and the Torah was seen as fluid, changing with the times, and open to interpretation that suited the current culture.

Conservative Judaism came later, in 1885. It was a middle-road response to the strictness of the Orthodox and the laxity of the Reform movements. Conservative Judaism does not mean that the people attending the congregations were conservative in a political sense; today Conservative Judaism's adherents are usually politically liberal. Conservative Judaism is more conservative with regards to religious practice and more liberal in thinking. Men and women sit together in services as a family. Men wore (and still wear) kippot and prayer shawls. Bar Mitzvah was a long-standing practice by this time, but the first Bat Mitzvah was Judith Kaplan, the daughter of American Rabbi Mordecai Kaplan, in 1922.

None of these developments in Judaism accept Yeshua as the Messiah. Some Jews look forward to a coming Messiah; others have scrapped the notion as an outdated concept and deny the need for a Messiah. For them, Judaism is a familial connection, a culture, a way of life. As a congregation of both Messianic Jews and

Messianic non-Jews, we know that no matter what the rabbis have ruled, Yeshua is the Messiah, and we can believe in Him and retain and appreciate our Jewishness, if we are Jewish, and/or gain a deeper and richer understanding of His!

Day 1:

1) Bible Memory: Memorize Proverbs 9:10.

2) Hebrew Word: זכר zachar – 1) remember, 2) male

3) Think about the lesson: Discuss with your parents: much of the development of denominations, whether in Judaism or in Christianity, have more to do with accommodating the worshipper's preferences to fit in with the world and/or comfort with tradition rather than what Adonai requires of us. Micah 6:8 reminds us what Adonai's focus is; may our focus be in line with His! Discussion notes:

_____
_____
_____

Day 2:

1) Bible Memory: Review Proverbs 9:10 and review three other verses.

2) Hebrew Word: זכר zachar – 1) remember, 2) male

3) Think about the lesson: Although there is nothing wrong with traditions that point to Yeshua, Yeshua warned us to keep our focus on Him. He is the only way to salvation. He is the only way for us to be in communion with our Creator God. He wants to be with us. He loves us so much that He sent His Son, Yeshua, to be our sin sacrifice. Through Him, we can have eternal life with Adonai. Pray about this.

Day 3:

1) Bible Memory: Review Proverbs 9:10 and review three other verses.

2) Hebrew Word: זכר zachar – 1) remember, 2) male

3) Think about the lesson: Research Baal Shem Tov and discuss with your parents how the Chasidim and other Orthodox Jewish groups maintain a visibly set apart status as Jews, both then and now. What do you notice?

_____
_____
_____

Day 4:

1) Bible Memory: Review Proverbs 9:10 and review three other verses.

2) Hebrew Word: זכר zachar – 1) remember, 2) male

3) Think about the lesson: Research the Enlightenment, and discuss with your parents how it led to the

development of Reform Judaism. What controversial issues might you find with Reform Judaism today?

_____

_____

_____

Day 5:

1) Bible Memory: Review Proverbs 9:10 and review three other verses.

2) Hebrew Word: זכר zachar – 1) remember, 2) male

3) Think about the lesson: Research Conservative Judaism, and discuss with your parents how this became a middle road between what many see as the two extremes of Orthodox and Reform Judaism. Also, research the first Bat Mitzvah. Who was she and what year was her Bat Mitzvah?

_____

_____

_____

Day 6:

1) Bible Memory: Review Proverbs 9:10 and review three other verses.

2) Hebrew Word: זכר zachar – 1) remember, 2) male

3) Think about the lesson: None of the major divisions of Judaism accept Yeshua as the Messiah. As Messianic Jews, we recognize who He is. We know He is our Savior. Regarding outside appearance and level of adherence to Torah commandments, we have all three of these groups represented within our Messianic Jewish congregation to a certain degree, as well as having representatives from non-Jewish Messianic groups. This makes the Body of Messiah unique, inclusive, and multi-cultural. Our primary focus is and should be on Yeshua. With various denominations in both Christianity and Judaism, and even among different Messianic congregations, we can observe that our different practices often reflect our own preferences and what makes us comfortable; many of our differences have nothing to do with what Yeshua commanded. Read what Yeshua said about our traditions in Mark 7:1-8. Then read Micah 6:8. Where does Adonai want our focus? On how we dress? On how well we stand apart from or blend in with our current culture? If not these, then what?

_____

_____

_____

LESSON 75
HISTORY: EXPELLED

Lesson Objective: Trace the expulsion and admittance of the Jews from and to different countries over the centuries.

Memory Verse: Psalm 56:3 When I am afraid, I will trust in you.

Hebrew Word: זָכַר zachar – 1) remember, 2) male

Lesson Summary:

There have been many excuses given over the millennia for hating the Jewish people. Some believe it is rightful judgment because Jews didn't follow God's rules, although non-Jews are just as guilty of not following God's rules. It is true that Adonai disciplines all of us for disobedience, but that is no reason to treat each other poorly. Others believe that Jews should be hated for not recognizing Yeshua as the Messiah. However, we know that Adonai is working even that together for our good according to Romans 11. Many have hated Jews for lending money at interest, a necessary job but one forbidden by the Catholic Church in past centuries. Just being different seems to have been a good excuse for some to hate. The Jews' refusal to convert to other religions led to many of the expulsions. This is admirable that so many Jewish people have held so firmly to Adonai for all these centuries! Additionally, Jews have been blamed and expelled for false charges such as causing illness, kidnappings for religious rituals, acts of terrorism, stealing, and the list goes on. These accusations are largely due to misinformation (telling and believing lies about Jews) and ignorance.

When we view the world through a Biblical lens, we see through the excuses and view the sheer hatred of Satan towards the Jewish people. He knew that from the Jewish people the Savior would arise, and whether or not the majority of our Jewish brothers or sisters accept Yeshua, they/we are beloved in His eyes. They/we are His brothers and sisters. Let Genesis 12:3 be a reminder of this!

Expulsion List:

Country and/or City	Date	Reason
Northern Israel and Samaria	722 BC	The Assyrians conquered Northern Israel and Samaria and dispersed the Jewish people
Jerusalem	586 BC	The Babylonians conquered Jerusalem and sent many of Jews, especially Jewish youth, to

		Babylon
Persia	475 BC	In Persia, Haman plots to kill and expel Jews
Rome	139 BC	Jews were proselytizing (telling everyone about Adonai and the coming Messiah and seeking converts to Judaism)
Jerusalem	70 AD	Rome squashes Jewish rebellion
Judea	135 AD	After the Battle of Bar Kokhba, Rome expels all Jews from Jerusalem and Judea and wiped the names off the maps (gave them Roman names – Aeolia Capitolina for Jerusalem and Syria Palestina for Judea)
Alexandria (in Egypt)	415 AD	"Ethnic cleansing"
Minorca (Spain)	418 AD	Jews had to convert or leave
Visigoth (France at that time)	612 AD	Jews had to convert or leave, and if they left, they had to leave behind all their possessions
Galilee	629 AD	The Byzantines put down another Jewish revolt, and the Jews were either killed or expelled
Medina and Khaybar in the Middle East	7th century AD	Muhammed expelled and/or killed members of Jewish tribes in these areas
Mainz (Germany)	1012 AD	Massacres due to Anti-Semitism
Europe, Middle East, and Jerusalem	1095-13th centuries AD	The Crusades swept across Europe and into Jerusalem, and Crusaders killed, robbed, or "converted " Jews along the way

Bavaria	1276 AD	Money lending and blood libel
France	12th-14th centuries AD	Repeated expulsions where Jews were forced to leave. They were required to leave behind all their possessions. Their possessions were used to enrich the rulers. Ramon Llul (1232-1315) is considered the first to officially create an expulsionist policy for Jews who would not convert to Christianity.
Naples (Italy)	1288 AD	Convert or leave
England	1290 AD	Anti-Semitism
Hungary	1360 AD	Jews were blamed for the Black Death
Bern, Switzerland	1392 AD	Christians were permitted to engage in money lending, so the Jewish moneylenders were no longer needed
Austria	1421 AD	Convert, leave, or be burned alive
Passau, Germany	1478 AD	Convert or leave; the synagogue was destroyed and a church built in its place
Ravenna, Italy	1491 AD	Synagogues destroyed
Spain, Sicily, Portugal, Italy	1492 AD	The Alhambra decree, issued by Ferdinand II and Isabella I, was the General Edict on the Expulsion of the Jews
Nuremburg	1499 AD	Jewish houses were destroyed to make room for the market, and the synagogue was destroyed for the church to be built in its place

Bavaria	1551 AD	Anti-Semitism
Milan	1597 AD	Power struggles and Jews were in the way
Frankfurt	1614 AD	As part of the Fettmilch Uprising
Vienna	1669-1670 AD	Mysterious deaths and fires were blamed on the Jews
Haiti	1683 AD	Code Noir decree issued by Louis XIV
Russia	1791 AD	Catherine the Great establishes the Pale of Settlement, deporting Jews to the west to live
Tennessee, Mississippi, and Kentucky	1862 AD	Jews were expelled here in the US by Ulysses S. Grant! (General Order No. 11) He accused Jews of running a black market Southern cotton industry. (Remember that this is during the Civil War; these are Southern states, and Grant was on the Northern side.)
Russia	1880-1910's AD	Pogroms in Russia caused many Jewish people to emigrate to the United States
Everywhere	1933-1948 AD	Anti-Semitism birthed the Holocaust. Jews were robbed, looted, pushed out of schools and jobs, expelled, moved into ghettos, sent to concentration camps, killed, synagogues were burned, and those who tried to escape by boat were often met with refusal of the new countries to take them in. Many on these boats died, too. The State of Israel was reestablished as the Jewish

		homeland in 1948, and the surrounding Arab nations responded immediately with war.

Day 1:

1) Bible Memory: Memorize Psalm 56:3.

2) Hebrew Word: זָכַר zachar – 1) remember, 2) male

3) Think about the lesson: With your parents, review the chart above and discuss.

Day 2:

1) Bible Memory: Review Psalm 56:3 and review three other verses.

2) Hebrew Word: זָכַר zachar – 1) remember, 2) male

3) Think about the lesson: Salvation for the world came through the Jewish people, for Yeshua was born a Jew. For this reason, Satan will try to get rid of the Jewish people at all times and in all places. When we stand up as Jews and/or for Jews, we are standing on Adonai's side and we can then have the opportunity to share the good news about Yeshua our Messiah with our brothers and sisters. Discuss with your parents.

Day 3:

1) Bible Memory: Review Psalm 56:3 and review three other verses.

2) Hebrew Word: זָכַר zachar – 1) remember, 2) male

3) Think about the lesson: Consider Genesis 12:3, pray, and record your thoughts:

_____

_____

_____

Day 4:

1) Bible Memory: Review Psalm 56:3 and review three other verses.

2) Hebrew Word: זָכַר zachar – 1) remember, 2) male

3) Think about the lesson: Read Revelation 12:17. What do you notice?

_____

_____

_____

Day 5:

1) Bible Memory: Review Psalm 56:3 and review three other verses.

2) Hebrew Word: זָכַר zachar – 1) remember, 2) male

3) Think about the lesson: Read John 15:18-25. What do you notice?

_____

_____

_____

_____

Day 6:

1) Bible Memory: Review Psalm 56:3 and review three other verses.

2) Hebrew Word: זָכַר zachar – 1) remember, 2) male

3) Think about the lesson: As a family, pray for the Jewish people worldwide, for safety and for salvation.

LESSON 76
HISTORY: ZIONISM AND THE REBIRTH OF ISRAEL

Lesson Objective: Be able to define Zionism, see the proponents and opponents of this move, know the reviver of the Hebrew language, and see the events that led up to the reestablishment of the state of Israel.

Memory Verse: Psalm 121:4 He who watches over Israel will neither slumber nor sleep.

Hebrew Word: יוֹסֵף – Yosef. The name Joseph means "He will add"

Lesson Summary:

Zionism: Started in 1897 by Theodore Herzl and continued later by Chaim Wiezmann, Zionism was a movement focused on the re-establishment of the Jewish nation in the land of Israel.

Zionists saw this move as a necessary response to increasing persecution, expulsions, and pressures to change their religion and culture.

1) They needed a total and drastic solution. Small changes within their local areas were not going to solve the problem.
2) The Jews would need to save themselves; no one else was going to do it.
3) Jews needed their own land where they would be the majority.
4) Only in their own land could they revive their own culture and language.

Zionists were secular, and their views conflicted with those of the religious Jews, who were waiting for the Messiah to come and save them and bring them into the Promised Land.

Today, Zionists are still in conflict with other groups, Jewish and non-Jewish, religious and secular, and Zionists themselves may be religious or secular now.

As Jews re-entered the land of Israel, Hebrew once again became a spoken language. Until that point, Hebrew was similar to Latin; it was spoken when reading sacred texts or prayers, but it was not spoken for day to day communication, except by those few Jews who still lived in the land of Israel, and there weren't many of them. Eliezer Ben Yehuda changed that, but it didn't happen overnight. It took a few decades. There were differences between Biblical Hebrew and Rabbinic Hebrew, and there were new words that were needed for items that did not exist and could not be described using Biblical Hebrew's limited vocabulary. When we make up new words, we often use words from a language we know, so words were borrowed from other languages that the Jewish people at the time spoke. Eliezer Ben Yehuda began the revival of Hebrew at home with his own family in 1881.

The Balfour Declaration, issued November 2, 1917 (during World War I), by Arthur Balfour of Great Britain, stated that Great Britain publically pledged to establish a national homeland for the Jewish people in Israel (which was called Palestine at the time, thanks to the Romans renaming it in 135 AD).

Jews trickled into Israel during these times, but it was dangerous to live there and scary to move from what they knew to what was unsure and undeveloped. Those who went to Israel often lived together in kibbutzim, which are collective communities where people live together and work together.

After World War II and the horrors of the Holocaust, many more Jewish people came to Israel, and on May 14, 1948, Israel announced to the world that they were a nation. The United States quickly supported this, and the Arab nations around them attacked just as quickly. However, The God who guards Israel neither slumbers nor sleeps, and Israel defeated her enemies!

Day 1:

1) Bible Memory: Memorize Psalm 121:4.

2) Hebrew Word: יוֹסֵף – Yosef. The name Joseph means "He will add"

3) Think about the lesson: Read Deuteronomy 1:8. What do you notice?

_____

_____

Day 2:

1) Bible Memory: Review Psalm 121:4 and review three other verses.

2) Hebrew Word: יוֹסֵף – Yosef. The name Joseph means "He will add"

3) Think about the lesson: Read Jeremiah 31. What do you notice?

_____

_____

_____

Day 3:

1) Bible Memory: Review Psalm 121:4 and review three other verses.

2) Hebrew Word: יוֹסֵף – Yosef. The name Joseph means "He will add"

3) Think about the lesson: Read Deuteronomy 30:1-5. What do you notice?

_____

_____

_____

Day 4:

1) Bible Memory: Review Psalm 121:4 and review three other verses.

2) Hebrew Word: יוֹסֵף – Yosef. The name Joseph means "He will add"

3) Think about the lesson: Read Isaiah 11:11-12. What do you notice?

_____

Day 5:

1) Bible Memory: Review Psalm 121:4 and review three other verses.

2) Hebrew Word: יוֹסֵף – Yosef. The name Joseph means "He will add"

3) Think about the lesson: The salvation that Yeshua offers is not just salvation from enemies here on earth; it is salvation from hell after death. When He saves us, He saves us here and now and forever. Yeshua is the Messiah that the ancient prophets announced and waited to see. We have seen Him come and go up to the Father. We know that He sacrificed Himself on our behalf. He took the punishment for our sins so that we could be saved. Read and discuss Revelation 21 with your parents. Discussion notes:

_____

_____

_____

_____

Day 6:

1) Bible Memory: Review Psalm 121:4 and review three other verses.

2) Hebrew Word: יוֹסֵף – Yosef. The name Joseph means "He will add"

3) Think about the lesson: Sometimes, Adonai wants us to wait on Him for deliverance; other times, He expects us to use the resources He has given us to do what is best for us, our families, and His people. With your family, discuss the views of the proponents and opponents of Zionism. Discussion notes:

_____

_____

_____

_____

LESSON 77
HISTORY: HITLER AND THE HOLOCAUST 1933-1945

Lesson Objective: Understand that this massive attack of the enemy is forever engrained in the hearts and minds of the Jewish people; Christians cannot hope to witness to Jews without addressing and praying for the healing of this hurt.

Memory Passage: Matthew 4:1-11 Then Yeshua was led by the Spirit into the desert to be tempted by the devil. After fasting forty days and forty nights, he was hungry. The tempter came to him and said, "If you are the Son of God, tell these stones to become bread." Yeshua answered, "It is written: Man does not live on bread alone, but on every word that comes from the mouth of God." Then the devil took him to the holy city and had him stand on the highest point of the temple. "If you are the Son of God," he said, "throw yourself down. For it is written: 'He will command his angels concerning you, and they will lift you up in their hands, so that you will not strike your foot against a stone.'" Yeshua answered him, "It is also written: do not put the Lord your God to the test." Again, the devil took him to a very high mountain and showed him all the kingdoms of the world and their splendor. "All this I will give you," he said, "if you will bow down and worship me." Yeshua said to him, "Away from me, Satan! For it is written: Worship the Lord your God and serve him only." Then the devil left him and angels came and attended him.

Hebrew Word: עֶשֶׂר eser - ten

Lesson Summary:

The anti-Semitism (hatred of Jews) we have seen so far in our lessons throughout Jewish History came to a peak from 1933-1945 and culminated in the worst attack on Jewish people ever in recorded history.

Earlier, Germany had started World War I (1914-1918), and as a result, after losing the war, was required to pay back enormous amounts of money to the countries it had attacked. Germany didn't have the money or resources to pay anything. This, along with other untenable requirements, led to Germany starting World War II.

As so many before her had also done, Germany found ways to place blame on the Jewish people for the plight of the Germans.

Thus began the Holocaust. Holocaust literally means a sacrifice by fire; it also means a huge loss of life. Under the leadership of Adolf Hitler, over 6 million Jews were murdered during the Holocaust (World War II).

Of note, one of the leading thrusts of the mindset behind the Holocaust was the concept of superior and inferior races, an idea born of evolutionist thinking. After studying the events of World War II and the Holocaust, consider a family discussion over the consequences of this mindset, or world view.

The following questions about the Holocaust can be answered from Gail Herman's book *What Was the Holocaust?* which is required reading for this lesson.

245

This lesson may be accompanied by reading other books about the Holocaust, such as Corrie ten Boom's *The Hiding Place*, which is a beautiful work that shows the love and care of a Christian family and the sacrifices they made to save Jewish people during the Holocaust. Additional books may be chosen at the discretion of parents for older readers, and this lesson may be extended several weeks if necessary.

Day 1:

1) Bible Memory: Memorize Matthew 4:1-2.

2) Hebrew Word: עֶשֶׂר eser - ten

3) Think about the lesson: Read and then answer the following questions over the Introduction and chapters 1-3 of *What Was the Holocaust?* by Gail Herman.

1) Define Holocaust _____

2) Define Anti-Semitism _____

3) Germany started World War I (1914-1918), and at the end was required to:

    1) _____

    2) _____

    3) _____

    4) _____

4) In 1919, Germany attempted to set up a democracy. It had a group of elected representatives, called the _____. The president was elected, and then the president chose a chancellor.

5) Germany didn't have the money it needed to pay back the billions of dollars (German marks) to the other countries, so the government tried to fix the problem by _____. This led to out of control inflation.

6) Guess who got blamed for Germany's problems? _____

7) When was Hitler born? _____

8) What kind of child was Adolf Hitler? _____

9) What happened to his parents? _____

10) How did Adolf Hitler get his ideas about the Jewish people?

_____

_____

11) What was Adolf Hitler known for?

_____

12) How did Hitler do serving in the military in World War I?

_____

13) What was the group Hitler joined? _____

14) Define "race."

_____

_____

15) Hitler was a charismatic leader and speaker. What does that mean?

_____

246

16) How did the Nazi party get its name?

17) What did Adolf Hitler do that got him locked up in prison?

18) What did he do while he was in prison?

19) What happened when Hitler ran for president?

20) How did the people respond the night Hitler was sworn in as Chancellor?

21) How many Jews were in Germany at the time? How many left after Hitler was sworn in? Why do you think more didn't leave?

Day 2:

1) Bible Memory: Review Matthew 4:1-2 and memorize Matthew 4:3-4.

2) Hebrew Word: עֶשֶׂר eser - ten

3) Think about the lesson: Read and then answer the following questions over chapters 4-5 of *What Was the Holocaust?* by Gail Herman.

1) What happened to the Reichstag building?

2) Hitler used this (the answer to #1) as an excuse to

3) What is a concentration camp?

4) What was the name of the first concentration camp? _____

5) How did Adolf Hitler gain full power? (p30)

    a. _____

    b. _____

6) List some of the ways that Hitler treated the Jewish people:

7) What was the Hitler Youth?

_____

_____

8) Think: How do you think the German children's views of Jewish people changed after the German children participated in the Hitler Youth? _____

9) Did Hitler abide by the World War I treaty? _____

10) When Hitler invaded Austria, how did the Austrians respond?

     a. _____

     b. _____

11) What was Kristallnacht?

_____

_____

12) Who did Hitler charge to pay for the damages done on Kristallnacht?

_____

13) Why didn't all the Jews leave?

     a. _____

     b. _____

14) What happened to the Jewish passengers on the *St. Louis?*

_____

15) Who were the Axis powers?

_____

_____

16) Who were the Allies?

_____

Day 3:

1) Bible Memory: Review Matthew 4:1-4 and memorize Matthew 4:5-6.

2) Hebrew Word: עֶשֶׂר eser - ten

3) Think about the lesson: Read and then answer the following questions over chapters 6-7 of *What Was the Holocaust?* by Gail Herman.

1) What was a ghetto?

_____

_____

2) What were some of the problems Jews suffered living in the ghettos?

_____

_____

3) What did Chaim receive as a gift from his parents at his bar mitzvah?

_____

4) What were the two reasons that the Nazis shaved prisoners' heads in the concentration camps?

a. _____

b. _____

5) The living conditions in the concentration camps were horrible. If working too slowly, prisoners could be _____. Bunk beds were shared with _____ or _____ people. Hundreds of people shared the same bathroom with only a _____ faucets. Toilets were long slabs with _____ cut out for seats. Prisoners had no clean _____ or soap or clean clothes. Prisoners woke at _____AM and stood outside in the cold for roll call, even the ones who had _____ during the night had to be carried out for roll call. They worked for _____ hours. What did they eat for breakfast and dinner?

_____

_____

6) How did some prisoners keep their sense of dignity and humanity in these conditions?

_____

_____

Day 4:

1) Bible Memory: Review Matthew 4:1-6 and memorize Matthew 4:7-8.

2) Hebrew Word: עֶשֶׂר eser - ten

3) Think about the lesson: Read and then answer the following questions over chapters 8-9 of *What Was the Holocaust?* by Gail Herman.

1) What was Hitler's "Final Solution?"

_____

_____

2) What is Zyklon B?

_____

_____

3) Poland became the land of _____ _____.

4) How were Jewish people rounded up and sent to the death camps?

_____

_____

5) What was the "trick?"

_____

_____

6) Many Jews fought back. They joined _____ groups that destroyed Nazi rail lines and blew up power stations.

7) Who was Oskar Schindler?

_____

_____

8) What did the Jews do in the Warsaw uprising?

    _____

    _____

9) How did the Nazis respond?

    _____

    _____

Day 5:

1) Bible Memory: Review Matthew 4:1-8 and memorize Matthew 4:9-11.

2) Hebrew Word: עֶשֶׂר eser - ten

3) Think about the lesson: Read and then answer the following questions over chapters 10-11 of *What Was the Holocaust?* by Gail Herman.

1) How did the Nazis try to hide their crimes from the world?

    _____

    _____

2) How did Adolf Hitler die? _____

3) When did Germany surrender? What was the month, day, and year? _____

4) Who was Adolf Eichmann?

    _____

5) After the war, when Jews tried to return home, they found that their homes had been destroyed, or taken over by others, and there was still violence against them. Those who didn't have anywhere to go were called _____ _____.

6) Where did they go? _____

7) Although it's painful to talk about, why is it important that people know about the Holocaust?

    _____

8) Martin Niemoller, a member of the Nazi party who spoke up against Hitler and ended up in a concentration camp himself along with Jews, Communists, Catholics, and more, said, "Then they came for me – And there was no one left to speak out for me." In your own words, think about what this means for us today when we see evil in the world. How should we respond?

    _____

    _____

    _____

Day 6:

1) Bible Memory: Review Matthew 4:1-11.

2) Hebrew Word: עֶשֶׂר eser - ten

3) Think about the lesson: Discuss what you have learned with your parents. Choose some other books to read over the next few weeks about the Holocaust and the people who experienced it. If possible, take a trip to a Holocaust museum and/or speak with survivors or their children or grandchildren about their experiences.

LESSON 78
HISTORY: WARS – 1967 AND 1973

Lesson Objective: Obedience leads to victory while disobedience can lead to defeat.

Memory Verse: Proverbs 3:5-6 Trust in the LORD with all your heart, and do not lean on your own understanding. In all your ways, acknowledge Him, and He will make your paths straight.

Hebrew: Cantillation – learntrope.com Set Aleph

Lesson Summary:

In 1967, Egypt closed the Strait of Tiran to Israel and to anyone bringing supplies to Israel. This was illegal. Egypt, based on false information from the Soviet Union, demanded that the UN troops leave the Sinai Peninsula and complained to the UN that Israel was amassing troops on the border. This was not true, but Israel soon realized that its surrounding neighbor nations were plotting against them, and Israel needed the straight open. Nasser of Egypt stated, "We knew that closing the Gulf of Aqaba meant war with Israel . . . if war comes, it will be total, and the objective will be Israel's destruction." On May 31, 1967, Iraqi President Abdul Rahmen Aref stated of Israel that Israel was a mistake that needed to be addressed. He vowed to "wipe Israel off the map."

On Monday, June 5, 1967, Israel preempted an attack. It attacked Egyptian airfields, demolishing them within hours. Israel also managed to turn their own planes around, refueling them and sending them out again, three times as fast as was normal, making it look like they had three times the air power they actually had. By Wednesday, June 7, Israel had claimed victory over the entire Sinai Peninsula, Jericho, Nablus, and Jerusalem. Moshe Dayan, who was part of the battle that reclaimed the Western Wall and Temple Mount, said, "We have unified Jerusalem, the divided capital of Israel. We have returned to the holiest of our holy places, never to depart from it again." It is fascinating to think that 1967 is a year of Jubilee – when land returns to its owners. A cease-fire was accepted on Friday, June 9, 1967.

The Six Day War and Yom Kippur War were both victories in the end, but the Yom Kippur War was a much tougher victory. The Yom Kippur War was launched against Israel by its enemies on the holiest day of the year – Yom Kippur – and there was a failure of intelligence that might have prepped Israel for what was to come. Initially, Israel lost many people, but after regrouping and counterattacking, they regained the Sinai Peninsula to the south and the Golan Heights to the north.

Day 1:

1) Bible Memory: Memorize Proverbs 3:5-6.
2) Hebrew: Cantillation – learntrope.com Set Aleph
3) Think about the lesson: With your parents, research the Six Day War. Record your notes:

_____

_____

_____

252

Day 2:

1) Bible Memory: Review Proverbs 3:5-6 and review three other verses.
2) Hebrew: Cantillation – learntrope.com Set Aleph
3) Think about the lesson: With your parents, research the Yom Kippur War. Record your notes:

_____

_____

_____

Day 3:

1) Bible Memory: Review Proverbs 3:5-6 and review three other verses.
2) Hebrew: Cantillation – learntrope.com Set Aleph
3) Think about the lesson: With your parents, research Moshe Dayan. Record your notes:

_____

_____

_____

Day 4:

1) Bible Memory: Review Proverbs 3:5-6 and review three other verses.
2) Hebrew: Cantillation – learntrope.com Set Aleph
3) Think about the lesson: With your parents, research Golda Meir. Record your notes:

_____

_____

_____

Day 5:

1) Bible Memory: Review Proverbs 3:5-6 and review three other verses.
2) Hebrew: Cantillation – learntrope.com Set Aleph
3) Think about the lesson: Read Joshua 6:20 (Jericho), Joshua 7:4, 10-12; 8:1-2 (Ai), and Judges 4:1-9 (Deborah and Barak). What do you notice?

_____

_____

Day 6:

1) Bible Memory: Review Proverbs 3:5-6 and review three other verses.
2) Hebrew: Cantillation – learntrope.com Set Aleph
3) Think about the lesson: Stay in fellowship with Yeshua. Walk in His ways. An easy victory can make us prideful and lax in our attentiveness to potential attack. Always keep on guard for potential spiritual attack, and walk in righteousness. Pray without ceasing so that you are always ready with a defense. Many soldiers speak of miraculous visions during these wars. Some met Yeshua as Savior

during these times. Yeshua gave himself, the right arm of God, on our behalf, that we might be saved. Turn to Him. Ask Him to be your Savior. He will save you from your sins.

LESSON 79
HISTORY: ISRAEL AND HER MUSLIM NEIGHBORS TODAY

Lesson Objective: Know that the Islamic goal for Israel is to "drive her into the sea."

Memory Verse: Isaiah 5:20 Woe to those who call evil good and good evil, who put lightness for dark and dark for lightness, who put bitter for sweet and sweet for bitter.

Hebrew: Cantillation – learntrope.com Set Bet

Lesson Summary:

Some would say it all started with the descendants of Ishmael versus the descendants of Isaac.

We've already studied the establishment of the Muslim faith, but we'll do a quick review before we look at Israel and Islam today. Islam was founded by Mohammed in the early 600's in Mecca. Although Mohammed was illiterate, he said that the Angel Gabriel gave him the words of the Koran to write down while he was holed up in a cave. Mohammed tried to preach to the Jews in his community, but they were not interested. He preached monotheism, or a belief in one God, named Allah, and he borrowed heavily from what he knew about the scriptures. Like Judaism, Islam rejects eating pork. Other kosher laws that are in the Bible are not included in Islam. Praying and fasting are part of both faiths. Muslims have five times of prayer established throughout the day; traditional Jews keep three. Judaism's primary day of fasting is Yom Kippur, whereas Muslims fast for the entire month of Ramadan, but only during the day. They can eat at night. Islam's statement of faith became, "There is no God but Allah, and Mohammed is his prophet."

Some today say that Allah is just another name for the Creator God of the Bible, but that is a lie. If we take a close look at the characters of each "God," we can see that they are not at all the same. The Muslim statement of faith is blasphemous. Islam recognizes that Yeshua existed; as any major religion must, given the obvious and overwhelming historical documentation that He lived and walked this earth. Yet they do not recognize Him for who He truly is. They say that he is a prophet, but not a prophet as great as Mohammed.

After Jews and Christians rejected Mohammed's preaching, he became violent and began spreading his new religion through war. Throughout the next four centuries, Islam spread by the sword. The central focus of Islam moved to Medina. The Medina period was characterized by bloodshed and domination. Islam sought to take over by forced conversion. Everyone must submit to Allah. Jihad is a holy war. When Islam states that it is a religion of peace, it is calling good evil and evil good. The Muslim idea of peace is that everyone is under Islamic rule and in submission to Allah. Yet, there is no peace with that either, for even in Muslim countries, Muslim factions war against each other. More Muslims have been killed in jihad than all others combined, and the others that Muslims have killed are many! There is no peace. Satan is behind Allah, and he is a liar. He hates the image of God in humans, and he wants to kill humans and drag their souls to hell before they have a chance to be saved.

In the 9th century in Iraq, Jews and Christians were dhimmis, or slaves, of the Muslims. Christians had to wear special belts that identified them, and Jews had to wear yellow stars that identified them. Hitler copied this idea centuries later and made Jews wear yellow stars during World War II. Dhimmis had to pay high taxes, and they were not allowed to practice their own religions.

By 1090, the Pope in Rome decided something had to be done. So, the Pope issued the first of the Crusades. The Crusades were successful in taking back Jerusalem for about 100 years, but then Saladin took Jerusalem back and held it under Islamic rule until Israel regained it in 1967.

(Recall our lessons on the Crusades – Jews were killed in the Christian quest to fight Islam).

Islam has a special fascination with holy places. Any place that is holy to a Jew or a Christian must be conquered. Any place that they have ever conquered before will be considered theirs forever. By the 1600's Islam covered more of the earth than the Roman Empire at its peak.

On September 11, 1683, Islam was stopped at the gates of Vienna. Notice that this date is important to Islam. What happened on a more recent September 11?

In 1924, the Islamic empire ended in Turkey, and women were given rights that they were earlier denied: they could vote, be educated, work, etc. This was huge, because women in Islam are considered to be property of men. They are not treated well and are not considered to have any rights.

In 1928, the Muslim Brotherhood was established in Egypt in order to fight to regain control. Currently, there are over 70 offshoots of the Muslim Brotherhood including Hamas and Al Qaida.

Jihad is waged on two fronts: military and political. Terrorism is just a small part of the world domination plan of Islam. Politically, Islamists will use the freedoms that Americans and Israelis enjoy to promote their agenda. Muslims seek to change our laws from the inside to guarantee special treatment, gain welfare benefits, and change the thinking of our youth through education. The ultimate objective of political Islam is to subjugate the entire world to Islam and bring everyone under sharia law.

The doctrine of taqiyya is the idea of wearing different "hats," meaning that it is ok within Islam to lie in order to advance Islam.

The doctrine of abrogation with regards to the teachings of the Koran, as explained by Major Nidal Hassan to his colleagues, is that where two verses contradict, the latter wipes out the former. Note that the former verses in the Koran, before Mohammed gave up on converting the Jews through preaching, are peaceful, whereas the latter verses are violent. The violent verses abrogate the former peaceful verses.

There are many moderate and peaceful Muslims, but their voices are silent.

Logic and reasonable discussion are not a part of Muslim culture and mindset. Those who regard Islam as a non-threatening religion and attempt to engage in peaceful discussion are regarded as "useful idiots."

Regarding Israel, past attempts to exchange land for peace have not been successful in achieving peace, and we know, based on what Muslim leaders say, that peace with Israel is not their intent.

Consider this quote (taken from jewishvirtuallibrary.org):

Ismail Haniyeh, Hamas Prime Minister:

"This intifada is not the result of despair. This intifada is a jihad, a holy war fought by the Palestinian people against the Zionist occupation. Only a holy war will drive the occupier out of Palestine." Israel Hayom, January 21, 2016

There are many more quotes at jewishvirtuallibrary.org, but please visit this site with your parents if you want to see more. Some quotes are quite violent.

Israel is a small country. At its narrowest point, one could walk across the width of the country. For survival, it's important for Israel to take every threat seriously, and sometimes preempting an attack is absolutely necessary for survival. Israelis take great care in attempting to live at peace with its neighbors, but we know, based on their own testimony, that their neighbors are enemies that do not recognize Israel's right to exist. Israelis take care to target enemies without harming civilians, but Muslims often locate their military and terrorist headquarters in the same places where young children and other innocent civilians would be harmed if Israel targeted leaders there.

In 1915, Great Britain promised independence in the land of Palestine for the Arabs who took up arms against their Turkish Ottoman rulers. Yet in 1917, in the Balfour Declaration, they declared this land a national homeland for the Jewish people. After the war, Great Britain chose to maintain the land for herself.

In1947, after World War II, the United Nations decided to divide the land of Palestine into two states: one Arab and one Jewish. The Jews agreed; the Arabs did not. When Israel declared its independence in 1948, 750,000 Arabs fled to other Arab nations, and five of the surrounding nations attacked Israel. Israel won. The Muslim Arabs who had fled to other Muslim countries became refugees.

In 1967, the Six Day War changed the map for Israel, gaining control of the Sinai Peninsula, the West Bank, the Gaza Strip, the Golan Heights, and all of Jerusalem.

The Palestinian Liberation Organization (PLO) was formed to demand a homeland for the Palestinians and the destruction of Israel.

In 1973, Egypt and Syria attach Israel in the Sinai and the Golan Heights. Israel wins and a cease fire is declared.

1979 saw a peace process between Israel and Egypt under President Carter, and Israel withdraws from the Sinai.

First Intifada – 1987-1990 – Palestinians want Israel to leave the West Bank and Gaza, so they do everything from throw rocks at Israelis to carry out suicide bombings.

257

1993-1994 – the Oslo Accords gave parts of the West Bank and Gaza to the Palestinians. Israel and Jordan signed a peace treaty.

Second Intifada - 2000-2005 – an attempt at an Israeli-Palestinian peace deal falls through, so the suicide bombings resume. Israel leaves the Gaza.

2006 – Hamas attacks Israel from Lebanon.

To this day, the attacks continue. Israel has built walls to stop and prevent some terrorist attacks, has developed weapons that can specifically target bad guys while leaving civilians unharmed, has developed its military defenses to be able to shoot rockets out of the sky to protect her people, and continues to lead the world in all types of innovations. Israel continues to help and medically treat her sick and injured neighbors.

Day 1:

1) Bible Memory: Memorize Isaiah 5:20.
2) Hebrew: Cantillation – learntrope.com Set Bet
3) Think about the lesson: Read Genesis chapter 16. What do you notice?

_____

_____

_____

Day 2:

1) Bible Memory: Review Isaiah 5:20 and review three other verses.
2) Hebrew: Cantillation – learntrope.com Set Bet
3) Think about the lesson: Read Genesis 25:12-18. What do you notice?

_____

_____

_____

Day 3:

1) Bible Memory: Review Isaiah 5:20 and review three other verses.
2) Hebrew: Cantillation – learntrope.com Set Bet
3) Think about the lesson: Discuss this week's memory verse with your parents. How does it apply to the tenuous relationship between Israel and her Islamic neighbors?

_____

_____

_____

Day 4:

1) Bible Memory: Review Isaiah 5:20 and review three other verses.
2) Hebrew: Cantillation – learntrope.com Set Bet
3) Think about the lesson: When Abraham had a child with Hagar outside of the will of God, it caused

problems for his family and for all the generations to follow. As we navigate this life, let us remember to pray continuously, so that we might stay in the will of God for our lives. When we come up against would-be attackers, let us stand for what is right, defend our families, and love our enemies (the way Israel does when her people care for the sick, poor, and injured of their enemy nations). In this way, we will be a witness to unbelievers.

Day 5:

1) Bible Memory: Review Isaiah 5:20 and review three other verses.
2) Hebrew: Cantillation – learntrope.com Set Bet
3) Think about the lesson: Even though most Israelis today do not see or recognize Yeshua as the Messiah, the active presence of God in the land of Israel is evident. Romans 11 promises us that Yeshua will be revealed to Israel when the fullness of the Gentiles comes in. We know that Yeshua is the Messiah, God's Son and right hand of salvation. He died for our sins so that we might have eternal life.

Day 6:

1) Bible Memory: Review Isaiah 5:20 and review three other verses.
2) Hebrew: Cantillation – learntrope.com Set Bet
3) Think about the lesson: With your parents, research current events in the Middle East. Record your notes:

_____

_____

_____

LESSON 80
HISTORY: THE UNITED STATES AND ISRAEL TODAY

Lesson Objective: See that President Trump recognized Jerusalem as Israel's capital and the Golan Heights as Israel's land.

Memory Verse: Proverbs 16:9 In his heart, a man plans his course, but the LORD determines his steps.

Hebrew: Cantillation – learntrope.com Set Gimel

Lesson Summary:

For the most part, the United States of America has been a friend and support to Israel; however, there are times in our history where we did not show friendship or support. We've already seen that during the Civil War, the southern states of Tennessee, Mississippi, and Kentucky expelled Jewish cotton farmers, and in World War II, the St. Louis, carrying 900 Jewish passengers from Europe, was turned away.

How we treat Israel as a nation depends largely on who we elect as leader of our nation. This is good to keep in mind for future years when you are old enough to vote.

After World War II, when Israel was reestablished, US President Truman was the first to officially recognize Israel as a legitimate nation; and now, within President Trump's term, Trump has moved the US embassy to Jerusalem, officially recognizing it as Israel's historic and modern capital, recognized the Golan Heights as legitimately belonging to Israel, disengaged from the Iran nuclear deal established by President Obama, and has created a new Israel-Palestine deal that may or may not end up being a win-win for Israelis and Palestinians both. The relationship between Israel and the United States is currently at an all-time high.

Day 1:

1) Bible Memory: Memorize Proverbs 16:9.
2) Hebrew: Cantillation – learntrope.com Set Gimel
3) Think about the lesson: Throughout this week, with your parents, study the modern Israeli-Palestinian conflict and research the current news.

Day 2:

1) Bible Memory: Review Proverbs 16:9 and review three other verses.
2) Hebrew: Cantillation – learntrope.com Set Gimel
4) Think about the lesson: With your parents, study the modern Israeli-Palestinian conflict and research the current news.

Day 3:

1) Bible Memory: Review Proverbs 16:9 and review three other verses.
2) Hebrew: Cantillation – learntrope.com Set Gimel
5) Think about the lesson: With your parents, study the modern Israeli-Palestinian conflict and research

the current news.

Day 4:

1) Bible Memory: Review Proverbs 16:9 and review three other verses.
2) Hebrew: Cantillation – learntrope.com Set Gimel
6) Think about the lesson: With your parents, study the modern Israeli-Palestinian conflict and research the current news.

Day 5:

1) Bible Memory: Review Proverbs 16:9 and review three other verses.
2) Hebrew: Cantillation – learntrope.com Set Gimel
7) Think about the lesson: With your parents, study the modern Israeli-Palestinian conflict and research the current news.

Day 6:

1) Bible Memory: Review Proverbs 16:9 and review three other verses.
2) Hebrew: Cantillation – learntrope.com Set Gimel
3) Think about the lesson: After this week's research and discussion with your parents, what are your thoughts about the current relationship between the United States and Israel? What hope might you see for the Israeli-Palestinian conflict? Or do you think it is unresolvable until Yeshua returns? For older students, you and your parents might consider researching the anti-Christ figures in Daniel and Revelation and comparing notes with modern-day proposals to resolve conflicts in the Middle East.

_____
_____
_____
_____
_____

LESSON 81
HISTORICAL TIMELINE OVERVIEW

Lesson Objective: Adonai is in control of the big picture.

Memory Verse: Psalm 115:3 Our God is in heaven; he does whatever pleases him.

Hebrew: Cantillation – learntrope.com Set Dalet

Lesson Summary:

We've covered a lot of history in this unit, and this is a good time to see an overview of it, so that you can get a timeline with historical highlights into your memory. Work on memorizing this timeline overview throughout the week:

About 6000 year ago – Creation

A little over 5000 years ago – the Flood

About 4000 years ago – Abraham, Isaac, and Jacob

Jacob's sons become the 12 tribes of Israel, time in Egypt – 400 years

Exodus to Promised Land – 40 years of wandering in the wilderness

Joshua – entrance into the Promised Land

First Judges, then Kings, King David, King Solomon, divided kingdom (900's BC)

Assyrians 722 BC

Babylonians, Diaspora 586 BC

Medes and Persians (Ahasuerus and Esther) 400's BC

Greeks 330's BC

Maccabean Revolt (Chanukah) 165-162 BC

Romans

Yeshua (4 BC – 30 AD)

Destruction of the 2nd Temple (70 AD), War of Bar Kochba (132-135 AD)

Development of Judaism, Mishnah and Talmud/Development of Christianity/Rise of Islam

Expulsions and Pogroms – many centuries in many locations

The Crusades 1099

World War I (1917-1918) and World War II (the Holocaust) 1933-1945

Israel re-established 1948

Six Day War 1967 and Yom Kippur War 1973

Intifadas 2000's

Israel today

Day 1:

1) Bible Memory: Memorize Psalm 115:3.
2) Hebrew: Cantillation – learntrope.com Set Dalet
3) Think about the lesson: Work on memorizing the dates and order of the topical words, names, and events in the timeline overview above.

Day 2:

1) Bible Memory: Review Psalm 115:3 and review three other verses.
2) Hebrew: Cantillation – learntrope.com Set Dalet
3) Think about the lesson: Continue memorizing the dates and order of the topical words, names, and events in the timeline overview above.

Day 3:

1) Bible Memory: Review Psalm 115:3 and review three other verses.
2) Hebrew: Cantillation – learntrope.com Set Dalet
3) Think about the lesson: Continue memorizing the dates and order of the topical words, names, and events in the timeline overview above. Write out the list and jot down details that you remember that go along with each topical word, name, or event. If you don't remember, look it up.

Day 4:

1) Bible Memory: Review Psalm 115:3 and review three other verses.
2) Hebrew: Cantillation – learntrope.com Set Dalet
3) Think about the lesson: Continue memorizing the dates and order of the topical words, names, and events in the timeline overview above. Write out the list and jot down details that you remember that go along with each topical word, name, or event. If you don't remember, look it up.

Day 5:

1) Bible Memory: Review Psalm 115:3 and review three other verses.

2) Hebrew: Cantillation – learntrope.com Set Dalet
3) Think about the lesson: Continue memorizing the dates and order of the topical words, names, and events in the timeline overview above. Write out the list and jot down details that you remember that go along with each topical word, name, or event. If you don't remember, look it up.

Day 6:

1) Bible Memory: Review Psalm 115:3 and review three other verses.
2) Hebrew: Cantillation – learntrope.com Set Dalet
3) Think about the lesson: Have your parents quiz you over the historical timeline overview.

SECTION 6 – A LIFE OF SERVICE

LESSON 82
GIFTS OF THE SPIRIT

Lesson Objective: Understand what the gifts of the Holy Spirit are that are given to you by God at the point of salvation through Yeshua the Messiah.

Memory Passage: Romans 12:4-8 Just as each one of us has one body with many members, and these members do not all have the same function, so in Messiah we who are many form one body, and each member belongs to all the others. We have different gifts, according to the grace given us. If a man's gift is prophesying, let him use it in proportion to his faith. If it is serving, let him serve; if it is teaching, let him teach; if it is encouraging, let him encourage; if it is contributing to the needs of others, let him give generously; if it is leadership, let him govern diligently; if it is showing mercy, let him do it cheerfully.

Hebrew: Cantillation – learntrope.com Set Hey

Lesson Summary:

We have spent the first five sections of this workbook learning about God, His Word, and His people. This learning is not just for us; it is for us to share with the world. God's Word is a light to the world. Those who have His light are like candles in a menorah that shine His light to others.

Just as Yeshua came to serve, not to be served, so we follow His example.

Many people in other religions or in no religion at all, believe in living a life of good works. It is good to do good things and to treat each other well, to be considerate and helpful, and to make positive changes in our communities.

Yet Isaiah 64:6 says that when we do righteous acts through our own power, "all our righteous acts are like filthy rags." Our own righteousness is nothing compared to the righteousness of God! For our righteous acts to be glorifying to God our Father, we need to do them through His power, not our own.

So how do we do righteous acts through God's power for His glory? We use the gifts of the Spirit that He gives us at the moment of our salvation through Yeshua our Messiah!

The gifts of the Holy Spirit, or Ruach HaKodesh, are above and beyond our natural-born gifts and talents. They are from God to be used for His purposes. We do not have access to the gifts of the Spirit without faith in Yeshua. They are a gift given to us with our salvation in Him.

There are many gifts of the Spirit listed in the Bible. This week's memory verse shows us seven; this week's assignments will show you more.

To truly make a difference in this world, we need the power of the Holy Spirit, and since we do not receive His power or His gifts without faith in Yeshua for our salvation, we must first approach Yeshua for salvation. Then, and only then, can we impact this world for the glory of God!

Day 1:

1) Bible Memory: Memorize Romans 12:4.
2) Hebrew: Cantillation – learntrope.com Set Hey
3) Think about the lesson: List the seven gifts of the Spirit in Romans 12:4-8.

_____
_____
_____
_____
_____
_____
_____
_____

Day 2:

1) Bible Memory: Memorize Romans 12:5 and review Romans 12:4.
2) Hebrew: Cantillation – learntrope.com Set Hey
3) Think about the lesson: Read 1 Corinthians 12:7-11. List the nine gifts of the Spirit you see in this passage.

_____
_____
_____
_____
_____
_____
_____
_____
_____

Day 3:

1) Bible Memory: Memorize Romans 12:6 and review Romans 12:4-5.
2) Hebrew: Cantillation – learntrope.com Set Hey
3) Think about the lesson: Read 1 Peter 4:10-11 and Ephesians 4:7-16. Which gifts do you see in each of these? And what is the purpose for the gifts?

_____
_____
_____
_____
_____
_____
_____

Day 4:

1) Bible Memory: Romans 12:7 and review Romans 12:4-6.
2) Hebrew: Cantillation – learntrope.com Set Hey
3) Think about the lesson: Read 1 Corinthians 12:27-31. List the eight gifts you see here.

_____
_____
_____
_____
_____
_____
_____
_____
_____

Day 5:

1) Bible Memory: Romans 12:8 and review Romans 12:4-7.
2) Hebrew: Cantillation – learntrope.com Set Hey
3) Think about the lesson: Read 1 Corinthians 13:1-3. When we become believers in and followers of Yeshua, and we are given the gifts of the Spirit, how should we use our gifts?

_____
_____

Day 6:

1) Bible Memory: Review Romans 12:4-8.
2) Hebrew: Cantillation – learntrope.com Set Hey
3) Think about the lesson: Read 1 Corinthians 12:12-26. Why do different people have different gifts? Explain how each individual makes up the body of Messiah. Why is it good that we each have different gifts?

_____
_____
_____
_____
_____
_____
_____

LESSON 83
EXAMINING GIFTS OF THE SPIRIT ACTIVE IN BIBLICAL ROLE MODELS

Lesson Objective: See different gifts of the Spirit in action in some of our favorite Biblical role models.

Bible Memory: Review all verses.

Hebrew: Cantillation – learntrope.com Set Vav

Lesson Summary:

A role model is someone we can look up to and imitate. The Bible gives us many examples of men and women who acted on the direction of God under the prompting of the Holy Spirit.

For example, consider Solomon, who prayed that God would give him supernatural wisdom to be a good leader. God was pleased with his request and answered that prayer. His story and one example of Solomon's wisdom is found in 1 Kings 3:5-28.

Moses and Deborah are two examples of good leadership fueled by the Spirit of God. Exodus 18:13-26 shows Moses taking leadership responsibility while also showing Jethro's gift for administration. The two complement each other well and demonstrate the way that we are to work together in the Body of Messiah. Deborah works with Barak in Judges 4:4-24. Deborah was the prophetess who judged Israel at that time, and Barak, the leader of the army, would not head into war without her.

Like Jethro, Nehemiah also had the gift of administration, and we see what he did with his gift in Nehemiah chapters 2-3.

Elijah and Elisha had the God-given gift of miracles. You can read about them in 1 Kings 18:16-46 and 2 Kings chapters 2-5.

Samuel and Dorcas are great examples of those with the gift of service. Samuel led the people as a selfless servant for years before they requested a king (1 Samuel 1:20-28, 3:1-21). Dorcas (Acts 9:36-41) had a servant's heart, hands, and eyes; she perceived needs and did what needed to be done to meet them.

Abigail (1 Samuel 25) is an amazing example of the gift of giving. With her clear vision prompted by the Spirit of God followed by fast action, she saved many from certain death.

The Good Samaritan (Luke 10:30-35) displayed the gift of mercy, going sacrificially above and beyond to make sure a hurt person was going to be alright.

Yeshua, being in very nature God Himself, obviously had all the gifts, but we see Him exercising the gift of healing in Mark 2:1-12.

These are just a few examples of Biblical role models we can emulate!

This week, we'll read many passages about more Biblical role models using their God-given gifts. As you read

268

each passage, you'll identify which gift or gifts you see being exercised. Use the following Gifts Box as a help for identification.

Service	Administration	Miracles	Teacher
Prophecy	Discernment	Tongues	Encourage
Giving	Healing	Mercy	Leader
Wisdom	Knowledge	Helps	Apostle
Faith	Evangelism	Pastor	

Day 1:

1) Bible Memory: Choose three verses to review.
2) Hebrew: Cantillation – learntrope.com Set Vav
3) Think about the lesson: Read Acts 10:44-48. What gift of the Spirit is evident here?

_____

Read 2 Samuel chapters 11-12 and Galatians 2:6-21. Which gift do Nathan and Paul use in these passages?

_____

_____

Day 2:

1) Bible Memory: Choose three verses to review.
2) Hebrew: Cantillation – learntrope.com Set Vav
3) Think about the lesson: Read Acts 3. What gift are Peter and John using?

_____

Read Acts 13-14. What gift are Paul and Barnabas using here?

_____

_____

Day 3:

1) Bible Memory: Choose three verses to review.
2) Hebrew: Cantillation – learntrope.com Set Vav
3) Think about the lesson: Read Nehemiah 8. Which gift is Ezra using?

_____

Read Proverbs 31. Which gifts do the Proverbs 31 woman use?

_____

_____

Day 4:

    1)   Bible Memory: Choose three verses to review.
    2)   Hebrew: Cantillation – learntrope.com Set Vav
    3)   Think about the lesson: Read Acts 6:1-7. Which gift do the deacons use here?

_____

        Read Acts 20:28-34 and 1 Peter 5:1-4. Which gift do these passages describe?

_____

Day 5:

    1)   Bible Memory: Choose three verses to review.
    2)   Hebrew: Cantillation – learntrope.com Set Vav
    3)   Think about the lesson: Read 1 Corinthians 14:3. Which gift do you see? _____
        Read Acts 20:17-38. Which gift is Paul using here? _____
        Read Matthew 8:1-13 and Hebrews 11. Which gift is shown in these passages? _____

Day 6:

    1)   Bible Memory: Choose three verses to review.
    2)   Hebrew: Cantillation – learntrope.com Set Vav
    3)   Think about the lesson: Read Acts 8:26-40. Which gift is Philip using? _____
        Read 1 Samuel 24. Which gift does David use? _____
        Read Acts 18:1-5 and 24-28. Which gift do Aquila and Priscilla use? _____
        Read Acts 17:10-12. Which gift do the Bereans exercise? _____

LESSON 84
IDENTIFYING AND DEVELOPING OUR OWN GIFTS AND TALENTS

Lesson Objective: Determine the specific gifts and talents you may have, those natural to you and those given supernaturally if you are a believer in Yeshua as the Messiah and have received the gifts of the Holy Spirit, or Ruach HaKodesh.

Bible Memory: Review all verses.

Hebrew: Cantillation – learntrope.com Set Zayn

Lesson Summary:

We've taken a look at some of the gifts of the Spirit that are revealed in the Bible, and we've seen some of those gifts in action in a few of our favorite Biblical role models. Now it's time to consider which gifts of the Spirit we may have. Before we begin, there are three things to remember:

1) There is a difference between natural-born gifts and talents, which we all have, and God-given spiritual gifts, which are only granted to us after we have placed our faith in Yeshua the Messiah. If we have not accepted Yeshua as our Lord and Savior, then we do not have the gifts of the Spirit. Our natural-born gifts and talents often dove-tail with our God-given gifts, but not always. For example, someone with the gift of singing can become quite popular on the secular scene, yet someone else with the same natural-born gift who is also a believer, can have that gift inspired by the Spirit of God for the purpose of leading worship. On the other hand, the gift of prophesy may be one that is given at a specific time for a specific purpose. Some gifts may not be natural-born, nor are they talents that can be honed.
2) The gifts of the Spirit are for God's purposes; they are not for us to misuse or manipulate. The focus is on God; not on us.
3) God gives different gifts to different people, some people have multiple gifts, and many gifts have a "season" during our lifetimes.

To begin considering which gifts of the Spirit you have, first make sure that you have accepted Yeshua as your Messiah. (Otherwise, you do not have the gifts of the Spirit.)

Second, there are many quizzes available online and in books that ask questions about you and your preferences; these quizzes are a good place to start if you want to determine what natural-born gifts, talents, and personality traits you have. Since many gifts of the Spirit dove-tail with your natural-born gifts, these quizzes are helpful. With your parents' guidance, you may choose to select one and take the test and determine your results.

Third, be in prayer for several day, weeks, or months, or however long it takes to get your answers, with regards to how God wants you to work for him in his kingdom. He will show you what to do and give you the words you need at the right time.

As you consider a life of service, you will be completing a service project during the course of this Bnei Mitzvah program. In the next lesson, you'll see some choices offered to get your mind rolling. You may know at this time exactly what you need to do, but chances are you have no idea yet what God wants you to do with your life, or even with the next few weeks. In that case, feel free to pray about it and choose to try different things as you embark on this adventure.

Day 1:

1) Bible Memory: Choose three verses to review.
2) Hebrew: Cantillation – learntrope.com Set Zayn
3) Think about the lesson: Discuss with your parents the gifts and talents you know that you have and what they see in you. What do you think? What gifts and talents, natural-born and Sprit-given, do you have?

_____
_____
_____
_____

Day 2:

1) Bible Memory: Choose three verses to review.
2) Hebrew: Cantillation – learntrope.com Set Zayn
3) Think about the lesson: Consider how your gifts and talents might be used.

_____
_____
_____
_____

Day 3:

1) Bible Memory: Choose three verses to review.
2) Hebrew: Cantillation – learntrope.com Set Zayn
3) Think about the lesson: What needs do you see in your congregation? In your community?

_____
_____
_____
_____
_____
_____

Day 4:

1) Bible Memory: Choose three verses to review.
2) Hebrew: Cantillation – learntrope.com Set Zayn
3) Think about the lesson: What specific needs in your congregation or community exist that you know you can meet?

_____
_____

_____
_____
_____

Day 5:

    1) Bible Memory: Choose three verses to review.
    2) Hebrew: Cantillation – learntrope.com Set Zayn
    3) Think about the lesson: Which Biblical role models do you get excited about and relate to? Which ones are your favorites and why?

_____
_____
_____
_____

Day 6:

    1) Bible Memory: Choose three verses to review.
    2) Hebrew: Cantillation – learntrope.com Set Zayn
    3) Think about the lesson: What do you believe your gifts and talents are? Is the Spirit of God prompting you in a certain area? If so, where? Pray before answering.

_____
_____
_____
_____
_____

LESSON 85
THE BAR OR BAT MITZVAH SERVICE PROJECT

Lesson Objective: Choose a service project to perform for your bar or bat mitzvah and go do it!

Bible Memory: Review all Bible memory verses.

Hebrew: Cantillation – learntrope.com Special Trope

Lesson Summary:

We've spent the last few weeks studying and discussing spiritual gifts, and now it's time to see how we can put those to use in a service project. Here are the guidelines:

1) Parents, you oversee this project, which may include driving, time, input, money, etc.
2) Projects should be specific rather than general, For example, being a good leader at school is general – we can't really tell whether or not we've been successful – whereas leading a group to accomplish a defined goal is specific.
3) Projects should have a set starting point and ending point, although the act of service may certainly continue after the defined ending point.
4) Projects should benefit the community, the congregation, and the Bar or Bat Mitzvah student.

The following is a list of service project ideas, grouped by the gifts of the Spirit categories we see in our Bible memory passage from Romans, to get you started. You are not limited to ideas on this list!

Prophecy ideas:
>   Start a blog, podcast, website, etc. to share the good news of Messiah
>   Organize a summer reading program to encourage children to read
>   Start a prayer group
>   Become a volunteer teen crisis counselor (older Bnei Mitzvah students)

Serving ideas:
>   Serve in the kitchen
>   Assist in a classroom
>   Organize a car wash to raise funds for a cause
>   Deliver meals through Meals on Wheels

Teaching ideas:
>   Assist in a classroom
>   Create a worksheet for a museum visit day
>   Write a book
>   Tutor younger children
>   Teach computer, tablet, or phone skills to the elderly

Encouragement ideas:
>   Send cards to soldiers overseas
>   Visit a nursing home to pray with the residents, and/or sing, dance, play an instrument, read a sotry, draw pictures, etc.
>   Perform dance, music, etc. for children in hospitals

Organize events to help new students make friends

Giving ideas:
Raise money for a cause
Collect items to donate to a homeless shelter, food bank, etc.
Send care packages to soldiers overseas
Mow someone's lawn who can't mow it themselves
Clean an elderly person's home
Sponsor a child living in a foreign country

Leadership ideas:
Organize a trip to the Perot museum and the ICR Discovery Center for Science and Earth History for a creation vs. evolution conversation
Organize and lead a youth prayer group, music team, dance group, etc.
Start a community garden
Organize a group to clean up a local trail, lake, or river

Compassion ideas:
Collect items to donate to a homeless shelter, food bank, etc.
Serve in a soup kitchen
Visit a nursing home to pray with the residents, and/or sing, dance, play an instrument, read a story, draw pictures, etc.
Build homes with Habitat for Humanity
Perform dance, music, etc. for children in hospitals
Take care of dogs and cats at an animal shelter
Become CPR certified and teach a safety class for children

Day 1:

1) Bible Memory: Choose five verses to review.
2) Hebrew: Cantillation – learntrope.com Special Trope
3) Think about the lesson: Choose a service project. What will you do?

_____

_____

Day 2:

1) Bible Memory: Choose five verses to review.
2) Hebrew: Cantillation – learntrope.com Special Trope
3) Think about the lesson: Set a starting point and an ending point. These will be

_____

Day 3:

1) Bible Memory: Choose five verses to review.
2) Hebrew: Cantillation – learntrope.com Special Trope
3) Think about the lesson: Discuss with your parents what you will need to accomplish this goal:

_____

_____

Day 4:

1) Bible Memory: Choose five verses to review.
2) Hebrew: Cantillation – learntrope.com Special Trope
3) Think about the lesson: How will your service project benefit your community? Your congregation? Yourself?

_____

_____

_____

Day 5:

1) Bible Memory: Choose five verses to review.
2) Hebrew: Cantillation – learntrope.com Special Trope
3) Think about the lesson: Gather what you need for your project. Take the time you need to do this.

Day 6:

1) Bible Memory: Choose five verses to review.
2) Hebrew: Cantillation – learntrope.com Special Trope
3) Think about the lesson: Complete your project. Take the time you need to do this.

MINI-DRASH NOTES

As part of your Bar or Bat Mitzvah, you will be offering a 5-10 minute long min-drash. You may choose your topic, as long as it is Biblical. It may relate to your Torah portion, but it does not have to. Your parents and/or teacher may help you, but they should not write it for you.

Made in the USA
Middletown, DE
04 March 2023

26198346R00172